The Causal Body and The Ego

by

Lieut.-Colonel Arthur E. Powell

THEOSOPHICAL PUBLISHING HOUSE
Quezon City, Metro Manila
Philippines

The views expressed in this book are those of the author, and must not be taken as necessarily those of The Theosophical Society.

3105

Published 1928

Reprinted 1956

Reprinted 1972

Reprinted 1978

Reprinted under arrangement with Theosophical Publishing House, Ltd., 68 Great Russell St., London, WC1B 3BU

DEDICATION

This book, like its three predecessors, is dedicated with gratitude and appreciation to those whose pains-taking labour and researches have provided the materials out of which it has been fashioned

CONTENTS

LIST OF DIAGRAMS

AUTHORS QUOTED

BOOK	AUTHOR	EDITION	ABBREVIATION
Ancient Wisdom	A. Besant	1897	*A W*
Chakras	C. W. Leadbeater	1927	*Ch*
Changing World	A. Besant	1909	*C W*
Clairvoyance	C. W. Leadbeater	1908	*C*
Death and After	A. Besant	1901	*D A*
Devachanic Plane	C. W. Leadbeater	1902	*D P*
Dreams	C. W. Leadbeater	1903	*D*
Evolution of Life and Form	A. Besant	1899	*E L F*
Gods in Exile	J. J. van der Leeuw	1926	*G E*
Hidden Life in Freemasonry	C. W. Leadbeater	1926	*H L F*
Hidden Side of Things, Vol. I.	C. W. Leadbeater	1913	*H S I*
Hidden Side of Things, Vol. II.	C. W. Leadbeater	1913	*H S II*
In the Outer Court	A. Besant	1910	*I O C*
Inner Life, Vol. I.	C. W. Leadbeater	1910	*I L I*
Inner Life, Vol. II.	C. W. Leadbeater	1911	*I L II*
Introduction to Yoga	A. Besant	1908	*I Y*
Karma	A. Besant	1897	*K*
Life After Death	C. W. Leadbeater	1917	*L A D*
Man and His Bodies	A. Besant	1900	*M B*
Man Visible and Invisible	C. W. Leadbeater	1902	*M V I*
Man: Whence, How and Whither.	Besant and Leadbeater.	1913	*M W H W*
Masters and the Path	C. W. Leadbeater	1925	*M P*
Monad	C. W. Leadbeater	1920	*M*
Nirvāna	G. S. Arundale	1926	*N*
Other Side of Death	C. W. Leadbeater	1904	*O S D*
Pedigree of Man	A. Besant	1908	*P M*
Reincarnation	A. Besant	1898	*R*
Science of the Sacraments	C. W. Leadbeater	1920	*S O S*
Self and Its Sheaths	A. Besant	1902	*S S*
Seven Principles of Man	A. Besant	1904	*S P*
Some Glimpses of Occultism	C. W. Leadbeater	1909	*S G O*
Study in Consciousness	A. Besant	1904	*S C*
Talks on the Path of Occultism.	Besant and Leadbeater.	1926	*T P O*
Talks with a Class	A. Besant	1921	*T C*
Text-book of Theosophy	C. W. Leadbeater	1914	*T B*
Theosophy	A. Besant	—	*T*
Theosophy and the New Psychology.	A. Besant	1909	*T N P*
Thought-Power	A. Besant	1903	*T P*

PUBLISHER'S PREFACE

The author's purpose in compiling the books in this series was to save students much time and labour by providing a condensed synthesis of the considerable literature on the respective subjects of each volume, coming mostly from the pens of Annie Besant and C. W. Leadbeater. The accompanying list shows the large number of books from which he drew. So far as possible the method adopted was to explain the form side first, before the life side: to describe the objective mechanism of phenomena and then the activities of consciousness that are expressed through the mechanism. There is no attempt to prove or even justify any of the statements. Marginal references give opportunity to refer to the sources.

The works of H. P. Blavatsky were not used because the author said that the necessary research in The Secret Doctrine and other writings would have been too vast a task for him to undertake. He added: "The debt to H. P. Blavatsky is greater than could ever be indicated by quotations from her monumental volumes. Had she not shown the way in the first instance, later investigators might never have found the trail at all."

INTRODUCTION

THIS book forms the fourth, and last, of the series of compilations dealing with the bodies of man. Throughout the series the same plan has been adopted. Approximately forty volumes, mostly those written by Dr. Annie Besant and by Bishop C. W. Leadbeater, have been thoroughly searched, the material thus found has been sorted, arranged and classified into its appropriate departments, so as to present to the student of modern Theosophy a coherent and sequential account of the finer bodies of man.

In addition, there has been incorporated a considerable amount of information regarding the planes, or worlds, associated with these four bodies of man. It is, therefore, probably near the truth to say that the gist of nearly everything that has been published by the two principal pioneers into the mysteries and complexities of the Ancient Wisdom, with the exception of certain clearly marked specialities (such as Occult Chemistry, for example) is to be found in these four books.

In 1913 appeared *Man: Whence, How and Whither?* In addition to these, two fascinating volumes, entitled *The Story of Atlantis* and *Lost Lemuria*, with maps of those continents, from the pen of W. Scott-Elliot, appeared in 1896 and 1904 respectively, describing in very full detail the races that inhabited those lands, and their civilisations.

In view of the fact that our occult knowledge, of planes finer than the physical, is likely to be enormously increased in the near future, it has seemed desirable to undertake the not inconsiderable task of arranging, in text-book form, such data as are already in our possession, before the total mass becomes too unwieldy to be handled in this manner. Moreover, by such orderly arrangement of our materials, we construct for ourselves an outline, or skeleton, into which further information can be built, as it becomes available.

As in the previous volumes, references to the sources of information have throughout been given in the margin, so that any student, who so desires, may verify for himself every statement made, at its original source. In the few cases where the compiler has stated his own unsupported views, the initials A. E. P. have been printed in the margin.

About two-thirds of the diagrams are original, the remainder having been taken, sometimes with slight modifications, from the works of Bishop Leadbeater, and a few from *A Study in Consciousness*, by Dr. Besant.

A further department of Theosophical knowledge, to a great extent self-contained, and therefore specialised, is that of the Scheme of Evolution in which man evolves: this includes Globes (such as the Earth), Rounds, Chains, Races, Sub-Races, and so forth. The writer hopes to compile a volume dealing with this section of technical Theosophy, in the near future.

A. E. P.

THE CAUSAL BODY

CHAPTER I

GENERAL DESCRIPTION

In the three preceding volumes of this series, viz., *The Etheric Double, The Astral Body* and *The Mental Body,* the life-history of each of the three lower vehicles of man has been studied. In these studies, it has been sufficient for us to take each of the three vehicles as we find it actually existing in man, and to examine its methods of functioning, the laws of its growth, its death, and then the formation, from the nucleus provided by the permanent atoms and mental unit, of new vehicles of the same kind, in order that man's evolution on the three lower planes may be continued.

When we come to study the causal body of man, we enter upon a new phase of our work, and must take a far wider sweep in our purview of man's evolution. The reason for this is, that whilst the etheric, astral and mental bodies exist for one human incarnation only, *i.e.,* are distinctly *mortal,* the causal body persists throughout the whole of a man's evolution, through many incarnations, and is therefore relatively *immortal.* We say *relatively* immortal advisedly because, as will be seen in due course, there is a point where a man, having completed his purely *normal* human evolution, commences his *supernormal* human evolution, and actually loses the causal body in which he has lived and evolved during the past ages of his growth.

Hence, in dealing with man's causal body, we are no longer standing within the personality, looking upon any vehicle of that personality, and seeing from its own standpoint how it is serving the evolution of the real man who uses it, but instead we must take up our stand by the side of the man himself, looking from above on the vehicles of the personality, and regarding them as so many temporary instruments fashioned for the use of the man himself, and discarded, as a broken tool is discarded, when they have served their purpose.

Furthermore, in order to make our study comprehensive, and to round it off in a manner that will be intellectually satisfactory, we must discover and study the origin and birth of the causal body, *i.e.*, how it was formed in the first instance. Finding that it *had* a beginning, we see at once, not only that it must have an end, but also that there must be some other form of consciousness which uses the causal body, much as the ego in the causal body uses the vehicles of the personality. This other form of consciousness is, of course, the human Monad. Hence, in order that we may fully comprehend the part which the causal body plays in the tremendous story of human evolution, we must study also the Monad.

Reverting to the birth or formation of the causal body, we are at once plunged into a consideration of the somewhat intricate subject of Group-Souls, with which we shall have to deal. Tracing the origin of Group-Souls, we are led back, step by step, to the Three Great Outpourings of the Divine Life, from which all forms of manifested life arise. Whilst studying the Three Outpourings, we must necessarily also consider to some extent the formation of the material world into which the Outpourings are projected.

Thus, in order that our study of the causal body may be a comprehensive one, we must describe, though in brief outline only, the formation of the field of evolution, the flow into that field of the great streams of life, the coming forth of the Monads, the building of the many kingdoms of life, and the plunging of the Monads, with the assistance of the permanent atoms, into the material universe, and the gradual development of the life in the Group-Souls until eventually, after æons of existence, the point of Individualisation is reached, when the causal body for the first time appears.

Thereafter our study will follow much the same lines as in the previous books of this series. We shall have to deal in turn with the functions of the causal body: its composition and structure; the nature of causal thought; the development and faculties of the causal body; the portion of the life after death spent in the causal body in the higher heaven-worlds.

Then we must pass to a fuller examination of the entity, the ego to wit, who inhabits and uses the causal body, projecting from it personality after personality into the cycle of reincarnation. We must examine what is known as Trishnā, the "thirst," which is the true cause of reincarnation; the permanent atoms and the mechanism of reincarnation; the attitude which the ego takes towards the whole process of reincarnation and to the personalities which he projects into the lower worlds.

The whole relationship of the ego to the personality, his link with it, and the way in which he uses it, must be carefully examined. A special chapter will be devoted to certain Sacramental aids towards strengthening and improving the link between the ego and the personality, and another chapter to the rationale of the memory of past lives.

Then we pass to describe, so far as is possible, the life of the ego on his own plane. This leads us on to Initiation into the Great White Brotherhood, when the causal body vanishes for the time. Some description of the buddhic consciousness must be attempted, and a succinct epitome of such facts as are known regarding the Second and Higher Initiations.

Finally, we conclude our long history with the relation of the ego to his "Father in Heaven," the Monad.

The field which this book attempts to cover is thus, as already said, a far greater one than that covered in any of the three preceding volumes of the series. The book will, it is hoped, enable the student of Theosophy to obtain a broad grasp of the wonderful panorama of human evolution, and to see in true perspective the part played by each of the four subtler bodies of man—the etheric, the astral, the mental and the causal.

CHAPTER II

THE FIELD OF EVOLUTION

S C 36. BY the "field of evolution" we mean the material universe in which evolution is to take place. Strictly speaking, life or spirit, and matter are not, in reality, separate and distinct existences, but rather are opposite poles of one noumenon; but for purposes of intellectual analysis and study it is convenient to consider these two aspects or poles almost as though they were separate and distinct, much in the same way that a builder, for example, considers, more or less separately, plans and sections of his buildings, although these plans and sections are merely abstractions from the one entity—the building itself.

S C 1–4. The field of evolution in our solar system consists of seven planes or worlds; these may be regarded as making up three groups: (1) the field of Logoic manifestation only; (2) the field of super-normal evolution; (3) the field of normal human, animal, vegetable, mineral and elemental evolution. These facts may be tabulated as shown on page 5.

S C 4. The Ādī and Anupādaka planes may be conceived as existing before the solar system is formed. The Ādī plane may be imagined as consisting of so much of the matter of space, symbolised by points, as the Logos marks out to form the material basis of the system He is about to produce.

The Anupādaka plane, symbolised by lines, we may imagine as consisting of this same matter, modified or coloured by His individual life, His all-ensouling consciousness, thus differing in some way from the corresponding plane in another solar system. These ideas may be roughly symbolised thus:—

The Fields of Evolution

Number.		Name		Field of Evolution.
Group.	Serial.	Sanskrit.	English.	
I.	1	Ādī	(*a*)	Logoic.
	2	Anupādaka	(*b*)	
II.	3	Ātmā	Spirit	Super-normal human, *i.e.*, " Initiates."
	4	Buddhi	Intuition	
III.	5	Manas	Mind	Normal human, animal, vegetable, mineral and elemental entities.
	6	Kāmā	Emotion	
	7	Sthūla	Physical Activity	

(*a*) No English equivalent exists: Ādī means literally " first."

(*b*) No English equivalent exists: Anupādaka means literally " without vesture."

First Stage	The Logos marks out His Universe on the Ādī plane.	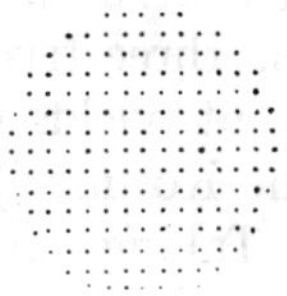
Second Stage	The Logos modifies this matter with His own individual life, on the Anupādaka plane.	

Diagram I.—The Beginning of a Universe.

This preparatory work may be illustrated in another S C 4-9.
way by two sets of symbols, one showing the threefold manifestation of the consciousness of the Logos, the other the threefold change in matter corresponding to the threefold change in consciousness.

Taking first the manifestation of consciousness, the site of the universe having been marked out (see Diagram II): (1) the Logos Himself appears as a point

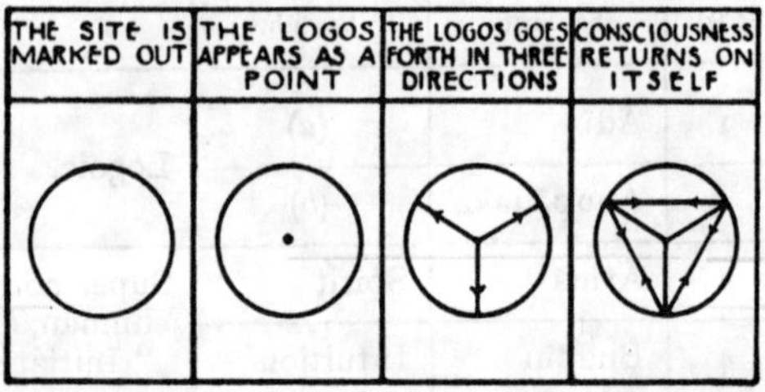

DIAGRAM II.—Manifestation of the Consciousness of the Logos.

within the sphere; (2) the Logos goes forth from that point in three directions to the circumference of the sphere or circle of matter; (3) the consciousness of the Logos returns on Itself, manifesting at each point of contact with the circle one of the three fundamental aspects of consciousness, known as Will, Wisdom and Activity, as well as by other terms. The joining of the three aspects, or phases of manifestation, at their outer points of contact with the circle, gives the basic triangle of contact with matter. This triangle, together with the three triangles formed by the lines traced by the point, yields the "divine tetractys," sometimes called the Kosmic Quaternary.

C 10–13. Taking now the changes set up in universal matter, corresponding to the manifestations of consciousness,

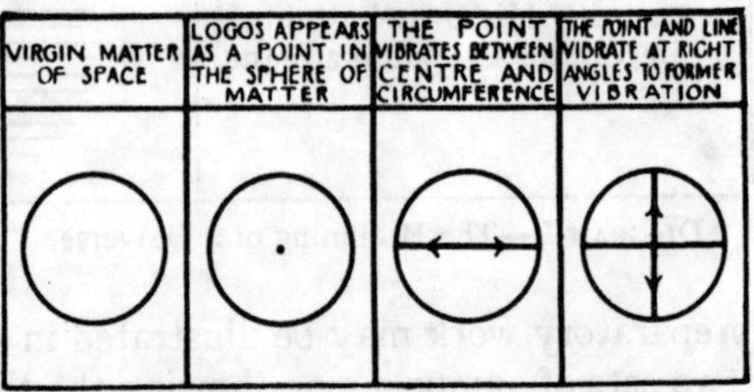

DIAGRAM III.—The Response of Matter.

we have, in the sphere of primordial substance, the virgin matter of space (see Diagram III): (1) the Logos appearing as a point irradiating the sphere of matter; (2) the point vibrating between centre and circumference, thus making the line which marks the drawing apart of spirit and matter; (3) the point, with the line revolving with it, vibrating at right angles to the former vibration, and forming the primordial Cross within the circle.

The Cross is thus said to "proceed" from the Father (the point) and the Son (the diameter), and represents the Third Logos, the Creative Mind, the divine Activity ready to manifest as Creator.

CHAPTER III

THE COMING FORTH OF THE MONADS

S C 13–14 : 48. *P M* 23–24 *S S* 18.

BEFORE considering the creative activity of the Third Logos, and the detailed preparation of the field of evolution, we must note the origination of the Monads, or units of consciousness, for whose evolution in matter the field of a universe is prepared. We shall return to their fuller consideration in a later chapter.

The myriads of these units, who are to be developed in the coming universe, are generated within the divine life, *before* the field for their evolution is formed. Of this forthgoing it has been written : " That willed : I shall multiply and be born " (*Chhandopanishat* VI. ii. 3) : thus the Many arise in the One by that act of will. The act of will is that of the First Logos, the undivided Lord, the Father.

The Monads are described as sparks of the Supreme Fire, as " Divine fragments." The Occult Catechism, quoted in *The Secret Doctrine*, I., 145, says : " ' Lift thy head, O Lanoo ; dost thou see one, or countless, lights above thee, burning in the dark midnight sky ?' ' I sense one Flame, O Gurudeva ; I see countless undetached sparks shining in it.' " The Flame is Īshvara, in His manifestation as the First Logos ; the undetached sparks are the Monads, human and other. The word " undetached " should be especially noted, as signifying that the Monads *are* the Logos Himself.

A Monad may thus be defined as a fragment of the divine life, separated off as an individual entity by rarest film of matter, matter so rare that, while it gives a separate form to each, it offers no obstacle to the free inter-communication of a life, thus encased, with the surrounding similar lives.

A Monad is thus not pure consciousness, pure Self, *I Y* 13 : 58
samvit. That is an abstraction. In the concrete universe there are always the Self and his sheaths, however tenuous the sheaths may be, so that a unit of consciousness is inseparable from matter. Hence a Monad is consciousness *plus* matter.

The Monad of Theosophy is the Jīvātmā of Indian philosophy, the Purusha of the Sāmkya, the particularised Self of the Vedānta.

The life of the Monads being thus of the First Logos, *S C* 13-15.
they may be described as Sons of the Father, just as *M* 1.
the Second Logos Himself is the Son of the Father; but the Monads are but younger Sons, with none of their divine powers capable of acting in matter denser than that of their own plane—the Anupādaka; while the Second Logos, with ages of evolution behind Him, stands ready to exercise His divine powers, "the first-born among many brethren."

Whilst the roots of their life are in the Ādī plane, the Monads themselves dwell on the Anupādaka plane, as yet without vehicles in which they can express themselves, awaiting the day of "manifestation of the Sons of God." There they remain, while the Third Logos begins the external work of manifestation, shaping the matter of the objective universe. This work will be described in the next chapter.

Diagram IV indicates the Monads, waiting on their own plane whilst the world in which they are to develop is being fashioned.

These Units of Consciousness, known as Monads, are *S C* 46.
described as the Sons, abiding from the beginning of a creative age, in the "bosom of the Father," who have not yet been "made perfect through suffering." Each of them is truly "equal to the Father as touching his Godhead, but inferior to the Father as touching his manhood"—in the words of the Athanasian Creed. Each of them is to go forth into matter in order to "render all things subject to himself" (1 Corinthians xv. 28). He is to be "sown in weakness" that he may be "raised in power" (*ibid.* xv. 43). From a static

condition, enfolding all divine potentialities, he is to become dynamic, unfolding all divine powers.

Whilst omniscient, omnipresent, on his own plane—the Anupādaka—he is unconscious, " senseless " on all the others ; he is to veil his glory in matter that blinds him, in order that he may become omniscient, omnipresent, on *all* planes, able to answer to all divine vibrations in the universe, instead of only to those of the highest levels.

S C 48 : 51–52. As the Monads derive their being from the First

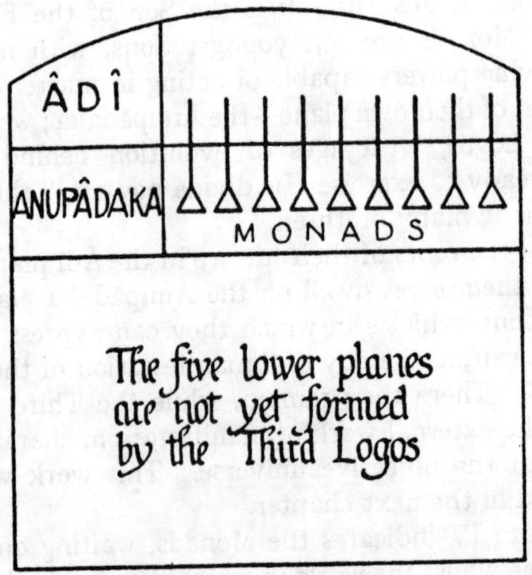

DIAGRAM IV.—The Coming Forth of the Monads.

Logos, His will to manifest is also their will. Hence the whole process of the evolution of the individual "I" is an activity chosen by the Monads themselves. We are here, in the worlds of matter, because we, as Monads, willed to live : we are Self-moved, Self-determined.

This divine impulse, striving ever after fuller manifestation of life, is seen everywhere in nature, and has often been spoken of as the Will-to-live. It appears in the seed, which pushes its growing point up towards the light, in the bud bursting its prison and expanding in the sunshine. It is the creative genius in the painter, the sculptor, the poet, the musician, the craftsman. The subtlest pleasure, the keenest savour of exquisite delight, derives from this urge, from within, to create. All things feel most alive when multiplying themselves by creation. To expand, to increase, results from the Will-to-live : the fruition is the Bliss of living, the joy of being alive.

CHAPTER IV

THE FORMATION OF THE FIVE PLANES

S C 17–21. CONTINUING now with the creative process, the Third
S D I 105. Logos, the Universal Mind, works on the matter of
M 3. space—Mūlaprakriti, the celestial Virgin Mary—throwing its three qualities of Tamas (Inertia), Rajas (Mobility), and Sattva (Rhythm) out of stable into unstable equilibrium, and therefore into continual motion in relation to each other.

The Third Logos thus creates the atoms of the five lower planes—Ātmā, Buddhi, Manas, Kāma and Sthūla: "Fohat electrifies into life and separates primordial stuff, or pregenetic matter, into atoms."

We may note, parenthetically, that there are three stages in the formation of these atoms :—

(1) The fixing of the limit within which the life of the Logos shall vibrate, this being known as the "divine measure" or Tanmātra, literally "the measure of That," "That" being the divine Spirit.

(2) The marking out of the axes of growth of the atom, the lines which determine its shape: these correspond with the axes of crystals.

(3) From the measurement of the vibration, and the angular relation of the axes with each other, the surface or wall of the atom is determined.

S C 25–26. Under the directive activity of the Third Logos, the
M V I 36. atoms of each plane are awakened to new powers and possibilities of attraction and repulsion, so that they aggregate into molecules, and simpler molecules into complex ones, until, on each of the five planes, six lower sub-planes are formed, making in all seven sub-planes on each plane.

The matter of the sub-planes so formed, however, is not that now existing: it is the more strongly attractive or cohesive energies of the Second Logos, the aspect of Wisdom or Love, which brings about the further integrations into the forms of matter with which we are acquainted.

Furthermore, the whirling currents in the atoms, known as spirillæ, are *not* made by the Third Logos, but by the Monads, with whom we shall deal presently. The spirillæ are developed into full activity in the course of evolution, normally one in each Round. S C 28–29.

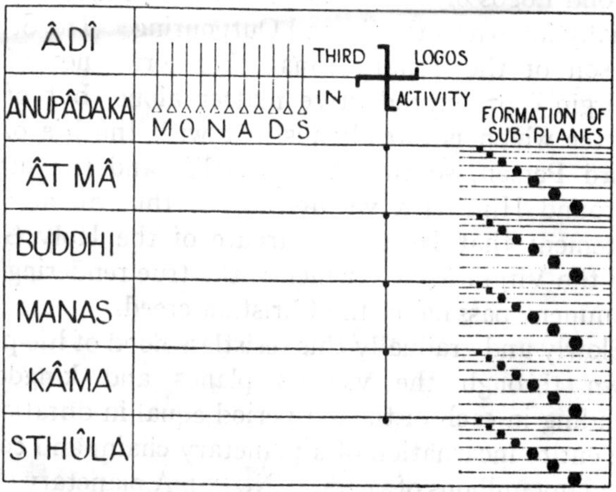

ÂDÎ
ANUPÂDAKA
MONADS
THIRD LOGOS IN ACTIVITY
FORMATION OF SUB-PLANES
ÂTMÂ
BUDDHI
MANAS
KÂMA
STHÛLA

DIAGRAM V.—The Formation of the Five Lower Planes.

Many of the practices of Yoga are directed to bring about the more rapid development of the spirillæ.

Thus in every atom lie involved innumerable possibilities of response to the three aspects of consciousness, and these possibilities are developed in the atom in the course of evolution. S C 31

This work of the Third Logos is usually spoken of as the First Life Wave, or First Outpouring.

Diagram V illustrates this work of the Third Logos or First Outpouring. We shall consider the matter a little further, and the *ascent* of the First Outpouring, in the next and later chapters, after we have dealt with the Second Outpouring.

CHAPTER V

THE KINGDOMS OF LIFE

M V I 37–40.
S C 69–72.
T B 28–32.
Ch. 13.
M 3–4.
T 85–86.
D P 88–92.

INTO the matter vivified by the Third Logos, the second great wave of the divine life descends, coming from the Second Logos or Second Person of the Trinity: this is usually known as the Second Outpouring. The Second Person of the Trinity thus takes form, not of the "virgin" or unproductive matter alone, but of the matter which is already instinct with the life of the Third Person, so that both the life and the matter surround Him as a vesture. It is thus an accurate statement that He is "incarnate of the Holy Ghost *and* the Virgin Mary," which is the true rendering of a prominent passage in the Christian creed.

Slowly and gradually this resistless flood of life pours down through the various planes and kingdoms, spending in each of them a period equal in duration to one entire incarnation of a planetary chain, and covering many millions of years. (NOTE: A planetary chain consists of seven globes of matter, of various grades, round which the stream of evolving lives passes seven complete times.)

At various stages of its descent, the life of the Second Outpouring is known by various names. As a whole, it is often spoken of as monadic essence, though this term is better confided to that portion of it which is clothed only in the *atomic* matter of the various planes. This name was originally given to it because it has become fit to provide permanent atoms to Monads.

When it ensouls matter of the lower sub-planes of each plane, *i.e.* all the sub-planes below the atomic, which consist of molecular matter, it is known as Elemental Essence. This name is borrowed from the writings of mediæval occultists, it having been bestowed by them on the matter of which the bodies of nature-spirits were composed: for they spoke of these as "Elementals," dividing them into classes belonging to the "Elements" of Fire, Air, Water and Earth.

When the Outpouring, or wave of the Divine Life—which in some previous æon has finished its downward evolution through the buddhic plane—pours down into the highest level of the mental plane, it ensouls great masses of the atomic mental matter. In this, its simplest condition, it does not combine the atoms into molecules in order to form a body for itself, but simply applies by its attraction an immense compressing force to them.

We may imagine the force, on first reaching this plane on its downward swoop, to be entirely unaccustomed to its vibrations, and unable at first to respond to them. During the æon which it will spend on this level, its evolution will consist in accustoming itself to vibrate at all rates which are possible there, so that at any moment it can ensoul and use any combination of the matter of that plane. During this long period of evolution it will have taken upon itself all possible combinations of the matter of the three arūpa (formless), or causal levels, but at the end of the time it returns to the atomic level—not, of course, as it was before, but bearing latent within it all the powers which it has gained.

The Wave of Life, then, having drawn together the matter of the causal plane, combines it into what at that level corresponds to substances, and of these substances builds forms which it inhabits. This is called the First Elemental Kingdom.

As we are here dealing with the monadic essence on its *downward* arc, progress for it means descent into matter instead of, as with us, ascent towards higher planes. Hence this essence, even on the causal plane, is less evolved than we are, not more so: but it would perhaps be more accurate to say that it is less *in*-volved, as its *e*-volution, in the strict sense of that term, has not yet commenced.

There are seven sub-divisions in the First Elemental Kingdom: the highest corresponds with the first subplane; the second, third and fourth correspond with the second sub-plane; the fifth, sixth and seventh correspond with the third sub-plane.

After spending a whole chain-period evolving through different forms at that level, the wave of life, which is all the time pressing steadily downwards, identifies itself so fully with those forms that, instead of occupying them and withdrawing from them periodically, it is able to hold them permanently and make them part of itself. When that stage is reached, it can proceed to the temporary occupation of forms at a still lower level. Accordingly it takes forms on the lower mental or rūpa (form) levels of the mental plane, and is known then as the Second Elemental Kingdom. The student should note that the ensouling life resides on the higher mental or causal level, while the vehicles through which it manifests are on the lower mental plane.

The Second Elemental Kingdom is divided into seven sub-divisions: the highest sub-division corresponds with the fourth sub-plane; the second and third divisions with the fifth sub-plane; the fourth and fifth sub-divisions with the sixth sub-plane; the sixth and seventh divisions with the seventh sub-plane.

For convenience of reference, the sub-divisions of the First and Second Elemental Kingdoms are tabulated thus:—

Plane.	Sub-Planes.	Elemental.	
		Sub-divisions.	Kingdoms.
Higher Mental	1	1	FIRST.
	2	2 : 3 : 4	
	3	5 : 6 : 7	
Lower Mental	4	1	SECOND.
	5	2 : 3	
	6	4 : 5	
	7	6 : 7	

After spending a whole chain-period at this stage, the continuous downward pressure has caused the process to repeat itself. Once more the life has identified itself with its forms, and has taken up its residence on the lower mental levels. Then it takes for itself forms of astral matter, and becomes the Third Elemental Kingdom.

As we saw in *The Astral Body* and *The Mental Body*, both mental and astral elemental essences are very intimately connected with man, entering largely into the composition of his vehicles.

After spending a whole chain-period in the Third Elemental Kingdom, the life again identifies itself with those forms, and so is able to ensoul the etheric part of the mineral kingdom, becoming the life which vivifies that kingdom.

In the course of the mineral evolution, the downward pressure again causes the life to identify itself with the etheric forms, and from those forms to ensoul the denser matter of such minerals as are perceptible to our senses.

What we know as the mineral kingdom includes, of course, not only what are usually called minerals, but also liquids, gases, and many etheric substances as yet unknown to Western orthodox science.

When in the mineral kingdom, the life is sometimes called "the mineral monad," just as at later stages it has been named "the vegetable monad" and "the animal monad." These titles, however, are somewhat misleading, because they seem to suggest that one great monad animates the entire kingdom, which is not the case, because even when the monadic essence first appears before us as the First Elemental Kingdom, it is already not one monad, but very many monads: not one great life-stream, but many parallel streams, each possessing characteristics of its own.

When the Outpouring has reached the central point of the mineral kingdom, the downward pressure ceases, and is replaced by an upward tendency. The "outbreathing" has ceased, and the "inbreathing" or indrawing has begun.

It will be noted that, if there were but one Outpouring of life, which passed from one kingdom to the next, there would be in existence at any given time one kingdom only. This, however, as we know, is not the case: the reason is, that the Logos sends out a constant succession of waves of life, so that at any given time we find a number of them in operation. Thus we ourselves represent one such wave; the wave that immediately followed our wave now ensouls the animal kingdom; the wave behind that is now in the vegetable kingdom; a fourth is in the mineral stage; whilst a fifth, sixth and seventh are represented by the three Elemental Kingdoms. All these are successive ripples of the same great Outpouring from the Second Aspect of the Logos.

The whole scheme tends increasingly towards differentiation, the streams as they descend from kingdom to kingdom dividing and sub-dividing more and more. It may be that before all this evolution takes place there is a point at which we may think of the great Outpouring as homogeneous, but of that nothing is known.

The process of sub-division continues until, at the end of the first great stage of evolution, it is finally divided into individualities, *i.e.* into men, each man being a separate and distinct soul, though at first, of course, an undeveloped soul.

S C 72–74. Looking at the work of the Second Life-Wave, or Second Outpouring, as a whole, we may fairly regard its downward sweep as concerned with the making of primary tissues, out of which in due time subtle and dense bodies will be formed. In certain ancient scriptures this process has been aptly called "weaving."

The materials, which are prepared by the Third Logos, are woven by the Second Logos into threads and fabrics out of which future garments—*i.e.* bodies—will be made.

The Third Logos may be thought of as the Chemist,

working as in a laboratory ; the Second Logos we may regard as the Weaver, working as in a manufactory. Materialistic as are these similes, they are useful as crutches for the understanding.

The Second Logos thus " weaves " various kinds of cloth, *i.e.*, of material, out of which will later be made the causal and mental bodies of men ; out of the cloth of astral matter, of desire-stuff, will later be made the astral bodies of men.

Thus are fashioned the materials of the mechanism of consciousness, the characteristics of each class of material being determined by the nature of the aggregations of particles—texture, colour, density, and so forth.

All this downward sweep of the life-wave through the planes, giving qualities to the many grades of matter, is a preparation for evolution, and is often, and more properly, called *in*volution. *S C* 74. *Ch* 16.

After the lowest stage of immersion in matter is reached, *both* the First and the Second Outpourings turn upwards, and begin their long ascent through the planes : this is evolution properly so called.

Diagram VI is an attempt to illustrate graphically the First Outpouring, from the Third Logos, forming the matter of the five lower planes, and the Second Outpouring which, taking the matter vivified by the Third Logos, moulds and ensouls it so as to produce the three Elemental Kingdoms and the Mineral Kingdom, and, in due succession, the vegetable and animal kingdoms.

There is indicated also on the diagram the Third Outpouring, from the First Logos, the Outpouring from which results the formation of individual entities, or human beings. With this, however, we shall deal more fully at a later stage of our study.

The student should take careful note of the exact position of the figures in Diagram VI, representing each kingdom. Thus the mineral is shown of full width in the denser part of the physical plane, showing that the life there, such as it is, has full control over the dense physical matter. But the band grows steadily narrower *M V I* 47–51.

as it mounts up through the etheric sub-planes, indicating that control over etheric matter is not yet perfectly developed.

The small point penetrating into the astral plane indicates that a little consciousness works through astral matter. This consciousness is the beginning of desire, expressed in the mineral kingdom as chemical affinity, etc. We shall refer to this again when we come to Mineral Group-Souls.

The band representing the vegetable kingdom has full width in the whole of the physical plane, dense as well as etheric. The portion representing astral con-

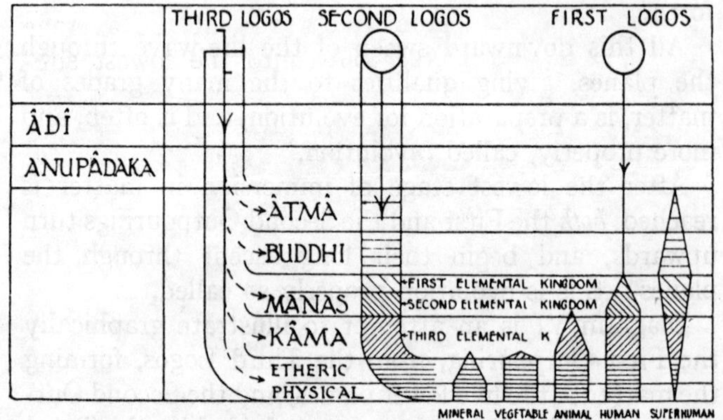

Diagram VI.—The Kingdoms of Life.

sciousness is, of course, much larger, because desire is much more fully developed in the vegetable than in the mineral kingdom. Students of plant life will know that many members of the vegetable kingdom exhibit a great deal of ingenuity and sagacity in attaining their ends, limited though those ends may seem to us, regarded from our point of view. The student is recommended in this connection to such books as *The Sagacity and Morality of Plants*, by J. E. Taylor.

In the animal kingdom the band shows that there is full development in the lowest astral sub-plane, showing that the animal is capable of experiencing to the fullest possible extent the lower desires ; but the narrowing of the band through the higher sub-planes shows that his capacity for the higher desires is much more limited. Nevertheless it does exist, so that it happens, in exceptional cases, that he may manifest an exceedingly high quality of affection and devotion.

The band representing the animal shows also that there is already a development of intelligence, which needs mental matter for its expression. It is now generally admitted that some animals, both domestic and wild, undoubtedly exercise the power of reasoning from cause to effect, although the lines along which their reason can work are naturally few and limited, nor is the faculty powerful as yet.

As the band is intended to represent the average animal, the point pierces only into the lowest subplane of the mental plane; with the highly developed domestic animal the point might readily extend even to the highest of the four lower levels, though of course it would remain only a point, and by no means the full width of the band.

As we are considering here the relative degrees of *M V I* 52–53.
consciousness in the various kingdoms, we may as well anticipate somewhat, and indicate the stage at which man has arrived. The band representing the human kingdom is seen to be of full width up to the lowest level of the mental plane, indicating that up to that level his reasoning faculty is fully developed. In the higher sub-divisions of the lower mental plane, the faculty of reason is not yet fully developed, as indicated by the narrowing of the band.

An entirely new factor, however, is introduced by the point on the higher mental or causal plane, because man possesses a causal body and a permanent reincarnating ego.

In the case of the great majority of men, the consciousness does not rise beyond the third mental subplane. Gradually only, as his development proceeds, the ego is able to raise his consciousness to the second or the first of the mental sub-planes.

The band on the extreme right-hand side represents *M V I* 64–65.

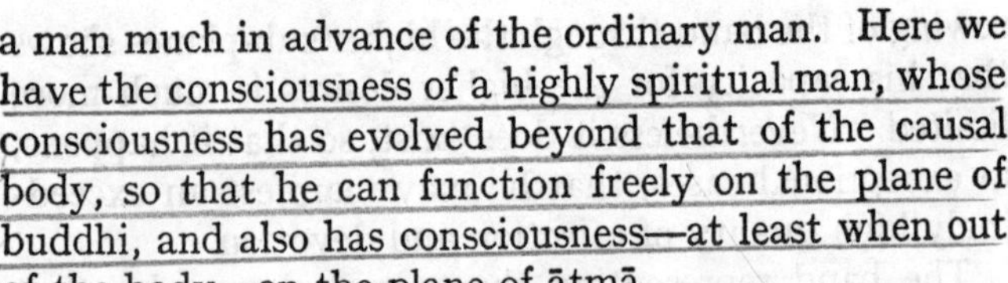

a man much in advance of the ordinary man. Here we have the consciousness of a highly spiritual man, whose consciousness has evolved beyond that of the causal body, so that he can function freely on the plane of buddhi, and also has consciousness—at least when out of the body—on the plane of ātmā.

It will be noted that the centre of his consciousness, indicated by the widest part of the band, is not, as in the case of most men, on the physical and astral planes, but between the higher mental and the buddhic planes. The higher mental and higher astral are much more developed than are their lower parts, and, although he still retains his physical body, yet this is indicated merely by a point, the explanation being that he holds it solely for the convenience of working in it, and not in any way because his thoughts and desires are fixed there. Such a man has transcended all karma which could bind him to incarnation, so that he takes the lower vehicles solely in order that through them he may be able to work for the good of humanity, and to pour out at those levels forces which otherwise could not descend so far.

S C 68. After this necessary digression, in order to explain the relative degrees of consciousness attained by each of the kingdoms of nature, it is important to note that the evolutionary process, which leads out into expression the *in*volved consciousness, has to begin by contacts received by its *outermost* vehicle, *i.e.*, it must begin on the physical plane. The consciousness can become aware of an outside only by impacts on its own outside. Until then it dreams within itself, as the faint inner thrillings ever outwelling from the Monad cause slight pressure in the Jīvātmā (Ātmā-Buddhi-Manas), like a spring of water beneath the earth, seeking an outlet.

With this process of ascent, and the Third Outpouring, which results in the formation of the causal body of man, we shall deal in succeeding chapters in due course.

Ch 13–14. Reverting to the Second Outpouring, we must note that it not only divides itself to an almost infinite degree, but also appears to differentiate itself, so that it comes through countless millions of channels on every plane and sub-plane. Thus, on the buddhic plane it appears as the Christ-principle in man; in man's mental and astral bodies it vivifies various layers of matter, appearing in the higher part of the astral as a noble emotion, in the lower part as a mere rush of life-force energising the matter of that body. In its lowest embodiment it rushes from the astral body into the etheric chakrams or force-centres, where it meets the Kundalinī welling up from the interior of the human body.

We may also note here, parenthetically, that Kundalinī, or the serpent-fire, which wells up from the interior of the human body, belongs to the First Outpouring, and exists on all planes of which we know anything. This force of Kundalinī is, of course, quite distinct from Prāna or Vitality, which belongs to the Second Outpouring, and also from Fohat, *i.e.*, from all forms of physical energy such as electricity, light, heat, etc. (*vide The Etheric Double, The Astral Body and The Mental Body, passim*). *Ch* 14–15.

Kundalinī in the human body comes from that "laboratory of the Holy Ghost" deep down in the earth, where are still being manufactured new chemical elements, showing increasing complexity of form, and more and more energetic internal life and activity.

But Kundalinī is *not* that portion of the First Outpouring engaged in the work of building chemical elements: it is more of the nature of a further development of the force which is in the living centre of such elements as radium. Kundalinī is part of the First Outpouring, *after* it has reached its lowest immersion in matter, and is once more ascending towards the heights from which it came.

It has already been mentioned that, speaking generally, the Life-Wave which descends through the worlds of matter, on its downward sweep, causes ever-increasing differentiation; on its upward return, however, it brings about reintegration into unity. *T* 85.

CHAPTER VI

THE ATTACHMENT OF THE ATOMS: I. HIGHER TRIAD

S C 58. THE Second Outpouring not only, as we saw in the preceding chapter, streams forth into the five planes, thereby bringing into existence the elemental and other kingdoms of life, but it brings also with it into activity the Monads, who, while ready to begin their evolution, have been waiting on the Anupādaka plane until the matter of the planes was prepared for them.

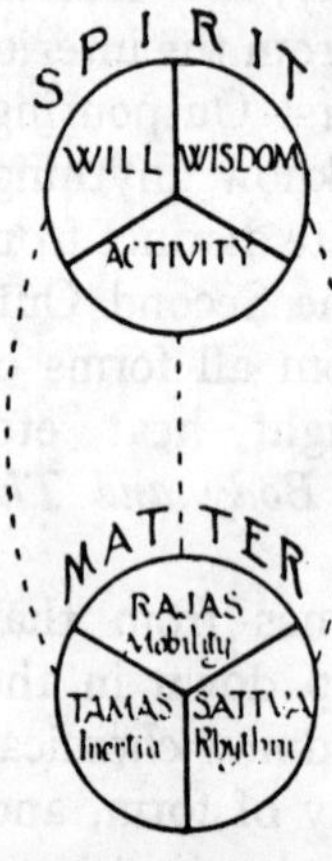

S C 59. I Y 57. To say that the Monads "go forth" would be somewhat inaccurate. It is rather that they shine forth, sending out their rays of life. They themselves remain ever "in the bosom of the Father," while their life-rays stream out into the ocean of matter, appropriating there, as we shall see in full detail presently, the materials necessary for their evolution in the lower planes.

DIAGRAM VII.—The Aspects of Consciousness and the Qualities of Matter.

The shining forth of the Monads has been graphically described by H. P. Blavatsky thus: "The primordial triangle (*i.e.*, the three-faced Monad of Will, Wisdom and Activity) as soon as it has reflected itself in the 'Heavenly Man' (*i.e.*, Ātmā-Buddhi-Manas), the highest of the lower seven—disappears, returning into 'Silence and Darkness.'"

I Y 57. The Monads themselves, therefore, remain ever beyond the fivefold universe, and in that sense are spectators. They dwell beyond the five planes of matter. They are the Self, standing Self-conscious, and Self-determined. They reign in changeless peace and live in eternity. But, as we have seen, they appropriate matter, taking to themselves atoms of the various planes.

The Monads are of seven types or "rays," just as SC 9: 94
matter also is of seven types or rays. The process by 75–79.
which the seven types arise is as follows: The three aspects of consciousness of the Logos or Universal Self, are Will (Ichchhā), Wisdom (Jnānam), and Activity (Kriyā). The three corresponding qualities in matter are Inertia (Tamas), Mobility (Rajas), and Rhythm (Sattva).

These are related as follows: The Aspect of Will imposes on matter the quality of Inertia or Tamas, the power of resistance, stability, quietude.

The Aspect of Activity gives to matter its responsiveness to action, Mobility or Rajas.

The Aspect of Wisdom gives to matter Rhythm or Sattva, harmony.

Diagram VII shows these correspondences.

Now every Monad has these three aspects of consciousness, the proportions of which may vary in different Monads in seven ways; thus :—

Predominant Aspect.	Secondary Aspect.	Tertiary Aspect.
Will	Wisdom	Activity
Will	Activity	Wisdom
Wisdom	Will	Activity
Wisdom	Activity	Will
Activity	Will	Wisdom
Activity	Wisdom	Will

The seventh variety is that in which the three aspects are equal.

The seven types of matter are similarly formed, by the varying proportions of the three qualities Tamas, Rajas and Sattva. The stream of life known as the Second Outpouring, in fact, is composed of seven streams, one of the seven types of matter-combinations being found in each of these seven streams.

Diagram VIII is an attempt to show the seven types of Monads with the seven corresponding types of matter.

M P 271. Another way of expressing the same truth, *viz.*, that each Monad belongs to one or other of the seven Rays, is to say that he came forth originally through one or other of the Seven Planetary Logoi, who may be regarded as centres of force within the Solar Logos, channels through which the force of the Solar Logos is poured out.

M P 274. Nevertheless, although, as has been said, each Monad belongs fundamentally to *one* Ray, yet he has within

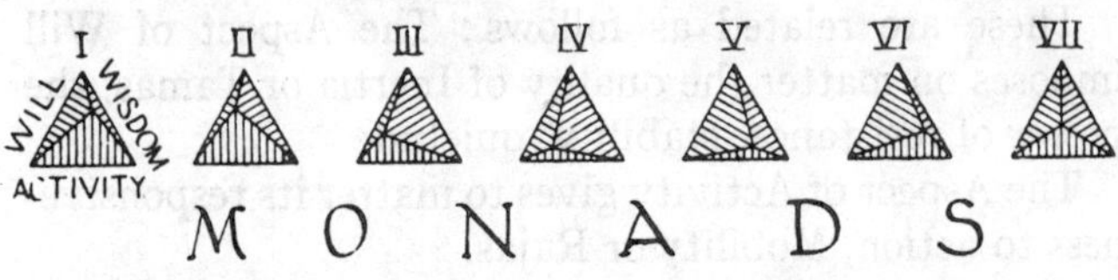

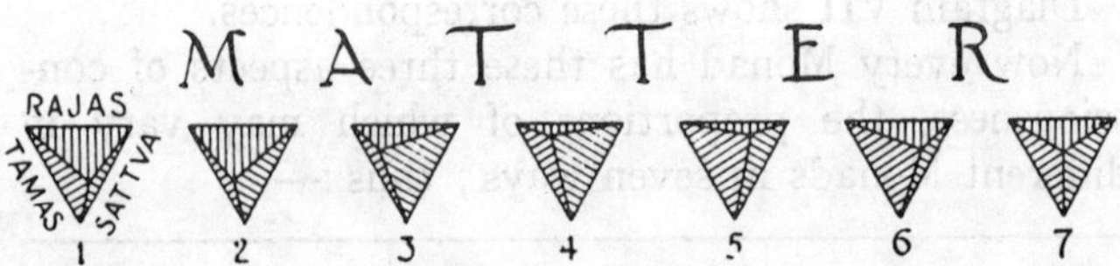

Diagram VIII.—The Seven Types of Monads and the Seven Types of Matter.

himself something of *all* the Rays. There is in him no ounce of force, no grain of matter, which is not actually part of one or other of the Seven Planetary Logoi. He is literally compacted of Their very substance, not of one, but of all, though always one predominates. Therefore, no slightest movement of any of these great Star Angels can occur without affecting to some extent every Monad, because they are bone of Their bone, flesh of Their flesh, Spirit of Their Spirit. This fact is, of course, the real basis of astrology.

M P 272. Furthermore, the bodies of those Monads, which originally came forth through a given Planetary Logos, will continue all through their evolution to have more of the particles of that Logos than of any other, and in this way men can be distinguished as primarily belonging to one or other of the seven Rays or Logoi.

M P 308–309.

Whilst the ordinary rule is that a Monad remains on the same Ray throughout the whole of his evolution, so that he eventually returns through the same Planetary Angel as that through which he first came forth, yet there are comparatively rare exceptions. For it is possible for a Monad to change his Ray, so that he will return through a Planetary Angel other than that through which he first emerged. Such transfers are usually to the First and Second Rays, there being relatively few persons on those two Rays at the lower levels of evolution.

S C 80–83: 75.

Before we can proceed to describe the method by which the atoms are attached to the Monads, there is still another factor with which we must first deal.

The Second Outpouring, in addition to its work of forming the Elemental and other Kingdoms, also brings with it evolved beings, at various stages of development, who form the normal and typical inhabitants of the three Elemental Kingdoms. These beings have been brought over by the Logos from a preceding evolution. They are now sent forth to inhabit the plane for which their development fits them; they co-operate with the work of the Logos, and later with man, in the general scheme of evolution. From them man derives his perishable bodies.

They are known in some religions as Angels, to Hindus as Devas—meaning literally, Shining Ones. Plato speaks of them as "Minor Gods." It is the translation of the word "deva" as "Gods" which has led to much misapprehension of Eastern thought. The "thirty-three crores (330 millions) of Gods" are not Gods in the Western sense of the term, but are Devas or Shining Ones.

Of these there are many grades, including representatives on each of the five lower planes, *i.e.*, those of Ātmā, Buddhi, Manas, Kāma, and the etheric part of the physical plane.

Their bodies are formed of the Elemental Essence of the Kingdom to which they belong, and are flashing and many-hued, changing form at the will of the entity himself. They form a vast host, ever actively at work, labouring at the Elemental Essence to improve its quality, taking it to form their own bodies, throwing it off again and taking other portions, so as to render it more sensitive.

In the First Elemental Kingdom, on the higher mental or causal plane, they make materials ready to clothe abstract thoughts. In the Second Elemental Kingdom, on the lower mental plane, they make materials ready to clothe concrete thoughts. In the Third Elemental Kingdom, on the astral plane, they prepare materials for the clothing of desires.

At the stage which we are now considering, this work of improving the Elemental Essence is the only work there is for them to do. Later on, they are also constantly busied in the shaping of forms, in aiding human egos on the way to incarnation in building their new bodies, bringing materials of the kind required, and helping in its arrangements. The less advanced the ego, the greater the directive work of the Devas. With animals they do almost all the work, and practically all with vegetables and minerals. They are the active agents of the Logos, carrying out all the details of His world-plan, and aiding the countless evolving lives to find materials they need for their clothing and use. Included with them are the vast numbers of the fairy kingdom, known as nature-spirits, trolls, gnomes, and by countless other names.

Some description of these hosts of beings is given in *The Astral Body* and *The Mental Body*, so that there is no need to describe them further here. All we are really concerned with at the moment is their origin, and the part they play in helping the Monads to commence their evolution in the lower planes.

The term Deva is, strictly speaking, not wide enough to cover *all* the living agencies which are employed in the work connected with the Monads and their long pilgrimage through the lower worlds. This work is carried out by no less than seven orders of beings, known collectively as Creative Hierarchies, the Monads themselves, curiously enough, being actually one of the seven.

For our present purposes, however, in order not to make the description too complicated and involved, we shall denote all these agencies by the single term Devas. In a later and separate chapter we shall to some extent go over the ground again more in detail, and give the names and functions (so far as these are known) of the seven Creative Hierarchies.

Thus we see that before any embodied consciousness, save that of the Logos and his Creative Hierarchies, could appear, or do anything at all, a vast preliminary work had to be accomplished, preparing the " form-side " of the field of evolution.

We now have the three factors needed to enable us to consider the attachment of the atoms to the Monads: these three are: (1) the atoms of the various planes; (2) the readiness of the Monads themselves on the Anupādaka plane; (3) the assistance of the Devas, without whom the Monads by themselves would be powerless to carry out their evolution.

A Monad, as we have seen, possesses three aspects of consciousness, each of which, when the time comes for the evolutionary process to begin, sets up what may be termed a vibratory wave, thus causing to vibrate the atomic matter of the planes of Ātmā, Buddhi, and Manas which surrounds him. *S C* 60–65. *P M* 26.

Devas from a previous universe, who have themselves passed through a similar experience before, guide the vibratory wave from the Will-aspect of the Monad to an atom of Ātmā, which thus becomes " attached " to the Monad, and is its Ātmic permanent atom, so called because it remains with the Monad throughout the whole process of evolution.

Similarly, the vibratory wave from the Wisdom-aspect of the Monad is guided by Devas to an atom of Buddhi, which becomes the Buddhic permanent atom.

Similarly, also, the vibratory wave from the Activity-aspect of the Monad is guided by Devas and attached to an atom of Manas, which becomes the third permanent atom. Thus is formed Ātmā-Buddhi-Manas, often called the Ray of the Monad.

Diagram IX illustrates the process just described.

A W 220-221. A graphic description of the process is as follows: from the luminous ocean of Ātmā a tiny thread of light is separated off from the rest by a film of buddhic matter, and from this hangs a spark which becomes enclosed in an egg-like casing of matter belonging to the formless levels of the mental plane. "The spark

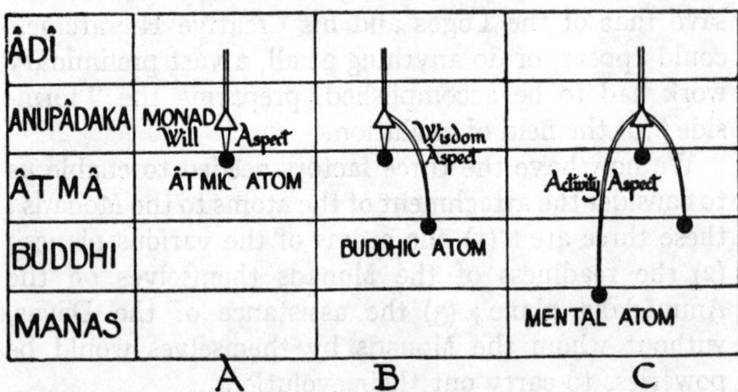

Diagram IX.—Attachment of the Ātmic, Buddhic and Mental Permanent Atoms.

hangs from the flame by the finest thread of Fohat." (*The Book of Dzyan*, vii, 5.)

S C 69. As said, those atoms which are attached to Monads become, and are called "permanent atoms"; H. P. Blavatsky spoke of them as "life-atoms" (*The Secret Doctrine*, ii, 709). The remainder of the atoms of the various planes, which are *not* attached to Monads, remain and continue to be called the Monadic Essence of each plane. The term is perhaps a little misleading, but it was given in the first instance, because (as mentioned in Chapter V) the essence at this stage is *suitable* to be attached to Monads as permanent atoms, though by no means all of it does actually become so attached.

Ātmā-Buddhi-Manas, the Ray of the Monad, is

known also by many other names; such as the Heavenly Man, the Spiritual Man, the Spiritual or Higher Triad, the Higher Self, the separated Self, and so on. The term Jīvātmā is also sometimes applied to it, though Jīvātmā, which may be rendered literally Life-Self, is of course equally applicable to the Monad. It is known also as the "manhood" of the Divine Son of the First Logos, animated by the "Godhead," *i.e.*, by the Monad. It may be regarded also as a vessel, into which the Monad pours his life.

Here we have the mystery of the Watcher, the

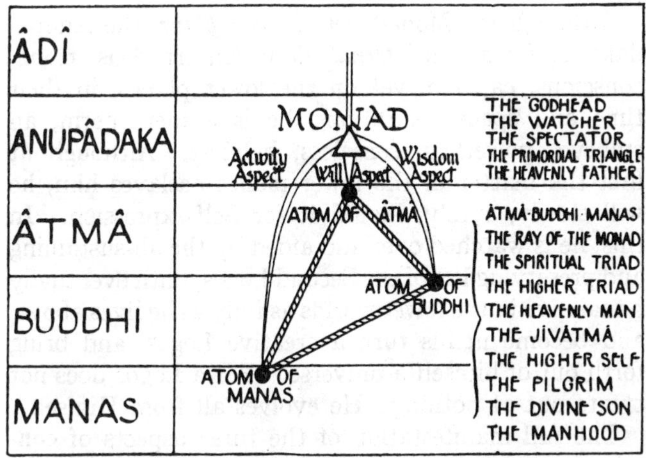

DIAGRAM X.—The Monad and the Higher Triad.

Spectator, the actionless Ātmā, *i.e.*, the Monad, who abides ever in his highest nature on his own plane, and lives in the world by his Ray (Ātmā-Buddhi-Manas), which in turn animates his "shadows," the lives or incarnations of the lower self on earth.

Diagram X illustrates the Monad and his Higher Triad.

It is important to remember that Ātmā-Buddhi-Manas, the Higher Triad, is identical in nature with the Monad, in fact *is* the Monad, though lessened in force by the veils of matter round it. This lessening of power must not blind us to the identity of nature, for it must ever be borne in mind that human consciousness is a unit, though its manifestations vary owing to the predominance of one or other of its aspects, and to the relative density of the materials in which an aspect is working at any given moment.

The Monad, having thus appropriated for his own use these three atoms, has begun his work. He himself in his own nature cannot descend below the Anupādaka plane; hence he is said to be in "Silence and Darkness," *i.e.*, unmanifest. But he lives and works in and by means of the atoms he has appropriated.

S C 65–66. Although the Monad, *on his own plane*, the Anupādaka, so far as his *internal* life is concerned, is strong, conscious, capable, yet on the lower planes, in their time and space limitations, he is a mere germ, an embryo, powerless, senseless, helpless. Although at first the matter of the lower planes enslaves him, he will slowly, surely, mould it for Self-expression. In this, he is watched over and aided by the all-sustaining and preserving life of the Second Logos, until eventually he can live in the lower worlds as fully as he lives above, and become in his turn a creative Logos, and bring forth out of himself a universe. For a Logos does not create out of nothing: He evolves all from Himself.

S C 57. The full manifestation of the three aspects of consciousness expressed by the Monad takes place in the same order as the manifestation of the triple Logos in the universe. The third aspect, Activity, revealed as the creative mind, as the gatherer of knowledge, is the first to perfect its vehicles. The second aspect, Wisdom, revealed as the Pure and Compassionate Reason, or Intuition, is the second to shine forth: this is the Krishna, the Christ, in man. The third aspect, Will, the divine Power of the Self, the Ātmā, is the last to reveal itself.

CHAPTER VII

THE ATTACHMENT OF THE ATOMS: II. LOWER TRIAD

THE spiritual Triad, Ātmā-Buddhi-Manas, having been formed, the warmth of the stream of Logoic life arouses within it faint thrillings of responsive life. After long preparation, a tiny thread, like a minute rootlet, a golden-coloured thread of life sheathed in buddhic matter, proceeds from the Triad. *S C* 85-90. *P M* 31.

This thread is sometimes called the Sūtrātmā, literally the Thread-Self, because the permanent particles will be threaded on it like beads on a string. The term, however, is used in various ways, but always to denote the idea of a thread connecting separate particles. Thus it is applied to the reincarnating Ego, as the thread on which many separate lives are strung: to the Second Logos, as the thread on which the beings in His universe are strung; and so on. It thus denotes a function, rather than a special entity or class of entities.

From each spiritual Triad appears one of these threads, which at first wave vaguely in the seven great streams of life. Then each of them is anchored, just as happened in the case of the Higher Triad, by the agency of the Devas, to a mental molecule, or unit as it is usually called, this being a particle of the fourth mental sub-plane, *i.e.*, the highest level of the lower mental plane.

Around this mental unit are gathered temporary aggregations of elemental essence of the Second Elemental Kingdom, scattering and regathering, over and over again. The vibrations of the essence gradually awaken the mental unit into faint responses, these again thrilling feebly upwards to the seed of consciousness in the Triad, producing therein vaguest internal movements.

The mental unit cannot be said to have always round it a form of its own, for there may be several or many mental units plunged into a given aggregation of essence, whilst other aggregations of essence may have only one mental unit in them, or none at all.

Thus, with inconceivable slowness, the mental units become possessors of certain qualities: *i.e.*, they acquire the power of vibrating in certain ways, which are connected with thinking, and will at a later stage make thoughts possible.

In this, they are helped by the Devas of the Second Elemental Kingdom, who direct upon them the vibrations to which they gradually begin to respond, and surround them with the elemental essence they, the Devas, throw off from their own bodies.

Furthermore, each of the seven typical groups is separated from the others by a delicate wall of monadic essence—atomic matter ensouled by the life of the Second Logos—the beginning of the wall of the future Group-Soul.

Diagram XI A illustrates the process just described.

The whole process is then repeated at the next lower level (*vide* Diagram XI B). The thread of life, ensheathed in buddhic matter, with the mental unit attached, pushes outward to the astral plane, where, by identically similar means, an astral atom is attached. Round this astral permanent atom gather temporary aggregations of elemental essence of the Third Elemental Kingdom, scattering and regathering as before.

Similar results follow, the astral atoms being gradually awakened to faint responses, these being passed upwards to the seed of consciousness, producing therein, once more, vaguest internal movements. Thus the astral permanent atoms acquire the power of vibrating in certain ways, connected with sensation, which will at a later stage make sensation possible. As before, the work is helped by the action of the Devas, of the Third Elemental Kingdom.

The separating wall of each of the seven groups now acquires a second layer, formed of astral monadic essence, thus approaching a stage nearer to the wall of the future Group-Soul.

Yet once more is the process repeated (*vide* Diagram XI c), when the great wave of life has passed onwards to the physical plane. The thread of life, sheathed in buddhic matter, with its attached mental unit and

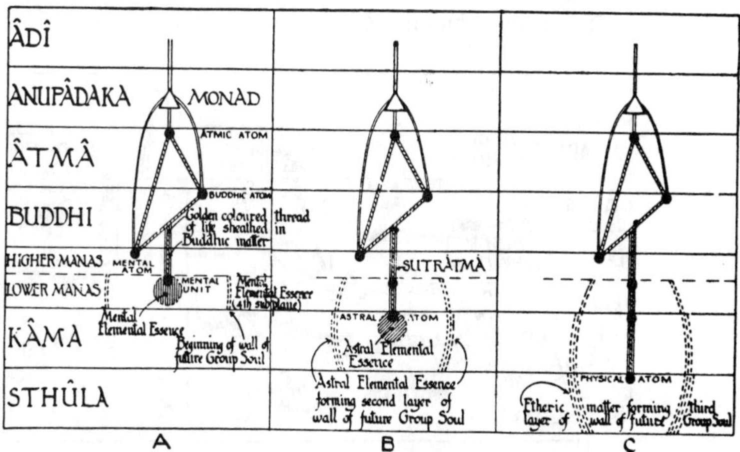

DIAGRAM XI.—Attachment of Mental Unit and Astral and Physical Permanent Atoms.

astral permanent atom, pushes outwards, and annexes a physical permanent atom. Round this atom etheric matter gathers, as before. The heavier physical matter, however, is more coherent than the subtler matter of the higher planes, and consequently a much longer term of life is observed.

Then, as the etheric types of the proto-metals, and later proto-metals, metals, non-metals and minerals are formed, the Devas of the etheric sub-planes submerge the physical permanent atoms into one or other of the seven etheric types to which they belong. Thus is begun the long physical evolution of the permanent atom.

Again, on the atomic sub-plane of the physical, a third layer is added to the separating wall which will form the envelope of the future Group-Soul.

In this manner is formed what is often called the Lower Triad, consisting of a mental unit, an astral permanent atom, and a physical permanent atom.

Diagram XII shows the stage which we have now reached, the Monad, with his three Aspects, having been provided with a Higher Triad of Ātmā-Buddhi-Manas, and the Higher Triad in its turn having been furnished with a Lower Triad of Lower-Manas-Kāma-Sthūla.

S C 93–96. It will be remembered that the matter of each plane

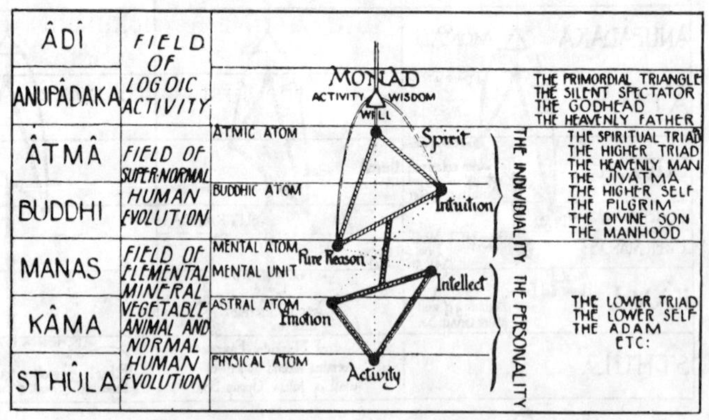

Diagram XII.—The Monad and His Atoms.

is of seven fundamental types, according to the dominance of one or other of the three great attributes of matter—Tamas, Rajas and Sattva. Hence the permanent atoms may be chosen from any one of these types. It appears, however, that each Monad chooses all his permanent atoms from the same type of matter. The choice is made by the Monad, although, as we have seen, the actual attachment is done by the Devas.

The Monad himself belongs, of course, to one of the seven fundamental types of Monads, and this is his first great determining characteristic, his fundamenta " colour," " key-note," or " temperament."

The Monad may choose to use his new pilgrimage

for the strengthening and increasing of this special characteristic, in which case the Devas will attach to his Sūtrātmā permanent atoms belonging to the group or type of matter corresponding to the type of the Monad. Such a choice would result in the secondary colour—that of the permanent atoms—emphasising and strengthening the first: in the later evolution, the powers and weaknesses of that doubled temperament would show themselves with great force.

On the other hand, the Monad may choose to use his new pilgrimage for the unfolding of another aspect of his nature. Then the Devas will attach to his Sūtrātmā atoms belonging to another matter-group, in which the aspect the Monad wishes to develop is predominant. This choice would result in the secondary "key-note" or "temperament" modifying the first, with corresponding results in later evolution. This latter choice is obviously by far more frequent, and it tends to greater complexity of character, especially in the final stages of human evolution, when the influence of the Monad makes itself felt more strongly.

Whilst the permanent atoms of both the Higher and the Lower Triads belong to the same type, the bodies of the Higher Triad, being, once formed, relatively permanent, reproduce definitely the key-note of their permanent atoms. But in the case of the bodies of the Lower Triad, various other causes operate in the determination of the choice of materials for these bodies.

The Monad can exert no *direct* action on the permanent atoms: nor could there be such direct action until the Higher Triad has reached a high stage of evolution. But the Monad can and does affect the Higher Triad, and through that exerts an *indirect* and continual action on the permanent atoms. *S C* 108–113: 103: 239–240.

The Higher Triad draws most of his energy, and all his directive capacity, from the Second Logos. But his own special activity does not concern itself with the shaping and building work of the Second Logos, being directed rather to the evolution of the atoms themselves, in association with the Third Logos. This energy from the Higher Triad confines itself to the atomic subplanes, and, until the Fourth Round, appears to spend itself chiefly on the permanent atoms.

S C 96–98: 105. The use of the permanent atoms is, of course, to preserve within themselves, as powers of vibration, the results of all the experiences through which they have passed. We may take the physical permanent atom as illustrating this process.

A physical impact of any kind will set up, in the physical body it strikes, vibrations corresponding to its own. These vibrations will be transmitted, by direct concussion if they are violent, and in all cases by the buddhic life-web, to the physical permanent atom.

Such a vibration, forced on the atom from outside, becomes in the atom a vibratory power, a tendency to repeat the vibration. Thus through the whole life of the physical body, every impact leaves its impression on the physical permanent atom. At the end of the life of the physical body, the physical permanent atom has in this way stored up innumerable powers of vibration.

The same process takes place in the case of the permanent atom or unit in each of the bodies of a man. Moreover, the student will by now be familiar with the fact that the permanent atoms—as their name implies—remain permanently with a human entity throughout the whole of his many incarnations, being, in fact, the *only* portions of his various bodies which survive and remain permanently with the evolving ego in the causal body.

The vortex, which is the atom, is the life of the Third Logos; the wall of the atom, gradually formed on the surface of this vortex, is made by the descent of the life of the Second Logos. But the Second Logos only faintly traces the outline of the spirillæ, as filmy channels: He does not vivify them.

It is the life of the Monad which, flowing down, vivifies the first of the spirillæ, making it a working part of the atom. This takes place in the First Round.

Similarly, in each successive Round, another of the spirillæ is vivified and brought into activity.

The first set of spirillæ is used by the prāna which affects the dense physical body; the second set with the prāna used by the etheric double; the third set by the prāna affecting the astral body, thus developing the power of sensation; the fourth set is used by the prāna of kāma-manas, making it fit to be used for the building of a brain as the instrument of thought.

As we are now in the Fourth Round, the normal number of spirillæ at work is four, both in the permanent atoms, and in the ordinary unattached atoms. But, in the case of a highly evolved man, the permanent atom may have five spirillæ at work, or even six. The fifth set of spirillæ will, in the normal course, be developed in the Fifth Round; but advanced people, as said, can by certain Yoga practices evolve even now both the fifth and sixth sets of spirillæ.

In addition to the permanent atoms themselves, the Monad also begins to work in a similar fashion on other atoms that are drawn round the permanent atom. Such vivification, however, is temporary only, as, when the physical body is broken up, these atoms return to the general store of atomic matter. They may then be taken up and used by some other Monad, being, of course, now more easily vivified again, on account of their former expereince.

This work takes place with all the permanent atoms of the Monad, such atoms thus evolving more rapidly than they would otherwise do, owing to their association with the Monad.

CHAPTER VIII

THE CREATIVE HIERARCHIES

As promised in Chapter VI, we now come to describe more in detail the hierarchies of beings, of various grades of power and intelligence, who build the universe, and help the Monads to undertake their vast pilgrimage through the worlds of matter.

The information at present available is somewhat fragmentary and ill-defined ; whilst recognising that this is so, we must endeavour to make the most of such few facts as are at our disposal

P M 7–8. We have already seen that the One Existence, the Supreme, from Whom all manifested life proceeds, expresses Himself in a threefold manner, as the Trimūrti, the Trinity This, of course, is recognised in practically every religion, under many names : *e.g.*, Sat, Chit, Ānanda : Brahmā, Vishnu, Shiva : Ichchhā, Jñāna, Kriyā : Cochmah, Binah, Kepher : Father, Son and Holy Spirit : Power, Wisdom, Love : Will, Wisdom, Activity, etc., etc.

P M 8–10. *S C* 49. Around the primary Trinity, in the light coming forth from Them, we find Those who are called the Seven. The Hindu speaks of the seven sons of Āditi : they have been called the Seven Spirits in the Sun : in Egypt they were known as the seven Mystery Gods : in Zoroastrianism they are named the seven Amshaspends : in Judaism they are the seven Sephiroth : among Christians and Muhammedans they are the seven Archangels, the seven Spirits before the Throne. In Theosophy they are usually termed the sever Planetary Logoi, each administering His own depar.-ment of the solar system. They have ever been identified with the seven sacred planets, the planets being their physical bodies.

Round the Seven, in a wider circle, there come the Creative Hierarchies, as they are called: the Twelve Creative Orders of the Universe. These are headed by the Twelve Great Gods, that appear in ancient stories, and that are symbolised in the familiar Signs of the Zodiac. For the Zodiac is a very ancient symbolic conception, in which the plan of the solar system is written.

When it is said that a planet "rules," or is the Lord of, one of the Signs of the Zodiac, the meaning is that the Planetary Spirit or Logos has dominion over one of the twelve Creative Hierarchies which, under His control and direction, build up His kingdom, and help the Monads to evolve.

The twelve Creative Hierarchies are thus intimately *P M* 6.
concerned with the building of the universe. These Hierarchies of Intelligence have, in past kalpas or universes, completed their own evolution, and thus become co-workers with the One Will, with Īshvara, in the shaping of a new universe, or Brahmānda. They are the Architects, the Builders of solar systems. They fill our solar system, and to them we human *S C* 50–51.
beings owe our evolution, spiritual, intellectual and physical. It is they who awaken the consciousness of the Monad and his Ray to the "dim sense of others," and of "I," and, with this, a thrill of longing for a more clearly defined sense of the "I" and of "others," this being the "individual Will-to-live," which leads them forth into the denser worlds, wherein alone such sharper definition becomes possible.

At the present stage of evolution, out of the twelve *P M* 10.
Creative Hierarchies, four have passed onward into liberation, and one is touching the threshold of liberation. Thus five have passed away from the ken of even the greatest and most developed Teachers of our world. There remain, therefore, seven only, with whom we have to deal.

Part of the work which some of them do, *viz.*, the attaching of the permanent atoms, has already been described in Chapters VI and VII. This will now be repeated, for the sake of completeness, with such few further particulars as are available, the whole work being classified into the departments for which each of the remaining seven Hierarchies is responsible.

A. The Arūpa Creative Orders

P M 11 : 25. 1. The First of the Arūpa, or Formless, Creative Orders, is described by words connected with fire. They are known as Formless Fiery Breaths, Lords of Fire, Divine Flames, Divine Fires, Fiery Lions, Lions of Life. They are described also as the Life and Heart of the universe, the Ātmā, the kosmic Will.

Through them comes the divine Ray of Paramātmā, that awakens Ātmā in the Monads.

2. The Second Order is twofold in its nature, and is known as the "twofold units," representing Fire and Ether. They stand for kosmic Buddhi, the Wisdom of the system, manifested Reason.

Their function is to arouse Buddhi in the Monads.

3. The Third Order is known as "the Triads," representing Fire, Ether and Water. They stand for Mahat, the kosmic Manas or Activity.

Their function is to awaken Manas in the Monads.

B. The Rūpa Creative Orders

P M 12–14 : 25. 4. The Fourth Creative Hierarchy consists of the Monads themselves.

At first sight, it may appear curious that the Monads themselves should be classed with the other Orders, but a little thought will show that the classification is a proper one, the Monads clearly having a great deal to do with their own evolution. It is by no means outer agencies alone that determine their involution and evolution. Let us briefly recapitulate some of the factors due to the Monads themselves.

S C 48 : 51. (1) Being of the First Logos, His will to manifest is also their will: they are self-moved.

S C 59 : 60 : 64. (2) It is the Monads who "shine forth," sending out their life, which builds the Ray or Higher Triad, and works through it.

(3) It is the Monads who choose the type of permanent atoms which are to be attached to them. *S C* 94.

(4) The Third Outpouring, resulting from which the causal body is formed, comes through the Monads themselves. *S C* 172–173.

(5) The Monads themselves pour down their life into and vivify the spirillæ in the atoms, both permanent and other. *S C* 110.

(6) The Monads, as evolution proceeds, steadily pour down more and more of their lives, gradually getting more closely into touch with their Rays—the Individuality, and also, through the Individuality, with the Personality. *S C* 95. *M P* 20: 179.

5. The Fifth Creative Hierarchy is named that of Makara, and has for its symbol the pentagon. In them the dual spiritual and dual physical aspects of nature appear, the positive and negative, at war with each other. They are the "rebels" of many myths and legends. Some of them are known as Asuras, and were the fruits of the First Chain. They are beings of great spiritual power and knowledge. Deep within themselves they hide the germ of Ahamkāra, the I-making faculty which is necessary for human evolution. *P M* 12–13.

The Fifth Hierarchy guides the vibratory wave from the Aspect of Ātmā of the Monad to an atom of Ātmā, which it attaches as a permanent atom. *P M* 26.

6. The Sixth Creative Hierarchy contains some who are known as Agnishvāttas, and also as the "sixfold Dhyānis." They are the fruit of the Second Planetary Chain. *P M* 13–14: 26.

This Hierarchy includes also great hosts of Devas.

They guide the vibratory wave from the Wisdom-aspect of the Monad to the Buddhic permanent atom.

Further, they give to man *all* but the Ātmā and the physical body, and so are called the "givers of the five middle principles." They guide the Monad in obtaining the permanent atoms (including, of course, the mental unit) connected with these principles, *i.e.*, Buddhi, Manas, Lower Manas, Kāma and the Etheric Double.

They have especially to deal with the intellectual evolution of man.

P M 14. 7. The Seventh Creative Hierarchy contains those known as Lunar Pitris, or Barhishad Pitris: these are the fruit of the Third Chain.

They have to do with the physical evolution of man.

Also belonging to the Seventh Hierarchy are vast hosts of Devas, the lower Nature-Spirits, who have to do with the actual building of the body of man.

For the convenience of the student, a tabular statement of the Creative Hierarchies is appended.

P M iv–vi: xi.

THE SEVEN CREATIVE HIERARCHIES

Class.	No.	Name.	Function of Evolution in Monads.	Notes.
A R	1	Fiery Breaths.	Awaken Ātmā.	
Ū P	2	Twofold Units.	Awaken Buddhi.	
A	3	Triads.	Awaken Manas.	
R Ū	4	Monads.	Will to manifest. Shine forth and build Ray. Choose type of permanent atoms. Channels for Third Outpouring. Vivify spirillæ of atoms. Influence Individuality and Personality.	
	5	Makara (including Asuras).	Attach atom of Ātmā.	Asuras were Fruit of First Chain.
P A	6	Agnishvāttas.	Give 5 " middle principles." Attach 4 permanent atoms and mental unit. Concerned with intellectual evolution of man.	Fruit of Second Chain.
	7	Barhishads.	Concerned with physical evolution of man.	Fruit of Third Chain.

CHAPTER IX

GROUP-SOULS

WE have now arrived at the stage where each Monad is provided with a Higher Triad, consisting of a permanent atom of the planes of Ātmā, Buddhi, and Manas, and a Lower Triad consisting of a mental unit, an astral and a physical permanent atom. These particles of matter are, of course, merely nuclei which enable the Monad, through his "ray," to come into touch with the various planes, and to build bodies or vehicles through which he can gather experiences from, and learn to express himself on, those planes of existence.

In order to understand the mechanism by which these results are achieved, we must next study the phenomena known as Group-Souls.

We have already seen that as the atoms of the Lower *S C* 87–89.
Triad are attached to the Sūtrātmā, or life-thread, thin films of matter come into existence, separating the seven main types of triads from one another. Thus are formed the seven primary groups or "rays" of triads which, by repeated division and sub-division, will give rise eventually to large numbers of Group-Souls in the various kingdoms of life.

These seven great types or "rays" of Group-Souls *T B* 37–38.
remain separate and distinct throughout all the viccissitudes of their evolution: that is to say, the seven types evolve in parallel streams, the streams never uniting or merging into one another. The seven types are clearly distinguishable in all the kingdoms, the successive forms taken by any one of them making a connected series of elementals, minerals, vegetables, or animals, as the case may be.

These seven Primary Group-Souls appear as vague, *S C* 115–116.
filmy forms, floating in the great ocean of matter as

balloons might float in the sea. They are seen first on the mental plane, becoming more clearly outlined on the astral plane, and still more so on the physical plane.

They float, one in each of the seven main streams of the Second Life-Wave.

Within each Primary Group-Soul there are, of course, innumerable Lower Triads, each connected by the radiant golden thread to its Higher Triad, these again depending from the overhanging Monad. As yet no golden life-web appears round the Triads ; this will not come into existence until the mineral kingdom is reached.

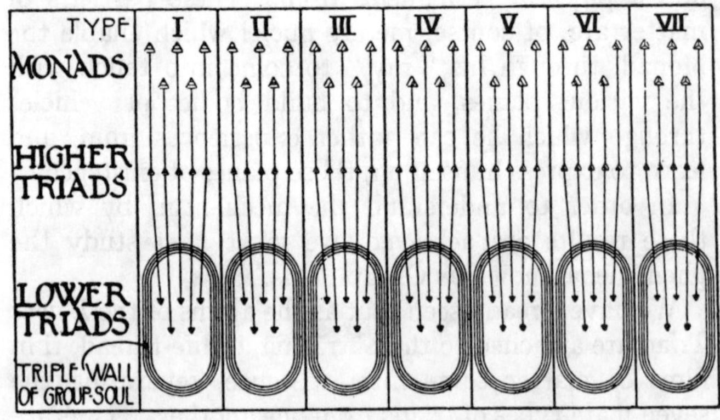

DIAGRAM XIII.—The Seven Primary Group-Souls.

Diagram XIII roughly illustrates the stage now reached. The very small number of Triads, which the limitations of space make it possible to show in the seven Group-Souls, must be considered as representing vastly larger numbers, with, of course, their connected higher Triads, and Monads.

The stage shown in the diagram is that at which the thin film or veil separating the seven Primary Group-Souls has received its three layers : these consist of mental elemental essence, astral monadic essence and atomic matter of the physical plane. As already stated, these films or veils will eventually form the containing walls or envelopes of the Group-Souls proper.

It should be noted that these envelopes are formed of matter of the same matter-group as that to which the Triads themselves belong.

The general plan of the evolutionary process—more *M V I* 40–
strictly the *in*volutionary process—is, as we have seen, 41.
a gradual differentiation of the great stream of divine life, until, after repeated division and sub-division, definite individualisation as a human being is attained, after which no further sub-division is possible, a human entity being an indivisible unit or "soul."

Group-Souls, which exist in the mineral, vegetable and animal kingdoms, thus represent intermediate stages leading up to complete differentiation into separate human entities or units. Hence, in the three kingdoms mentioned, we do not find one soul in a block of mineral, or a plant, or an animal. Instead of this, we find one block of life—if we may use such a term—ensouling a vast quantity of mineral substance, a large number of plants or trees, or a number of animals. Into the details of these we will enter later, confining ourselves for the moment to a consideration of the general function and purpose of the Group-Souls.

The best physical analogy of a Group-Soul is perhaps *M V I* 42–
the oriental one of water in a bucket. If a glassful of 43. *T B* 35.
water be taken from the bucket, it represents the soul— *M P* 16–17.
or portion of soul—of, say, a single plant or animal. For the time being, the water in the glass is quite separate from that in the bucket, and, moreover, it takes the shape of the glass which contains it.

So may a portion of a Group-Soul occupy and vivify a vegetable or animal form.

An animal, during its life on the physical plane, and for some time after that in the astral world—has a soul, just as separate as a man's; but, when the animal comes to the end of its astral life, that soul does not reincarnate in a single body, but returns to the group-soul, which is a kind of reservoir of soul-matter.

The death of the animal would thus, in our analogy, be represented by pouring the water from the glass back into the bucket. Just as the water from the glass becomes thoroughly mixed and united with the water in the bucket, so does the portion of soul from the particular animal become mixed and incorporated with the total soul in the Group-Soul. And just as it would not be possible to take again from the bucket another glassful consisting of the same molecules of water, so is it not possible for the same portion of the total soul in the Group-Soul to inhabit another particular animal form.

Continuing the analogy further, it is clear that we could fill many glasses with water from the bucket at the same time : equally is it possible for many animal forms to be ensouled and vivified by the same Group-Soul.

Further, if we suppose that any given glassful of water becomes coloured with a distinctive hue of its own, then, when the water is poured back into the bucket, that colouring matter will be distributed throughout the whole of the water in the bucket, the colour of all the water in the bucket being thereby to some extent modified.

If we consider the colouring matter to represent experiences or qualities acquired by a particular animal, then, when the portion of soul vivifying that animal returns to its parent Group-Soul, those experiences or qualities will become part of the general stock of the whole Group-Soul and be shared by every other part of it equally, though in a lesser degree than that in which the experience existed in the particular animal to whom it occurred ; *i.e.*, we may say that the experiences concentrated in a particular animal are spread, in a diluted form, over the whole of the Group-Soul to which the animal is attached.

S C 118 There is an exact resemblance between the Group-Soul in the Mineral, Vegetable and Animal Kingdoms, and a human child in its prenatal life. Just as the human child is nourished by the life-stream of the mother, so does the protective envelope of the Group-Soul nourish the lives within it, receiving and distributing the experiences gathered in.

The circulating life is that of the parent: the young plants or animals are not yet ready for individual life, but must depend on the parent for nourishment. Thus the germinating lives of mineral, vegetable, and animal are nourished by the envelope of elemental and monadic essence, thrilling with Logic life.

The evolution of the lives in these early stages in the Group-Soul depends upon three factors: (*a*) first, and chiefly, the cherishing life of the Logos; (*b*) the co-operating guidance of the Devas; (*c*) their own blind pressure against the limits of the enclosing form. *S C* 117–118.

The general mechanism of the process by which, through these three agencies, the vibratory powers of the atoms in the Lower Triads are awakened, is as follows:— *S C* 121–123.

The Second Logos, acting in the envelope of the Group-Soul, energises the physical permanent atoms. These are plunged, by the action of the Devas, into the various conditions offered by the mineral kingdom, where each atom is attached to many mineral particles. The experiences—consisting of heat, cold, blows, pressure, shaking, etc.—through which the mineral substances pass, are conveyed to the attached physical permanent atoms, thus arousing vague answers of sympathetic vibration from the deeply slumbering consciousness within.

When any permanent atom has reached a certain responsiveness, or when a mineral form, *i.e.*, the particles to which the permanent atom is attached, is broken up, the Group-Soul withdraws that atom into itself.

The experiences acquired by that atom—*i.e.*, the vibrations it has been forced to execute—remain in it as powers of vibrating in particular ways, as vibratory powers, in short. Then the permanent atom, having lost its embodiment in the mineral form, remains, as we might say, naked in its Group-Soul: here it continues to repeat the vibrations it has learnt, repeating its life-experiences, and thus setting up pulses which run through the envelope of the Group-Soul, and are thereby conveyed to the other permanent atoms contained in that Group-Soul. Thus each permanent atom affects and helps all the others.

S C 123. *M V I* 44. *T B* 36. Now another important phenomenon arises. It is clear that those permanent atoms which have had experiences similar in character will be affected more strongly by each other than will be those whose experiences have been different. Thus a certain segregation will take place within the Group-Soul, and presently a filmy separating wall will grow inwards from the envelope, dividing these segregated groups from each other.

Reverting to the simile of the water in the bucket, we may conceive of a scarcely perceptible film forming itself across the bucket. At first the water filters through this barrier to some extent ; but nevertheless the glasses of water taken out from one side of that barrier are always returned to the same side, so that by degrees the water on one side becomes differentiated from the water on the other side. Then the barrier gradually densifies, and becomes impenetrable, so that eventually there are two distinct portions of water instead of one.

In similar fashion, the Group-Soul after a time divides itself by fission, and forms two Group-Souls. The process is repeated over and over again, producing an ever-increasing number of Group-Souls, with contents showing a correspondingly ever-increasing distinction of consciousness, while, of course, still sharing certain fundamental characteristics.

S C 126–128. The laws according to which permanent atoms in a Group-Soul are plunged into the kingdoms of nature are as yet by no means clear. There are indications that the evolution of the mineral, vegetable and the lowest part of the animal kingdom belongs rather to the evolution of the earth itself than to that of the Triads, representing the Monads, who are evolving in the solar system and who come, in due course, to the earth to pursue their evolution by utilising the conditions it affords.

Thus, grass and small plants of every kind seem to be related to the earth itself much as man's hairs are related to his body, and not to be connected with the Monads and their Triads. The life in grass, etc., appears to be that of the Second Logos, which holds them together as forms, whilst the life in the atoms and molecules composing them is, of course, that of the Third Logos, modified not only by the Planetary Logos of our system of Chains, but also by a somewhat obscure entity known as the Spirit of the Earth. Thus these kingdoms, while offering a field for the evolution of Monads and their Triads, do not appear to exist by any means solely for that purpose.

Hence we find permanent atoms scattered through the vegetable and mineral kingdoms, though we do not as yet understand the reasons governing their distribution. A permanent atom, for example, may be found in a pearl, a ruby, or a diamond ; many will be found scattered through veins of ore, and so on. But, on the other hand, much mineral substance does not seem to contain any permanent atoms.

Similarly with short-lived plants. But in plants of long continuance, such as trees, permanent atoms are constantly found. But here again the life of the tree seems to be more closely related to the Deva evolution than to the evolution of the consciousness to which the permanent atom is attached.

It is, therefore, rather as though advantage were taken of the evolution of life and consciousness in the tree for the benefit of the permanent atom. The permanent atom may thus be said to be there more as a parasite, profiting by the more highly evolved life in which it is bathed. The student must recognise that at the moment our knowledge on these matters is extremely fragmentary.

Having now studied the general nature and functions of Group-Souls, we can pass on to consider more in detail Mineral, Vegetable and Animal Group-Souls, commencing with the Mineral Group-Soul.

CHAPTER X

MINERAL GROUP-SOULS

S C 114–116. Diagram XIV is an attempt to illustrate a Mineral Group-Soul. It will be seen that the wall or envelope of the Group-Soul has three layers: the outermost is composed of physical atomic matter; the central one of astral monadic essence; the innermost one of mental elemental essence, *i.e.*, matter of the fourth mental sub-plane.

A Mineral Group-Soul may thus be defined as a collection of Triads, enclosed in a triple envelope consisting of mental elemental essence, astral monadic essence, and physical atomic matter.

Within the Group-Soul are shown some Lower Triads, attached, of course, to their respective Higher Triads, these again being linked to their over-shadowing Monads. These Triads within the Group-Soul are not at the moment plunged into any mineral substance.

Below the Group-Soul are shown a number of irregular shapes, which are intended to represent groups or blocks of mineral substances. Within some of these blocks are to be seen some Lower Triads, the lines rising upwards from these indicating that they belong to their parent Group-Soul hovering over them.

S C 122. On the extreme right of the diagram is shown a block of mineral substance which is supposed to have been in some way shattered, so that it is broken up into fragments. The Lower Triad, which previously was immersed in it, is shown in the act of withdrawal towards its parent Group-Soul, as described on p. 49.

S C 119. The habitat of the Mineral Group-Soul may be said to be that of its densest envelope, *i.e.*, the physical: in other words, the most active working of the Mineral Group-Soul is on the physical plane.

Every Lower Triad has to pass through the mineral kingdom, this being the place where matter reaches its grossest form, and where the great Life-Wave reaches the limit of its descent, and turns to begin its upward climbing. *S C* 117.

Furthermore, it is physical consciousness that is the first to be awakened: it is on the physical plane that life must turn definitely outwards and recognise contacts with the external world. The consciousness gradually learns to recognise the impacts from without, to refer them to the outer world, and to realise as its own the changes which it undergoes in consequence of those impacts. In other words, it is on the physical plane that consciousness first becomes Self-consciousness. *S C* 120–121: 169.

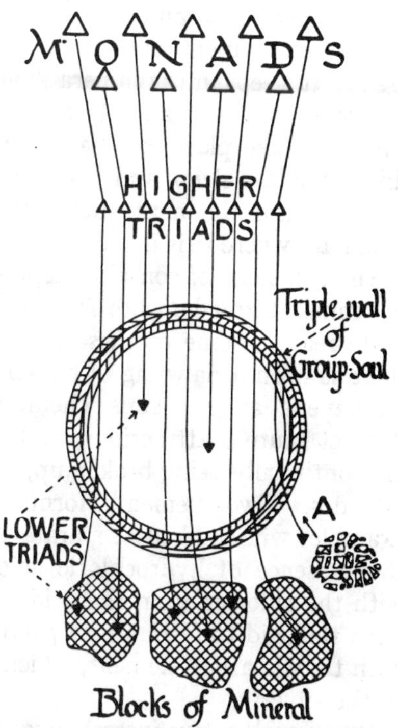

DIAGRAM XIV.—A Mineral Group-Soul.

By prolonged experiences, the consciousness feels the pleasure or pain arising from the impacts, identifies itself with that pleasure or pain, and begins to regard as *not itself* that which touches its external surface. Thus is formed the first rough distinction between "Not-I" and "I."

As experiences accumulate, the "I" will retreat ever inwards, throughout the whole of its future evolution, one veil of matter after another being relegated outwards as belonging to the "Not-I." But, while its connotations steadily change, the fundamental distinction between subject and object ever remains. "I" is the consciousness which wills, thinks, feels, acts; "Not-I" is that *about* which the consciousness wills, thinks, feels or acts.

Consciousness thus awakens on the physical plane, as we have said, and its expression is through the physical permanent atom. In this atom it lies sleeping: "It sleeps in the mineral," according to the well-known aphorism; and therein some degree of awakening must take place, so that it may be roused out of this dreamless sleep, and become sufficiently active to pass on into the next stage—that of the vegetable kingdom, where it is destined to "dream."

S C 123–125. The responses of consciousness to external stimuli in the mineral kingdom are far greater than many may quite realise, some of these responses indicating that there is even a dawning of consciousness in the astral permanent atom. Thus chemical elements exhibit distinct mutual attractions, and chemical compounds are continually being broken up, when another element intrudes. Two elements forming a silver salt, for example, will suddenly separate from one another, in the presence of hydrochloric acid, the silver uniting with the chlorine from the acid, leaving the hydrogen from the acid to form a new partnership or compound with the discarded element, which formerly was united to the silver.

When such active interchanges take place, there is a slight stir in the astral atom, in consequence of the violent physical vibrations set up by the formation of, and wrenching apart of, intimate ties.

Thus astral consciousness is slowly aroused from the physical, a little cloud of astral matter being drawn round the astral permanent atom by these slight thrillings. This astral matter is, however, very loosely held, and seems to be quite unorganised.

At this stage, there does not seem to be any vibration in the mental unit.

S O S 407.
T B 37.
M P 277. No detailed list has as yet been made of minerals,

plants or animals, of the seven Rays or types; but the following list of jewels and minerals is a beginning of the classification which will no doubt some day be made.

Ray.	Jewel at Head of Ray.	Other Jewels on same Ray.
1	Diamond .	Rock Crystal.
2	Sapphire .	Lapis Lazuli, Turquoise, Sodalite.
3	Emerald .	Aquamarine, Jade, Malachite.
4	Jasper .	Chalcedony, Agate, Serpentine.
5	Topaz .	Citrine, Steatite.
6	Ruby .	Tourmaline, Garnet, Carnelian, Carbuncle, Thulite, Rhodonite.
7	Amethyst .	Porphyry, Violane.

CHAPTER XI

VEGETABLE GROUP-SOULS

S C 119. A VEGETABLE Group-Soul is illustrated in Diagram XV. It will be observed that the wall of the Group-Soul has now two layers only; the outer one is composed of astral monadic essence, *i.e.*, of astral atomic matter; the inner one of mental elemental essence, of matter of the fourth mental sub-plane. The physical layer, which the envelope of the Mineral Group-Soul possessed, has thus disappeared, as though absorbed, by the contents of the Group-Soul, for the strengthening of their own etheric bodies.

Within the Group-Soul are shown some Lower Triads, attached to their respective Higher Triads, these being again linked with their over-shadowing Monads. The Lower Triads within the Group-Soul are not at the moment directly associated with any plant life.

Below the Group-Soul are shown a number of forms which are intended to indicate groups of plants or vegetable lives. Within some of them are found some Lower Triads, the lines between these and the Group-Soul indicating that they belong to the parent Group-Soul which hovers over them.

As in the case of the Mineral Group-Soul, at A, on the extreme right of the diagram, there is shown a plant form which is supposed to have been destroyed as an organism; the Lower Triad, which was embedded in it, is released, on the destruction of the form, the Group-Soul then withdrawing it back into itself, as indicated by the arrow in the diagram.

The activity of the Group-Soul is now transferred from the physical to the astral plane, its work being the nourishment of the astral bodies of the lives it contains.

Precisely as in the case of the Mineral Group-Souls, we may repeat that it is not to be supposed that every blade of grass, every plant, every tree, has a permanent atom within it, evolving to humanity during the life of our system. It is rather that the vegetable kingdom, which exists on its own account, and for other purposes, also affords the field of evolution for these permanent atoms, the Devas guiding the permanent atoms to one plant-form after another, so that they may experience the vibrations that affect the vegetable world, and again store up these as vibratory powers in themselves, as they did whilst they were embedded in the mineral kingdom. S C 125.

The method of interchange of vibrations, and consequently of segregation, continue as before. The Group-Souls therefore constantly divide and sub-divide, becoming thus not only more numerous, but also more different from one another in their leading characteristics.

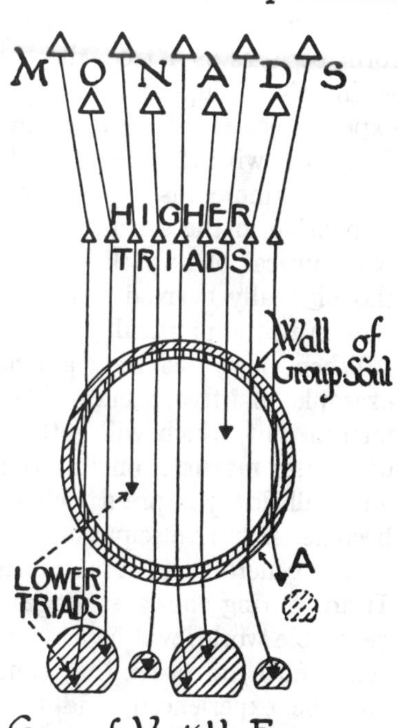

DIAGRAM XV.—A Vegetable Group-Soul.

During the time that is spent in the vegetable kingdom, there is more activity perceptible in the astral permanent atom, than was the case during the period spent in the mineral kingdom. In consequence, the astral permanent atom attracts round itself astral matter, which is arranged by the Devas in a rather more definite way. In the long life of a forest tree, S C 128.

the growing aggregation of astral matter develops itself in all directions as the astral form of the tree. That astral form experiences vibrations, which cause "massive" pleasure or discomfort, set up in the physical tree by sunshine and storm, wind and rain, heat and cold, etc., these experiences being passed on, to some extent, to the permanent atom embedded in that particular tree. As stated before, when the tree-form perishes as a tree, the permanent atom retreats within the Group-Soul, taking with it its rich store of experiences, which it shares, in the manner previously described, with the other Triads in the Group-Soul.

S C 128–130. Furthermore, as the consciousness becomes more responsive in the astral, it sends little thrills down to the physical plane; these give rise to feelings which, though really derived from the astral, are yet felt as though in the physical.

When there has been a long separate life, as, for example, in a tree, there will be a slight arousing of the mental unit, which will gather round it a little cloud of mental matter; on this the recurrence of seasons, etc., will slowly impress itself as a faint memory, which becomes a dim anticipation.

As a general rule, in fact, it appears that each Lower Triad, during the later stages of its evolution in the vegetable world, will have a prolonged experience in a single form, in order that some thrills of mental life may be experienced, and the Lower Triad thus be prepared to profit, in due time, by the wandering life of an animal. The rule, however, is not universal, for it also appears that, in some cases, the passage into the animal kingdom is made at an earlier stage, so that the first thrill in the mental unit occurs in some of the stationary forms of animal life, and in very lowly animal organisms. For conditions, similar to those described as existing in the mineral and vegetable kingdoms, appear to prevail also in the lowest types of animals. In other words, the kingdoms appear to overlap to some extent.

CHAPTER XII

ANIMAL GROUP-SOULS

AN Animal Group-Soul is illustrated in Diagram XVI. As will be seen from the diagram, the envelope of the Group-Soul now has but a single layer, consisting of elemental essence of the fourth mental sub-plane. The astral layer, which the Vegetable Group-Soul possessed, has been absorbed, for the strengthening of the vague astral bodies of the Triads within the Group-Soul. S C 116: 119.

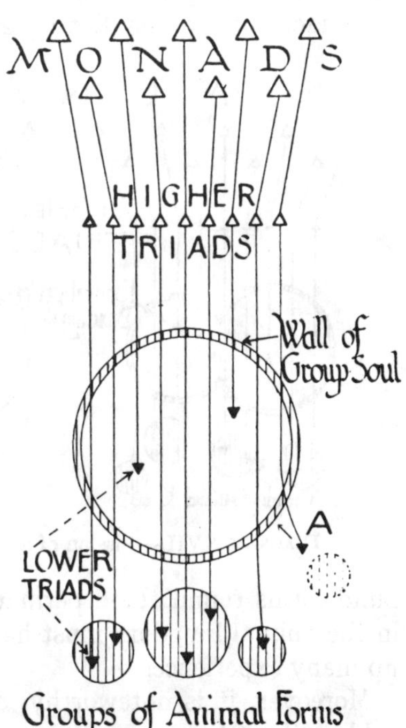

DIAGRAM XVI.—An Animal Group-Soul.

The activity of the Group-Soul is now transferred a plane higher, to the lower mental plane, and it nourishes the inchoate mental bodies of the contained Triads, thus gradually strengthening these into outlines less vague.

Diagram XVI is on lines exactly similar to those of Diagrams XIV and XV. At A is an animal form which, as a form, has been destroyed. Consequently, the Lower Triad from it is being withdrawn into the Group-Soul, as indicated by the arrow in the diagram.

S C 129–130. Just as in the earlier kingdoms, the Devas guide the Triads into animal forms. Also, as in the mineral and vegetable kingdoms, the lower forms of animal life, such as microbes, amœbæ, hydræ, etc., show a permanent atom only as a visitor, now and again, and obviously in no way depend upon it for their own life and growth, nor do they break up when the permanent atom is withdrawn. These animal forms are thus merely hosts, which from time to time receive permanent atoms as passing guests: in no sense are they bodies formed round a permanent atom.

In fact, before the Devas, at a much later stage,

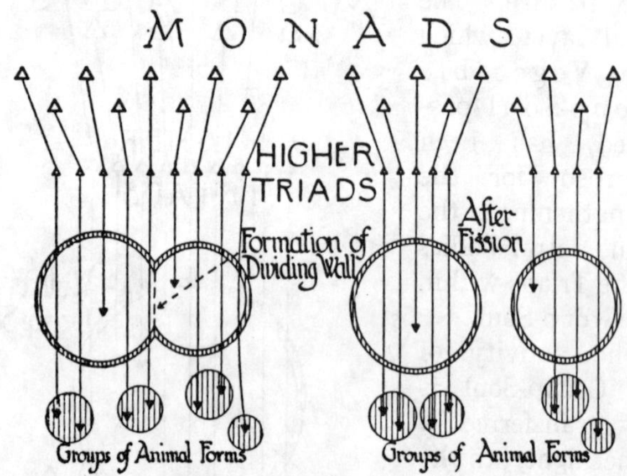

DIAGRAM XVII.—Fission of an Animal Group-Soul.

build forms round these permanent atoms, the atoms in the animal kingdom must have received and stored up many experiences.

Moreover, it is noteworthy, at this stage, that the golden life-web in no way represents the organisation of the body of the *host*. The life-web seems rather to act as rootlets act in soil, attaching to themselves particles of soil and sucking from them the nourishment they require for the organism they serve.

S C 130–131 : 114. Needless to say, in the animal kingdom, the permanent atoms receive far more varied vibrations than in the lower kingdoms: consequently, they differentiate more quickly. As this differentiation proceeds, the multiplication of Group-Souls goes on with increasing rapidity, the number of Lower Triads in any one Group-Soul of course steadily diminishing.

Diagram XVII illustrates the fission of an animal Group-Soul. Mineral and vegetable Group-Souls, as already described, also divide by a similar process of fission.

Again and again the Group-Soul divides, until eventually each Lower Triad possesses its own separate envelope. The Triad is still within the enveloping case of elemental essence, which protects and nourishes it. It is drawing near to "Individualisation," and the term Group-Soul is no longer strictly applicable to it, because one Lower Triad clearly is not a "group." It is a single Lower Triad which has separated off from the "group" to which previously it belonged.

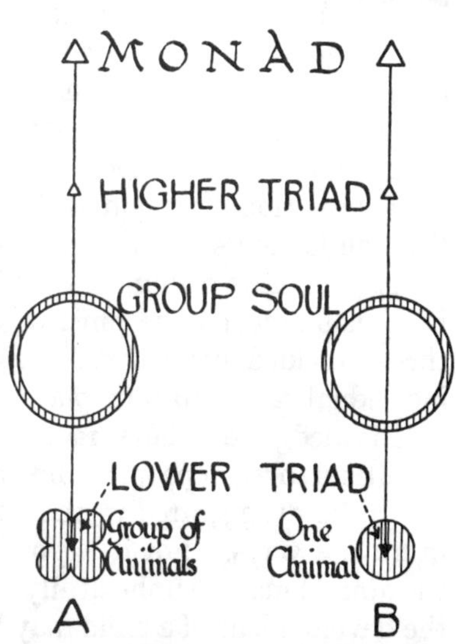

DIAGRAM XVIII.—Animal Group-Soul containing one Lower Triad—
(A) Attached to a group of animals.
(B) Attached to one animal.

Diagram XVIIIA shows the stage which has now been reached: in the Group-Soul envelope there is but one Lower Triad; but there are still several animal forms attached to the Group-Soul. The next stage is reached when there is only *one* animal form attached to the Group-Soul. This is indicated in Diagram XVIIIB. Large numbers of the higher domestic animals have reached this stage, and have really become separate entities, incarnating in a succession of animal bodies; although they have not as yet, of course, attained to the possession of a causal body—the true mark of individualisation.

S C 132–133. Before passing on to describe the very interesting process of individualisation, we may here note an analogy between the animal, when it is approaching individualisation, and the human ante-natal life. The animal at this stage corresponds to the last two months of the human fœtus.

Now it is known that a seven-months child may be born, and may survive, but it will be stronger, healthier, more vigorous, if it profits yet another two months by its mother's shielding and nourishing life. So is it also better, for the normal development of the ego, that it should not burst too soon the envelope of the Group-Soul, but should remain within it, still absorbing life through it, and strengthening from its constituents the finest part of its own mental body. When that mental body has reached the limit of growth possible, under these shielded conditions, then the time is ripe for individualisation to take place.

Knowledge of these facts has sometimes caused occultists to warn people, who are very fond of animals, not to be exaggerated in their affection, or to show it in unwise ways. For it is possible that the growth of the animal may be unhealthily forced—just as we know the development of a child may be unhealthily forced—and the individualisation of the animal thus be hastened out of due time. It is obviously far better to let an animal develop naturally, until it is fully ready for individualisation, than to force it artificially, and cause it to become an individual before it is really ready to stand by itself, and live in the world as a separate human entity.

M V I 45: 61. *T B* 38–39. It must be recollected that we are at present little more than half-way through the Fourth Round of the Fourth Chain, *i.e.*, a little more than half-way through the evolution of this Chain of worlds, and that it is only at the end of this evolution that the animal kingdom is expected to attain humanity. Hence, any animal which is now attaining, or even approaching individualisation, must be very remarkably in advance of the others, and the number of such cases is consequently very small. Nevertheless, they do occasionally occur. Close association with man is necessary to produce this result.

We may note two factors at work: (1) the emotions and thoughts of the man act constantly upon those of the animal, and tend to raise him to a higher level both emotionally and intellectually; (2) the animal, if kindly treated, develops devoted affection for his human friend, and also unfolds his intellectual powers in trying to understand that friend and to anticipate his wishes.

It has been found that individualisation, which lifts an entity definitely from the animal kingdom into the human, can take place only from certain kinds of animals—one for each of the seven great types or "rays." In fact, it is only among domesticated creatures, and by no means among all classes even of these, that individualisation occurs. Of these classes, we already know certainly the elephant, the monkey, the dog and the cat. The horse is possibly a fifth. *M V I* 45: 61. *T B* 37–38. *I L II* 380.

Up to each of these heads of types leads a long line of wild animals, which has not yet been fully investigated. It is known, however, that wolves, foxes, jackals and all such creatures culminate in the dog: lions, tigers, leopards, jaguars and ocelots culminate in the domestic cat.

It should be noted also that an animal of any given type, that individualises into a human being, will become a man of that same type, and of no other.

Both bees and ants (which, together with wheat, were brought from Venus by the Lords of the Flame) live in a manner quite different from purely terrestrial creatures, in that with them a Group-Soul animates the entire ant or bee community, so that the community acts with a single will, and its different units are actually members of one body, in the sense in which hands and feet are members of the human frame. It *I L II* 368–369.

might indeed be said of them that they have not only a Group-Soul, but a group-body also.

The investigations of M. Maeterlinck appear to confirm the above fully. He writes :—

" The population of the hive, the ant-hill and the termitary, seems to be one individual, one single living creature, whose organs, composed of innumerable cells, are disseminated only in appearance, but remain always subject to the same energy or vital personality, the same central law. By virtue of this collective immortality, the decease of hundreds of termites, that are immediately succeeded by others, does nor affect or touch the central being. For millions of years the same insect has gone on living, with the result that not a single one of its experiences has been lost. There has been no interruption of its existence, or disappearance of its memories ; an individual memory has remained, and this has never ceased to function or to centralise every acquisition of the collective soul. They bathe in the same vital fluid as the cells of our own being ; but in their case this fluid would seem to be much more diffuse, more elastic, more subtle, more psychical or more ethereal than that of our body. And this central unity is no doubt bound up with the universal soul of the bee, and probably with what is actually *the* universal soul." [1]

I L II 379–380. With regard to the numbers of separate creatures attached to a Group-Soul, there may be quadrillions of flies or mosquitoes ; hundreds of thousands of rabbits or sparrows ; a few thousands of such animals as the lion, tiger, leopard, deer, wolf or wild boar. Among domesticated animals such as sheep and oxen the number is still smaller.

In the case of the seven animals from whom individualisation is possible, there are usually only a few hundred attached to each Group-Soul, and, as their development continues, they break up rapidly. Whilst there may be a thousand pariah dogs attached to one Group-Soul, in the case of the really intelligent pet dog

[1] From *The Life of the White Ant,* by Maurice Maeterlinck, pp. 199–20.

or cat, there may be not more than ten or twelve bodies over which the Group-Soul hovers.

Animal Group-Souls are greatly affected and assisted by the influences which the Masters of Wisdom are continually pouring out, affecting to some extent everything within a wide radius. *I L I* 35.

CHAPTER XIII

INDIVIDUALISATION: ITS MECHANISM AND PURPOSE

C 170–172. WE have now arrived at the stage where a change of vast importance to the evolving life is about to take place—viz., the individualisation of the animal, the formation of the causal body, the entry into the human kingdom.

In order to understand the whole phenomenon, and to recognise its full significance, let us briefly recapitulate the stages already passed. We saw first that the Monads, which derive their being from the First Logos, come forth and dwell on the Anupādaka plane during all the ages over which we have glanced. With the help of the Devas, each Monad has appropriated to himself the three permanent atoms which represent him as a Jīvātmā on the planes of Ātmā, Buddhi and Manas, these three forming the Higher Triad. In addition, to each Higher Triad has been attached also a Lower Triad, consisting of a Mental Unit, and an Astral and a Physical Permanent Atom.

The Lower Triad has been plunged successively into the earlier kingdoms of life, shielded and nourished by its Group-Soul. By repeated sub-division, brought about by differentiation of experience, each Lower Triad has now become possessed of an envelope or sac to itself, derived from the original Group-Soul. After a succession of experiences in a series of single animal forms, the Lower Triad is at length sufficiently awakened to warrant a further step being taken in the evolutionary scheme, a step which will bring to it a further instalment, if we may use such an expression, or aspect, of the Divine Life.

Just as the human fœtus is nourished by the mother in her womb until such time as the child is strong enough to live its own independent existence in the outer world, so is the Triad shielded and nourished by the Group-Soul, the medium by which the Second Logos protects and nourishes His infant children, until the Triad is strong enough to be launched into the outer world as a self-contained unit of life, pursuing its own independent evolution.

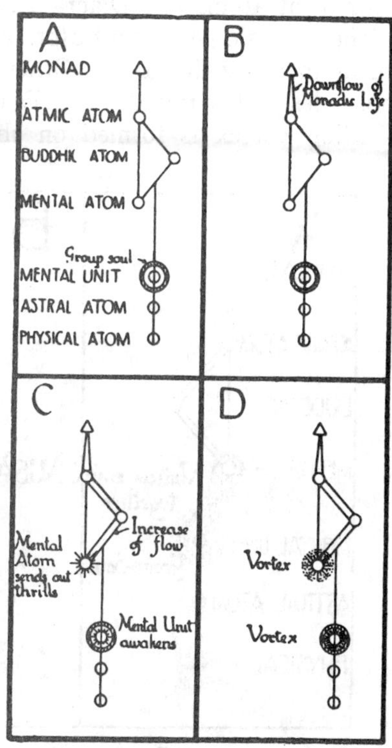

DIAGRAM XIX.—Individualisation.

Thus is reached the term of the ante-natal life of the Jīvātmā (the Higher Triad of Ātmā-Buddhi-Manas) enclosing the life of the Monad, the time being now ripe for his birth into the lower world. The mother-life of the Second Logos has built for him the bodies in which he can live as a separate entity in the world of forms, and he has to come into direct possession of those bodies, and take up his human evolution.

Up to this point, all the communication of the Monad with the lower planes has been through the Sūtrātmā, or thread-self, on which the permanent atoms are strung (see Diagram XIX A). But now the time has come for a fuller communication than is represented by this delicate thread in its original form. The Sūtrātmā accordingly widens out (see Diagram XIX B), the Ray from the Monad glows and increases, assuming more the form of a funnel : "the thread between the Silent

S C 172–173: 119–120.

Watcher and his shadow becomes more strong and radiant" (*The Secret Doctrine*, I., 285).

This downflow of monadic life is accompanied by much increased flow between the buddhic and manasic permanent atoms (see Diagram XIX C).

The manasic permanent atom awakens, sending out thrills in every direction. Other manasic atoms and molecules gather round it (see Diagram XIX D), and a whirling vortex is formed on the three upper sub-

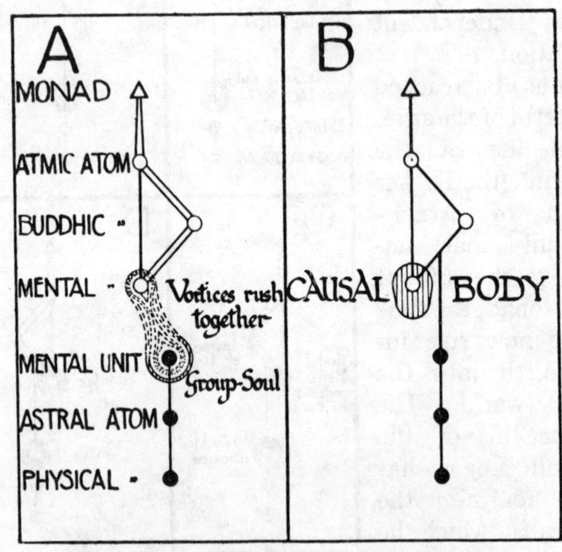

DIAGRAM XX.—Formation of Causal Body.

planes of the mental plane. A similar whirling motion takes place in the cloudy mass surrounding the mental unit which, as we have seen, is enveloped in the Group-Soul.

The wall of the Group-Soul is then torn asunder, and caught up into the vortex above (see Diagram XX A). Here it is disintegrated, being resolved into matter of the third mental sub-plane, and, as the whirlpool subsides, it is formed into a delicate, filmy envelope, this being the causal body (see Diagram XX B).

M V I 60–61. In describing this process, the illustration usually given in the East is that of the water-spout. There we have a great cloud hovering above the sea, on the surface of which waves are constantly forming and moving. Presently from the cloud is extended an inverted cone of violently whirling vapour, like a great finger.

Underneath this, a vortex is rapidly formed in the ocean ; but instead of being a depression in its surface, as in the ordinary whirlpool, it is a whirling cone rising above that surface.

Steadily the two draw closer and closer together, until they come so near that the power of attraction is strong enough to overleap the intervening space, and suddenly a great column of mingled water and vapour is formed, where nothing of the kind existed before.

In just the same way, animal Group-Souls are constantly throwing parts of themselves into incarnation, like the temporary waves on the surface of the sea. At last, after the process of differentiation has continued to the maximum possible, a time comes when one of these waves rises high enough to enable the hovering cloud to effect a junction with it. Then it is drawn up into a new existence, neither in the cloud nor in the sea, but between the two, and partaking of the nature of both. Thus it is separated from the Group-Soul, of which hitherto it has formed a part, and falls back again into the sea no more. Technically expressed, the life of the animal, working in lower mental matter, is whirled up to meet the downpouring life of the Monad, expressed through higher mental or causal matter.

We may thus think of the Monad as waiting on his
own high plane, while the lower bodies are being *M B* 76.
formed, round the atoms attached to him, brooding *T* 35.
over them through long ages of slow evolution. When they are sufficiently evolved, he flashes down and takes possession of them, to use them for his own evolution. As he meets the upward-growing, unfolding mind-stuff, he comes into union with it, fertilising it, and, at the point of union, forms the causal body, the vehicle of the individual.

S C 173. *I L I* 149. The downflow of life, resulting in the formation of the causal body, is known as the Third Life-Wave, or Third Outpouring, and derives from the First Logos, the eternal all-loving Father—from Whom came also, as we have seen, the Monads themselves in the first instance.

The action of the three Outpourings in producing an individual human being is graphically represented in the well-known diagram opposite page 38 in *Man Visible and Invisible*, and on page 16 of *The Chakras*. This diagram we have ventured to modify slightly (see Diagram XXI), in accordance with the further information given in *The Chakras*, and in *The Masters and the Path*.

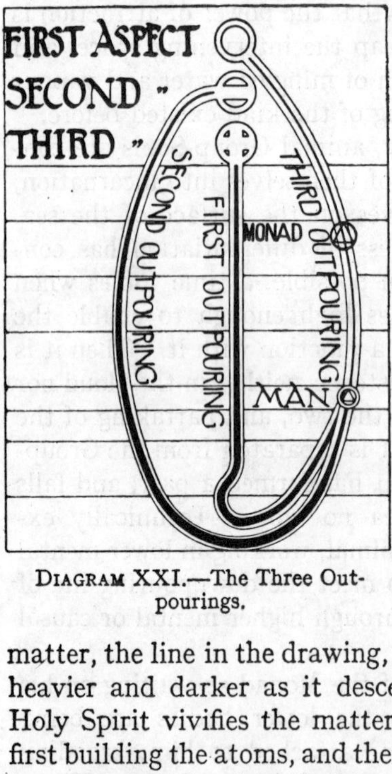

DIAGRAM XXI.—The Three Outpourings.

The explanation of Diagram XXI is as follows:—

Ch. 15–16. *M P* 174–175. The First Life-Wave or Outpouring, from the Third Logos or Aspect, plunges straight down into matter, the line in the drawing, indicating this, growing heavier and darker as it descends, showing how the Holy Spirit vivifies the matter of the various planes, first building the atoms, and then aggregating the atoms into elements (as described in Chapter V).

Into that matter so vivified the Second Life-Wave, or Outpouring, from the Second Logos or Aspect, God the Son, descends through the First, Second and Third Elemental Kingdoms, down to the mineral kingdom; then it ascends through the vegetable and animal to the human kingdom, where it meets the downward-reaching power of the First Logos—the Third Outpouring, from the First Logos or Aspect.

Meanwhile the force of the Third Logos, the First Outpouring, from the Third Aspect, after touching its lowest point, also rises again. On this path of return or ascent, it is Kundalinī, and it works in the bodies of evolving creatures in intimate contact with the Primary or Life-Force, the two acting together to bring the creature to the point where it can receive the Outpouring of the First Logos, and become an ego, a human being, and still carry on the vehicles even after that. Thus we may say that we draw God's mighty power from the earth beneath as well as from heaven above, and are children of earth as well as of the sun. The two Forces meet in us, and work together for our evolution. We cannot have one without the other, but if one is greatly in excess there are serious dangers. Hence, incidentally, the risk of any development of the deeper layers of Kundalinī before the life in the man is pure and refined.

Whilst all three Outpourings are truly the actual *M P* 176.
Life of God Himself, yet there is a vital and important distinction between the First and Second Outpourings on the one hand and the Third Outpouring on the other hand. For the First and Second Outpourings have come down slowly and gradually through all the sub-planes, drawing round themselves the matter of each of these, and enmeshing themselves in it so thoroughly that it is scarcely possible to discern them for what they are, to recognise them as Divine Life at all.

But the Third Outpouring flashes straight down from its source *without* involving itself in any way in the intermediate matter. It is the pure white light, uncontaminated by anything through which it has passed.

Furthermore, although in the diagram, as originally published, the Third Outpouring was shown as coming forth *directly* from the Logos, yet it has in fact (as we saw in Chapter IV) issued from Him long ago, and is hovering at an intermediate point, *i.e.*, on the second or Anupādaka plane, where we know it as the Monad. We have, therefore, ventured to modify the original diagram by inserting the triangle, representative of the Monad, in its appropriate place in the stream of the Third Outpouring.

S P 69. *I L I* 108–109. This "monadic inflow," resulting in the evolution of the Monad from the animal into the human kingdom, continued up to the middle of the Fourth Race (the Atlantean), the human population thus continually receiving fresh recruits. This point represents the middle of the scheme of evolution in our Planetary Chain, and, after it has passed, very few animals attain individualisation. An animal who does succeed in individualising is as far in advance of his fellows as is the human being who attains Adeptship in advance of the average man. Both are doing, at the middle point of evolution, what they are expected to be able to do only at the end of it. Those who achieve only at the normal time, at the end of the seventh round, will approach their goal so gradually that there will be little or no struggle.

The Secret Doctrine, I., 205, refers to this matter when it states that after the "central turning point" of the cycle of evolution, "no more Monads can enter the human kingdom. The door is closed for this cycle."

T B 39. The student will observe that the Third Outpouring differs from the others in another important respect, in that whilst the First and Second Outpourings affect thousands or millions simultaneously, the Third Outpouring comes to each one individually, only as that one is ready to receive it.

The Third Outpouring, as we have seen, has already descended as far as the buddhic world, but comes no farther until the upward leap is made by the soul of the animal from below. Then the two flash together, and form the ego, as a permanent individuality, in the manner described.

Whilst we speak of the individuality of man as being

permanent, it must be understood that such permanence is relative only, for at a far later stage in evolution the man transcends it, and reaches back to the divine unity from which he came. This matter will be dealt with in a later chapter.

Recapitulating briefly, we see that the Logos sends *T* 87.
forth three mighty waves of His Life, through His three Aspects in succession: the first shapes and ensouls matter; the second imparts qualities and builds forms; the third carries down the human Monad to unite with the forms prepared by the second.

The student should note that previous to individuali- *T B* 39–40.
sation, the fragment of the Group-Soul has played the *M V I* 63–64.
part of the ensouling force. After individualisation, *M* 4.
however, that which was the Group-Soul is converted *M P* 17–18.
into the causal body, thus becoming the vehicle which is ensouled by the Divine Spark which has descended into it from the higher world.

Thus that which hitherto has been the ensouling life *M P* 18.
becomes in turn the ensouled, for it builds itself into a form, symbolised in ancient mythology by the Greek idea of the Crater or Cup, and by the mediæval story of the Holy Grail. For the Grail or Cup is the perfected result of all that lower evolution, into which is poured the wine of the Divine Life, so that the soul of man may be born. Thus, as has been said, that which had previously been the animal *soul* becomes in the case of man the causal *body*, occupied by the ego or human soul. All that has been learned in its evolution is thus transferred to this new centre of life.

Now that the causal body has been formed, the *S C* 173–174.
Higher or Spiritual Triad has a permanent vehicle for further evolution. When the consciousness in due time becomes able to function freely in this vehicle, the Higher Triad will be able to control and direct, far more effectively than before, the evolution of the lower vehicles.

The earlier efforts at control are not, of course, of a very intelligent description, any more than the first movements of an infant are intelligent; although we know that there is an intelligence connected with them. The Monad is now, quite literally, born on the physical plane; but he must be regarded as a baby there, a true Individuality, but an infant ego, and he will have to pass through an immense period of time before his power over the physical body will be anything but infantile.

I C C 56–57. The Soul or Ego we may consider as that which individualises the Universal Spirit, which focusses the Universal Light into a single point; which is, as it were, a receptacle into which is poured the Spirit; so that that which in Itself is universal, poured into this receptacle *appears* as separate: always identical in its essence, but separated in its manifestation. The purpose of this separation is, as we have seen, that an individual may develop and grow; that there may be an individualised life potent on every plane of the Universe; that it may know on the physical and other planes as it knows on the spiritual planes, and have no break in consciousness; that it may make for itself the vehicles that it needs for acquiring consciousness beyond its own plane, and then may gradually purify them one by one until they no longer act as blinds or as hindrances, but as pure and translucent media through which all knowledge on every plane may come.

I O C 57–58. The process of individualisation, however, should not be conceived as merely the making of a form or receptacle, and then pouring something into it, so that that which is poured at once takes the definite outline and shape of the vessel. The real phenomenon is more analogous to the building of a solar system from a nebula. Out of the primeval matter of space, a slight mist first appears, too delicate almost to be called even a mist: the mist grows gradually denser as the particles aggregate more closely together; eventually shapes are formed within the mist, which, as time goes on, become more and more definite, until a system is formed, with a central sun and planets around it.

So is the coming of Spirit into individualisation. It

is like the faint appearance of a shadow in the universal void; the shadow becomes a mist, which grows clearer and more definite, until eventually an individual comes into existence. The Soul, or individual, is thus not a thing complete at first, plunging like a diver into the ocean of matter: rather is it slowly densified and builded, until out of the Universal it becomes the individual, which ever grows as its evolution proceeds.

Thus the Third Outpouring makes within each man that distinctive "spirit of the man which goeth upward," in contradistinction to "the spirit of the beast which goeth downward"—which, being interpreted, means that while the soul of the animal pours back after the death of the body into the Group-Soul to which it belongs, the divine spirit in man cannot so fall back again, but rises ever onward and upward towards the Divinity from Whom it came. *M V I* 59–60.

As has already been stated, the divine life represented by the Third Life Wave appears to be unable of itself to descend lower than the Buddhic plane, where it hovers like a mighty cloud, waiting for an opportunity of effecting a junction with the life of the Second Outpouring, which is rising to meet it.

Now although this cloud seems to exercise a constant attraction upon the essence below it, yet the effort which makes the union possible must be made from below. With the nature of this effort we shall deal in the next chapter.

The junction of the Third with the First and Second Outpourings is the beginning of the intellectual evolution, the coming of the Ego to take possession of his physical tabernacle, and to link to that tabernacle the Spirit which has brooded over it, which has by its subtle influence shaped and fashioned it. *P M* 4–5.

Of this, H. P. Blavatsky says: "There exists in nature a triple evolutionary scheme, for the formation of the three periodical Upādhis; or rather three separate schemes of evolution, which in our system are inextricably interwoven and interblended at every point. . . . I. The Monadic, as the name implies, is concerned with the growth and development into still higher phases of activity of the Monads, in conjunction with : II. The Intellectual, represented by the Mānasa-Dhyānis (the Solar Devas, or the Agnishvātta Pitris), the ' givers of intelligence and consciousness ' to man ; and : III. The Physical, represented by the Chhāyas of the Lunar Pitris, round which Nature has concreted the present physical body. . . . It is the union of these three streams in him, which makes him the complex being he now is " (*The Secret Doctrine*, I., 203, 204).

P M 22. " Man " has been well defined in Occultism as that being in the universe, in whatever part of the universe he may be, in whom highest Spirit and lowest Matter are joined together by *intelligence*, thus ultimately making a manifested God, who will go forth to conquer through the illimitable future that stretches before him.

R 11. Man himself, the reincarnating ego, should preferably be considered as the *Thinker*, rather than as *Mind ;* for the word Thinker suggests an individual Entity, whereas the word Mind suggests rather a vague, diffused generality.

P M 15-17. If we consider the phases of involution and evolution in broad outline, we may think of them as consisting of seven stages. During three the Spirit descends. As it descends, it broods over Matter, imparting qualities, powers and attributes. The fourth stage stands alone, for in it Matter, now imbued with various powers and attributes, comes into manifold relations with the informing Spirit, which now enters it. This is the great battle of the universe, the conflict between Spirit and Matter, the battle of Kurukshetra, of the vast hosts of the opposing armies. In this part of the field is the point of balance. The Spirit, coming into innumerable relations with Matter, is at first overpowered ; then comes the point of balance, when neither has the advantage over the other ; then slowly the Spirit begins to triumph over Matter, so that, when the fourth stage is over, Spirit is master of Matter, and is ready for his ascent through the three stages that complete the seven.

In these, the Spirit organises the Matter which he has mastered and ensouled, turns it to his own purposes, shapes it for his own expression, so that Matter may become the means whereby all the powers of the Spirit shall be made manifest and active. The last three stages are thus taken up by that spiritual ascent. In tabular form, the seven stages may be indicated thus :—

I, II, III.	Descent	Qualities imparted	Materialisation	Involution
IV.	Turning-point : Balance	Relationships established	Conflict	Changing from Involution to Evolution
V, VI, VII.	Ascent	Organisms built	Spiritualisation	Evolution

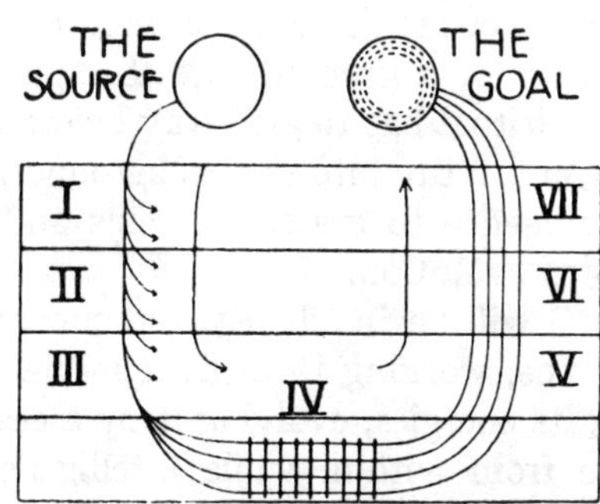

DIAGRAM XXII.—The seven Stages of Involution and Evolution.

The 7 Stages of Involution and Evolution

During Stages I, II and III Spirit descends, imparting qualities (indicated by the arrows branching out laterally) to Matter.

During Stage IV Spirit and Matter are in conflict, indicated by the two opposing arrows, and by the cross-lines, symbolising the battleground of life.

During Stages V, VI and VII Spirit ascends, gradually attaining mastery over Matter.

The Diagram also attempts to portray the splitting up of the line of Spirit, multiplicity thus emerging from unity, and the return of Spirit to the level of its source, enriched by its experiences with, and mastery over, matter.

Diagram XXII is an attempt to illustrate the same ideas in graphic form.

The principle, of which this is a particular example, is one which recurs over and over again throughout the processes of nature: for example, in the cycle of human reincarnation. The student is therefore recommended to grasp the principle clearly, as it should help him in his understanding of many other portions of the "Ancient Wisdom."

I P O 260. The whole course of the movement downwards into matter is called in India the *pravritti mārga*, or the path of outgoing. When the lowest point necessary has been reached, the man enters upon the *nivritti mārga*, or the path of return. The man returns from his day's work of harvesting, bearing his sheaves with him, in the shape of the fully awakened consciousness, which enables him to be far more useful than he could have been before his descent into matter.

P M 38–39. In the course of man's development, the intellectual evolution must for a time obscure the spiritual evolution. The spiritual has to give way before the rush of intelligence, and retire into the background for a while, leaving intelligence to grasp the reins and guide the next stages of evolution.

The Monad will begin silently and subtly to inform the intelligence, working through it indirectly, stimulating it by its energies, evolving it by a ceaseless flow of influence from within, while intelligence grapples with the lower vehicles, to be at first conquered and enslaved, but eventually to master them and to rule.

Thus for a time the spirit is obscured, maturing in silence, while the warrior intellect carries on the struggle: the time will eventually come when intellect will lay its spoils at the feet of spirit, and man, becoming divine, shall reign on 'earth,' *i.e.*, on the lower planes, as their master, no longer their slave.

A W 223–224. The intellect is essentially the separative principle in man, that marks off the "I" from the "not I," that is conscious of itself, and sees all else as outside itself and alien. It is the combative, struggling, self-assertive principle, and, from the plane of the intellect downwards, the world presents a scene of conflict, bitter in proportion as the intellect mingles in it. Even the passion-nature is spontaneously combative only when it is stirred by the feeling of desire, and finds anything standing between itself and the object of its desire. It becomes more and more aggressive as the mind inspires its activity, for then it seeks to provide for the gratification of future desires, and tries to appropriate more and more from the stores of nature. But the intellect appears to be spontaneously combative, its very nature being to assert itself as different from others. Hence we find in intellect the root of separateness, the ever-springing source of divisions among men.

Unity, on the other hand, is at once felt when the buddhic plane is reached. But with that we shall deal in a much later chapter.

The student, however, must not form the idea that man is *only* that which functions as mind or intellect in his causal body. In essence, as we have seen, man is a Spark of the Divine Fire, *i.e.*, the Monad, and that Monad manifests its three aspects as Spirit in the world of Ātmā, as Intuition in the world of Buddhi, and as Intelligence in the world of Manas. It is *these three aspects taken together which constitute the ego* which inhabits the causal body, which was built from the fragment of the Group-Soul. Thus man, as we know him, though in reality a Monad residing in the monadic world, shows himself as an ego in the higher mental world, manifesting the three aspects of himself which we designate Spirit, Intuition and Intelligence. *T B* 41-42.

The ego is the man during the human stage of evolution; he is the nearest correspondence, in fact, to the ordinary and somewhat unscientific conception of the soul. He lives unchanged (except for his growth) from the moment of individualisation until humanity is transcended and merged in divinity. He is in no way affected by what we call birth and death, for what we commonly consider as his life is, of course, only a day in his real life. The lower bodies, which are born and die, are merely garments, which he puts on for the purposes of a certain part of his evolution.

T 25. A concise way of stating the case is to say that man *is* an immortal individuality, who *has* a mortal personality.

T P O 17. In the whole of man's existence, there are three definite changes which outweigh all others in importance and significance. (1) The first of these is when he individualises and enters the human kingdom, emerging from the animal, and beginning his career as an ego. (2) The second is the passing of the First of the great Initiations. (3) The third is the attainment of Adeptship. With (2) and (3) we shall deal in later chapters: here we are concerned only with (1)—the attainment of individualisation.

I L I 84–86. *M V I* 68–69. To gain this individuality is the aim of animal evolution, and its development serves a definite purpose. That purpose is to make a strong individual centre, through which eventually the force of the Logos can be poured out.

When such a centre is first formed, it is of course merely a baby ego, weak and uncertain. In order that it may become strong and definite, it has to be fenced round by *selfishness*—the intense selfishness of the savage. For many lives a strong wall of this selfishness has to be maintained, so that within it the centre may grow more and more definite.

Selfishness may therefore be regarded as a kind of scaffolding, which is absolutely necessary for the erection of the building, but which must be destroyed as soon as the building is completed, in order that the building may serve the purpose for which it was erected. The scaffolding is unbeautiful, and, if it were not removed, the building would be uninhabitable: yet, without the scaffolding, there would have been no building at all.

The object of the creation of the centre being that, through it, the force of the Logos should radiate out upon the world, such radiation would be quite impossible if the selfishness persisted; nevertheless, without the selfishness in the earlier stages a strong centre could never have been established.

Hence, in the light of this analogy, we see that even the most unlovely of qualities has its place in the scheme of evolution—*at the right time.* For many men, however, its work is over, and they should rid themselves of selfishness completely. It is useless and foolish to be angry with men who are selfish, for their conduct implies that what was in the savage a necessary virtue is still persisting into the civilised condition. A wiser attitude to adopt towards the selfish is to regard them as anachronisms—survivals from prehistoric savagery, men behind the times.

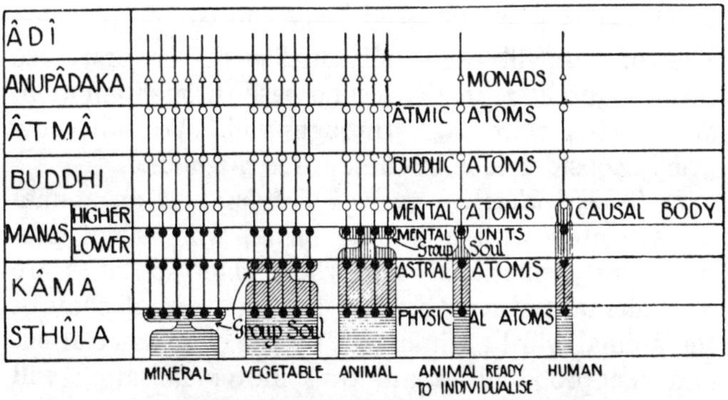

Diagram XXIII.—From Mineral to Man.

Diagram XXIII summarises the results of the last four chapters, showing the relative positions in the evolutionary scheme of the stages we know as the Mineral Group-Soul, the Vegetable Group-Soul, the Animal Group-Soul, the Animal ready to Individualise, and the Human Being in his Causal Body.

CHAPTER XIV

METHODS AND DEGREES OF INDIVIDUALISATION

I L II 372–373. It was said in the preceding chapter that the effort, resulting from which individualisation takes place, must be made from below, *i.e.*, by the animal. This effort may take place in one of three distinct ways, and so exercise a very far-reaching effect on the whole future life of the entity concerned.

When an ego is formed, the three aspects of the Higher Triad, *i.e.*, Ātmā, Buddhi and Manas, must all be called forth: the first connection, however, may be made through any one of the three, as follows :—

(1) Between the lower mind and the higher.
(2) Between the astral body and Buddhi.
(3) Between the physical body and Ātmā.

The animal will thus individualise in the first case through intellect, in the second case through emotion, and in the third case through will. We will now briefly consider each of these three methods.

L II 374. I. *Individualisation through Intellect.*—If an animal is associated with a human being, who is not predominantly emotional, but whose chief activities are of a mental nature, then the nascent mental body of the animal will be stimulated by the close association, and the probabilities are that individualisation will take place through the mind, as the result of mental efforts made by the animal to understand his master.

II. *Individualisation through Emotion.*—If, on the other hand, the master be an emotional man, full of strong affections, the probability is that the animal will develop chiefly through his astral body, and that the final breaking of the link with the group-soul will be due to some sudden outrush of intense affection, which will reach the buddhic aspect of the floating Monad belonging to it, and will thus cause the formation of the ego.

III. *Individualisation through Will.*—In yet a third *I L II* 375.
case, if the master be a man of great spirituality, or of intensely strong will, while the animal will develop great affection and admiration for him, it will yet be the *will* within the animal which is principally stimulated. This will show itself in the physical body by intense activity, and indomitable resolution to achieve whatever the creature may attempt, especially in the service of his master.

We thus see that the character and type of the *I L II* 374.
master will have a great influence on the destiny of the animal. The greater portion of the work is, of course, done without any direct volition on either side, simply by the incessant and inevitable action due to the proximity of the two entities concerned. The astral and mental vibrations of the man are far stronger and more complex than those of the animal, and they are consequently exercising a never-ceasing pressure upon the latter.

The student should avoid the error of thinking that *I L II* 375–
the " distance " between Ātmā and the physical body 376.
is greater than that between the lower mind and the higher mind, or between the astral and the buddhic principles. It is not a question of distance in space at all, but rather of the conveying of a sympathetic vibration from the reflection to the original. Looking at the matter in this way, it is clear that each reflection must be in some direct connection with its original, whatever the " distance " between them may be—in closer connection than it is with any object which is out of the direct line, no matter how much nearer in space the latter object may be.

The desire of the animal to rise constitutes a steady *I L II* 376–
upward pressure along all the lines mentioned, and the 378.
point at which that pressure finally breaks through the restrictions, and forms the required link between the Monad and the personality, determines certain

characteristics of the new ego which thus comes into existence.

The actual formation of the link is usually instantaneous, in the case of individualisation through affection or will : it is more gradual when it takes place through intellect. This also makes a considerable difference in the current of the future evolution of the entity.

Out of a great mass of people who were individualised at a certain point in the Moon-Chain, those who had attained individualisation gradually, by intellectual development, came into incarnation on the earth about a million years ago : since then they have taken an average interval between lives of about 1,200 years.

Those of the group who had attained individualisation through an instantaneous uprush of affection, or of will, came into terrestrial incarnation about 600,000 years ago; they have taken an average interval between incarnations of about 700 years. The condition of both groups at the present time is nevertheless about the same.

It appears that those who individualised through affection are able to generate, if anything, slightly *more* force than those who individualised through intellect. But a better description of the difference between the two classes is to say they produce a different *kind* of force. The shorter interval between lives is due to the fact that this group takes its bliss in a much more concentrated form, and therefore works out the result of an equal expenditure of force in much less time.

In fact, it appears probable that the period of the respective entries of these two groups upon terrestrial life was especially arranged in order that, after running through about the same number of incarnations, they might arrive at the same point, and be able to work together. The necessity of bringing groups of people into incarnation together, in order not only that they may work out mutual karmic interrelations, but also that they may all learn to labour together towards one great end, is evidently a dominant factor in regulating the rate of the expenditure of force.

Besides the differences in the *method* of individualisa- *I L II* 379–
tion, there are also differences in the *degree* of indivi- 381.
dualisation, owing to the stage at which it takes place. For it makes a great deal of difference at what stage of development of the animal individualisation occurs. Thus, for example, if a pariah dog were to individualise —as is presumably possible—it could be only a very low type of individualisation. Probably it would at most be nothing more than a separated fragment of the group-soul, with a Monad hovering over it, connected perhaps by a line or two of spiritual matter.

A case of this kind would correspond to the "lunar *I L II* 324.
animal-men"—those egos who individualised from the earliest stage of the animal kingdom, at which individualisation was possible. They commenced their human life without anything which could properly be called a causal body, but with the Monad floating above a personality, to which it was linked only by certain threads of nirvānic matter. It was they who, in the first round of the Earth-period, filled the forms made by the Lords of the Moon, thus doing pioneer work for all the kingdoms.

A really intelligent and affectionate pet dog or cat, *I L II* 381.
on the other hand, whose owner looks after him properly, and makes a friend of him, would certainly, when he individualised, obtain a causal body at least equivalent to that of the First Order of Moon-Men.

Various intermediate types of domestic animals would produce the "basket-work" causal body, such as that obtained by the Second Order of Moon-Men.

The last-named class of egos had not yet fully *I L II* 322.
developed a causal body, but had what might be described as the skeleton of such a vehicle—a number of interlacing streams of force, which indicated the outline of the ovoid that was yet to come. They had consequently a somewhat curious appearance, almost as though they were enclosed in a kind of basket-work of the higher mental matter.

M W H W 72. The determining cause of these different causal bodies lies in the stage at which individualisation takes place. If the animal, a dog, for example, has been for a long time in contact with man, and is one of a small group of 10 or 20, then, on individualising, a complete causal body is formed. If there are about 100 in the group—the sheep-dog stage—a basket-work causal body is formed. If there are several hundreds—the pariah-dog stage—there is formed the indication of a causal body made by the connecting lines.

I L II 381–383. The amount of real work done in the attainment of any given level in evolution is practically always the same, but in some cases more is done in one kingdom and less in another. For the various kingdoms of nature overlap a good deal, so that an animal who reached the summit of intelligence and affection possible in the animal kingdom, would skip over the absolutely primitive conditions of humanity, and show himself as a first-class individuality from the beginning of his human career. On the other hand, one who leaves the animal kingdom at a lower level will have to begin correspondingly lower down in the scale of humanity.

This is the explanation of a remark once made by a Master, when referring to the cruelty and superstition shown by the great mass of humanity: "They have individualised too soon; they are not yet worthy of the human form."

I L II 383–387. The three methods of individualisation—through intellect, affection and will—are the normal methods. Occasionally, however, individualisation is attained in other ways, which we may call abnormal or irregular ways.

For example, at the beginning of the Seventh Round of the Moon-Chain, a certain group of beings were at the point of individualisation, and were drawn towards it by their association with some of the perfected inhabitants, whom we call the Lords of the Moon. An unfortunate twist, however, entered into their development, and they began to take so great a pride in their intellectual advance, that that became the prominent feature in their character. They worked, not so much to gain the approval or affection of their masters, as to show their advantage over their fellow-animals, and to excite their envy.

This latter motive pushed them on to make the efforts resulting in individualisation, and so the causal bodies which were formed showed almost no colour but orange. They were allowed to individualise, apparently because if they had continued in the animal kingdom any further, they would have become worse instead of better.

This detachment—or " ship-load," as it is sometimes called—numbered about two millions. They individualised by pride, and, though clever enough in their way, possessed but little of any other quality.

The members of this orange ship-load, from Planet A of the Moon-Chain, declined to enter the vehicles provided for them in the Earth-Chain, while the golden-coloured egos from Globe B, and the rose-coloured egos from Globe C, accepted the conditions, entered into the vehicles, and fulfilled their destiny.

All through their history these orange egos caused trouble to themselves and to others, owing to their arrogance and unruliness. They have been described as turbulent and aggressive, independent and separative, prone to discontent and eager for change.

Some of the cleverest of them became the notorious " Lords of the Dark Face " in Atlantis, and later world-devastating conquerors, caring nothing for the thousands who were slain or starved in the course of the gratification of their mad ambition, or, later still, unscrupulous millionaires, aptly termed " Napoleons of finance."

Another abnormal method of individualising is *I L II* 387–389.
through fear. In some cases animals which have been cruelly treated by man have developed cunning by their strenuous efforts to understand and avoid the cruelty, so that they have broken away from the

Group-Soul, and produced an ego possessing only a very low type of intellectuality.

A variant of this class is the type of ego in which the cruelty has produced hatred, instead of fear. This is the explanation of the fiendishly cruel and bloodthirsty savages, of whom we sometimes hear, of the inquisitors of the Middle Ages, and of child-torturers at the present day.

Yet another variant is the entity who is individualised by an intense desire for power over others, such as is sometimes shown by the chief bull of a herd. An ego developed in such a way often manifests great cruelty, and appears to take pleasure in it, probably because to torture others is a manifestation of his power over them.

On the other hand, those who have individualised at a comparatively low level along one of the regular lines—as by affection, for example—provide us with a type of equally primitive, but joyous and good-natured, savages. Such savages are so only in name, for they are kindly, as are many of the tribes in some of the islands of the South Seas.

CHAPTER XV

FUNCTIONS OF THE CAUSAL BODY

THE causal body owes its name to the fact that in it reside the causes which manifest themselves as effects in the lower planes.

T N P 35.
M B 75–77.
T 36.
T B 45.
D 19.

For it is the experiences of past lives, stored in the causal body, which are the *cause* of the general attitude taken up towards life, and the actions undertaken.

In Samskrit, the causal body is known as the Kārana Sharīra, Kārana meaning cause.

Briefly, we may say that the causal body has two main functions :—

(1) To act as a vehicle for the Ego : the causal body is the " body of Manas," the form-aspect of the individual, the true man, the Thinker.

(2) To act as a receptacle or storehouse for the essence of the man's experiences in his various incarnations. The causal body is that into which is woven everything which can endure, and in which are stored the germs of qualities, to be carried over to the next incarnation. Hence one sees that the lower manifestation of the man, *i.e.*, his expression in his mental, astral and physical bodies, depends ultimately upon the growth and development of the real man himself, the one " for whom the hour never strikes."

As we have seen in Chapter XIII., there is no *man*, no real *human* being, until the causal body comes into existence. Every individual being must necessarily have a causal body : it is, in fact, the possession of a causal body which constitutes individuality.

The immense amount of work done, in the long æons preceding the birth of the causal body, is devoted to developing and building the matter of the physical, astral and lower mental planes, until it becomes a fit habitation for the divine spirit to dwell in as a *man*.

At its inception, the causal body, or form-aspect of the true man, is described as a delicate film of subtlest matter, just visible, marking where the individual begins his separate life. That delicate, almost colourless, film of subtlest matter, is the body which will last through the whole of the human evolution: on this, as on a thread—the thread-self, or Sūtrātmā, as it is sometimes called—will all the future incarnations be strung.

The causal body, as said, is the receptacle of all that is enduring—*i.e.*, *only* that which is noble and harmonious, and in accordance with the law of the spirit; for every great and noble thought, every pure and lofty emotion, is carried up, and its essence worked into the substance of the causal body. Hence the condition of the causal body is a true register—the *only true* register—of the growth of the man, of the stage of evolution to which he has attained.

M B 7–8. All the various bodies of man should be regarded as casings or vehicles, enabling the Self to function in some definite region of the universe. Just as a man may use a carriage on land, a ship on the sea, a balloon in the air, to travel from one place to another, and yet in all places remain himself, so does the Self, the real man, utilise his various bodies, each for its appropriate purposes, yet remains all the time himself, no matter in what vehicle he may be functioning at any given moment. Relatively to the man, all these bodies are transient, they are his instruments or servants; they wear out and are renewed, time after time, and adapted to his varying needs, and his ever-growing powers.

T P 20. More specifically, because mind is fundamentally dual in its functioning, so man needs, and is provided with, two mind-bodies. As we saw in *The Mental Body*, the mental body serves for the concrete mind, which deals with concrete thoughts; the causal body similarly is the organ for abstract thinking.

In the Thinker, residing in the causal body, are all the powers that we class as Mind, *i.e.*, memory, intuition, will. The Thinker gathers up all the experiences of the earth-lives, through which he passes, to be transmuted within himself, by his own divine alchemy, into that essence of experience and knowledge which is Wisdom. Even in one brief earth-life we distinguish between the knowledge we acquire and the wisdom we gradually—often too rarely—distil from that knowledge. Wisdom is the fruitage of a life's experience, the crowning possession of the aged. In a much fuller and richer sense, Wisdom is the fruitage of many incarnations, the produce of much experience and knowledge. In the Thinker, thus, is the store of experiences, reaped in all our past lives, harvested through many rebirths. *R* 14–15.

In the classification of the bodies of man as "sheaths," the causal body is known as the discriminating sheath, as in the following table :— *S S* 30 : 70–71.

Principle in man.	Kosha or Sheath.	
	Samskrit.	English.
Buddhi . .	Ānandamayakosha	Bliss sheath.
Higher Manas .	Vijñānamayakosha	Discriminating sheath.
Lower Manas and Kāma . .	Manomayakosha .	Feeling sheath.
Prāna . . .	Prānamayakosha .	Vitality sheath.
Sthūla . . .	Annamayakosha .	Food sheath.

In the word Vijñānamayakosha, the particle "Vi" implies the discriminating, separating, and arranging of things, for that is the peculiar function of this sheath. Into the Vijñānamayakosha, or causal body, experiences from the Manomayakosha are reflected as ideal concepts. The Manomayakosha collects and elaborates, the Vijñānamayakosh aarranges and discriminates. The lower bodies receive and deal with sensations, perceptions, the making and elaborating of ideas, but it is the work of the causal body to arrange these, discriminate between them, and perform the work of abstract reasoning from them, dealing with pure ideas, separated from the concrete presentations. *S S* 89–91. *R* 21.

In the causal body we thus have the abstract, not the concrete, the pure internal working, no longer confused by the senses, nor in any way interfered with by the outer world. Here there is pure intelligence, clear vision, intelligence unmoved by the senses, intelligence tranquil, strong, serene.

In the causal body also lies the creative power of meditation, the energies that grow out of one-pointed contemplation. This is the creative sheath of man, for Manas in man corresponds in the Kosmos to Mahat, the Universal Mind, Divine Ideation, the moulding, directing force which is the creative power, from which all comes forth. In this sheath of man exist all forms that can come forth, to which objective reality may be given by this creative power.

S P 52–53. *The Secret Doctrine* (I., 312) says: "Kriyāshakti: the mysterious power of thought which enables it to produce external, perceptible, phenomenal results by its own inherent energy. The ancients held that *any idea will manifest itself externally if one's attention be deeply concentrated upon it.* Similarly an *intense volition will be followed by the desired results.*" This, of course, is the secret of all true "magic."

E L F 14. *A W* 216. Intelligence in man is thus, as said, the reflection of Brahmā, of the Universal Mind, the creative energy. The creative faculty of imagination in man, which at present works in subtle matter, will, when man becomes perfect, work in grosser matter as well, because, as said, the imaginative power in man is the reflection of the power that created the universe. Brahmā meditated, and all forms came forth: so, in the creative power of mind lies every possibility of form.

T P O 357: 194. Hence H. P. Blavatsky sometimes calls manas the deva-ego, or the divine as distinguished from the personal self. Higher manas is divine because it has positive thought, which is kriyāshakti, the power of doing things. Manas, mind, is thus, by its very nature, *activity.* All work is really done by thought-power; the sculptor's hand does not do the work, but the thought-power directing that hand does it. For it is a truism to say that thought precedes action. Whilst there are occasions on which a man may act, as we say, without thinking, yet even so his action is the result of *previous* thought; he has set up a habit of thought along a certain line and acts instinctively in agreement with that line of thought.

Higher manas is divine because, as said, it is a positive thinker, using the quality of its own life, which shines from within. That is what is meant by the word divine, from *div*, to shine.

The outgoing energy of Ātmā, working in the causal body, is the force which dominates and moulds everything that is external to it. The outgoing energy of Ātmā, working in the Manomayakosha, on the other hand, is Desire, and its characteristic is that it is attracted by external objects and its direction is governed from without. But Ātmā, working in the causal body, is Will, dealing no longer with choice directed from without, but with choice initiated from within, moulded on the internal images by a process of discriminative reflection. Thus the outgoing energy is, in the causal body, *guided from within* in its direction, whereas in the lower bodies it is *attracted from without*. This is the essential difference between Will and Desire. The will, moreover, is essentially a quality of the ego, not of the personality. *S S* 91–92. *S G O* 227.

The Chit, or intelligence aspect of man is the first to be evolved: this is the analysing faculty which perceives multiplicity and differences; then comes Ānanda, the wisdom that realises the unity of things, and that accomplishes union, thus finding the joy or bliss that is at the heart of life; lastly, comes the third or highest aspect, Sat, self-existence, the Unity that is beyond even union. *E L F* 14.

In the cycle of the Races, the Fifth Race is developing the Chit, or Intelligence aspect; the Sixth will develop the Ānanda, the union or bliss aspect, the "Kingdom of Happiness"; the Seventh will develop the Sat, or Self-existence aspect. *E L F* 15: 18.

CHAPTER XVI

COMPOSITION AND STRUCTURE

T B 20–21 : 45. *T P O* 194. THE causal body consists of matter of the first, second and third sub-planes of the mental plane.

T 82. *I L II* 261. The student will recollect that an atom of mental matter contains 49^4 or 5,764,801—approximately, say, $5\frac{3}{4}$ millions—of "bubbles in koilon."

In ordinary people the causal body is not yet fully active, and consequently only that matter which belongs to the third sub-plane is vivified. As the ego, during the long course of his evolution, unfolds his latent possibilities, the higher matter is gradually brought into activity; but it is only in the perfected men whom we call Adepts, or Masters, that it is developed to its fullest extent.

T B 46 : 60. *M B* 86. *D* 19. *A W* 168–171. It is difficult to describe a causal body fully, because the senses belonging to the causal world are altogether different from and higher than those we employ at the physical level. Such memory of the appearance of a causal body, as it is possible for a clairvoyant to bring into his physical brain, represents it as ovoid, that being, in fact, the shape of all the higher bodies, and as surrounding the physical body of the man, extending to a distance of about 18 inches from the surface of the physical body.

I L I 401–402. A human being, who has just individualised from the animal kingdom, has a causal body of minimum size.

In the case of primitive man, the causal body resembles a bubble and gives the impression of being empty. It is a mere colourless film, just sufficient, apparently, to hold itself together and make a reincarnating entity, but no more. Although it is filled with higher mental matter, this is not yet brought into activity, and so it remains colourless and transparent.

As the man develops, this matter is gradually stirred into alertness by vibrations which reach it from the lower bodies. This comes but slowly, because the activities of man in the earlier stages of his evolution are not of a character to obtain expression in matter so fine as that of the causal body. But, when a man reaches the stage where he is capable either of abstract thought, or of unselfish emotion, the matter of the causal body is aroused into response.

The vibrations thus aroused show themselves in the causal body as colours, so that, instead of being a mere transparent bubble, it gradually becomes a sphere filled with matter of the most lovely and delicate hues, an object beautiful beyond all conception.

The student will be familiar with the meaning of the various colours, from his study of the same phenomenon in the astral and the mental bodies. Thus pale *T B* 47. rose expresses unselfish affection; yellow indicates high intellectual power; blue betokens devotion; sympathy is expressed by green; and luminous lilac-blue typifies the higher spirituality. These same colours in the denser bodies are, of course, far less delicate and also less living.

Although, in the course of his evolution in the lower *T B* 47: 58, *M V I* 74. *I L I* 261–262. *T P O* 194: 500. worlds, a man often introduces into his vehicles qualities which are undesirable, and entirely inappropriate for his life as an ego—such, for example, as pride, irritability, sensuality—yet none of these can be expressed in the causal body. Diagram XXIV may help to make clear the reason for this important phenomenon. Each section of the astral body acts strongly upon matter of the corresponding mental sub-plane. Hence, as the coarser vibrations of the astral body are expressed only in the lower sub-planes of the astral world, they will affect the mental body only, not the causal body. *The causal body, therefore, is affected only by the three higher portions of the astral body, and the vibrations in those portions represent only good qualities.*

The practical effect of this is that the man can build

into his ego, that is, into his true self, nothing but good qualities. The evil qualities which he develops are,

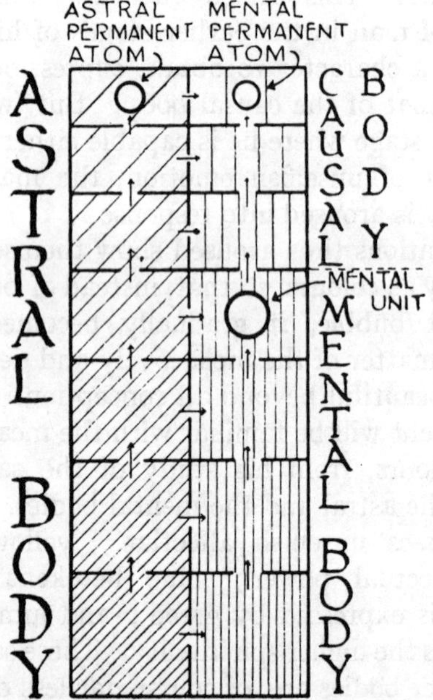

DIAGRAM XXIV.—Effect of Astral on Mental and Causal Bodies.

DIAGRAM XXIV.—The sub-planes of the astral and mental planes are here shown as of diminishing size, in order to illustrate the fact of their increasing fineness as we rise from the lower to the higher levels.

Openings between adjacent sub-planes of each plane indicate that certain of the " vibrations " of a given sub-plane can be transmitted to the sub-plane immediately above. These openings or gateways become narrower and narrower, indicating that only the finest vibrations can pass onwards to the higher levels.

Openings between each sub-plane of the astral plane and the corresponding sub-plane of the mental plane, indicate that there is also a possibility of an astral vibration being communicated, at a higher octave, to the corresponding mental sub-plane.

The diagram further illustrates that the mental body is more directly affected by the four lower levels of the astral plane, whilst the causal body is affected by only the three higher levels of astral matter.

from the point of view of the ego, only transitory, and must be thrown aside as the man advances, because he no longer has within him matter which can express them.

For coloured illustrations of causal bodies at various degrees of development, the student is referred to *Man Visible and Invisible*, by Bishop C. W. Leadbeater, as follows :—

Causal body of savage . .	Plate V, page 66
Causal body of average man .	Plate VIII, page 91
Causal body of developed man	Plate XXI, page 118
Causal body of Arhat . .	Plate XXVI, page 138

As already said, the causal body of an undeveloped *M V I* 66–
savage is like a gigantic soap-bubble, transparent yet 67.
iridescent. It is almost empty in appearance, what little there is within it representing certain qualities which may already have been evolved within the Group-Soul, of which it previously formed a part. The faint indications of these rates of vibrations are observable within the young causal body as dawning gleams of colour.

It might perhaps have been thought that the causal *I L II* 250.
body of a primitive man would be very small at first ; but this is not the case ; his causal body is the same size as any other ; it does at a later stage increase in size, but not until it has first been vivified and filled with active matter.

In the case of an average man, there is a distinct *M V I* 92–
increase in the content of the great ovoid film. A 93.
certain amount of exceedingly delicate and ethereal colour now exists within it, though it is still less than half filled. Something of the higher intellect is visible, and something of the power of devotion and unselfish love. There is also a faint tint of that exceedingly delicate violet which indicates the capacity of love and devotion turned towards the highest ideal, and also a faint hint of the clear green of sympathy and compassion.

As soon as the man begins to develop in spirituality, *D* 19–20.
or even higher intellect, a change takes place. The real individual then begins to have a persisting character of his own, apart from that moulded in each of his personalities in turn by training, and by surrounding cir-

cumstances. This character shows itself in the size, colour, luminosity, and definiteness of the causal body, just as that of the personality shows itself in the mental body, except that the higher vehicle is naturally subtler and more beautiful.

M V I 118–121. *M B* 86. *D P* 80–81.

In the case of the spiritually developed man, an enormous change is noticed. The glorious iridescent film is now completely filled with the most lovely colours, typifying the higher forms of love, devotion and sympathy, aided by an intellect refined and spiritualised, and by aspirations reaching ever towards the divine. Some of these colours have no place in the physical plane spectrum.

The inconceivably fine and delicate matter of such a causal body is intensely alive, and pulsating with living fire, forming a radiant globe of flashing colours, its high vibrations sending ripples of changing hues over its surface—hues of which earth knows nothing—brilliant, soft and luminous beyond the power of language to describe.

Such a causal body is filled with living fire, drawn from a still higher plane, with which it appears to be connected by a quivering thread of intense light—the Sutrātmā—vividly recalling to mind the stanzas of Dzyan: " The spark hangs from the flame by the finest thread of Fohat." As the soul grows, and is able to receive more and more from the inexhaustible ocean of the Divine Spirit, which pours down through the thread as a channel, the channel expands, and gives wider passage to the flood, till, on the next sub-plane, it might be imaged as a water-spout connecting earth and sky, and higher still as itself a globe, through which rushes the living spring, until the causal body seems to melt into the inpouring light. As the stanza says: " The thread between the watcher and his shadow becomes more strong and radiant with every change. The morning sunlight has changed into noon-day glory. This is thy present wheel, said the flame to the spark. Thou art myself, my image and my shadow. I have clothed myself in thee, and thou art my *vāhan* to the day 'Be-with-us,' when thou shalt re-become myself and others, thyself and me."

M V I 120–122. *T B* 48. *I L II* 247.

It was said above that in the undeveloped man the causal body is at first almost empty, and as the man develops, the ovoid gradually fills up. When it is completely filled, not only will it commence to grow in size but, in addition, streams of force will flow out in various directions. This, in fact, is one of the grandest characteristics of the developed man—his capacity to serve as a channel for higher force. For his attitude of helpfulness, and readiness to give, make it possible for the divine strength to descend upon him in a steady stream, and, through him, reach many who are not yet strong enough to receive it directly.

Furthermore, from the upper part of the causal body there ascends a crown of brilliant sparks, indicating the activity of spiritual aspiration, and of course adding very greatly to the beauty and dignity of the man's appearance. No matter how the lower man may be occupied on the physical plane, this stream of sparks rises constantly. The reason for this is that once the soul or ego of man is awakened upon his own level, and is beginning to understand something of himself, and his relation to the Divine, he looks ever upwards towards the source from which he came, quite irrespective of any activities which he may be inspiring on lower planes.

It must be remembered that even the noblest personality is but a very small and partial expression of the real higher self; so that as soon as the higher self begins to look round him, he finds almost unlimited possibilities opening before him, of which in this cramped physical life we can form no idea.

This very upward rushing of spiritual aspiration, which makes so glorious a crown for the developed man, is itself the channel through which the divine power descends: so that the fuller and stronger his aspirations become, the larger is the measure of the grace from on high.

M V I 137-139. *T B* 48.

In the case of the causal body of an Arhat. *i.e.*, of one

who has passed the Fourth of the great Initiations—the colours have two characteristics, which are irreconcilable on the physical plane. They are more delicate and ethereal than any that have been previously described: yet at the same time they are fuller, more brilliant and more luminous. The size of the causal body is many times larger than that of the physical body, and there is displayed magnificent development of the highest types of intellect, love and devotion, great wealth of sympathy, and highest spirituality.

The bands of colours are arranged now in concentric rings, while through these, and extending beyond them, there are streams of white light, radiating outwards from the centre. The outrush of Divine influence is thus enormously intensified, for the man has become an almost perfect channel for the life and power of the Logos. Not only does the glory radiate from him in white light, but all the colours of the rainbow play round him, in ever changing gleams like mother-of-pearl. Hence there is something in that radiation to strengthen the highest qualities in every person who approaches him, no matter what those qualities may be. None can come within the range of his influence without being the better for it; he shines upon all around him like the sun, for, like that luminary, he has become a manifestation of the Logos.

M V I 135–137. *T B* 48. *M B* 86. The causal body of an Adept or Master has enormously increased in size, and shines with a sun-like splendour far beyond all imagination in its glorious loveliness. Of the beauty and form of colour here, as Bishop Leadbeater states, no words can speak, for mortal language has no terms in which those radiant spheres may be described. Such a vehicle would be a separate study in itself, but one quite beyond the powers of any but those who are already far on the Path.

As in the case of the causal body of an Arhat, the colours no longer move in whirling clouds, but are arranged in great concentric shells, yet penetrated everywhere by radiations of living light, always pouring forth from Him as a centre.

The order of the colours varies according to the type to which the Adept belongs, so that there are several well-marked varieties amid their glory. A perfectly accurate tradition of this fact has been preserved in many of the roughly drawn pictures of the Lord Buddha, which may be seen upon temple walls in Ceylon. The Great Teacher is usually represented there surrounded by an aura; and, although the colouring and general arrangement of those surroundings would be very inaccurate, and even impossible, if intended for the aura of an ordinary man, or even for that of one who is of the rank of a Master, yet it is a rough and material representation of the actual higher vehicle of the Adept of that particular type, to which this Great One belongs.

The causal body is sometimes called the "auric egg." But, when H. P. Blavatsky spoke of the sacred auric egg, it seems probable that she meant the four permanent atoms—more accurately, the physical and astral permanent atoms, the mental unit, and the mental permanent atom—within an envelope of matter of the ātmic or nirvānic plane.

D. 15.
M 15.
I L I 347–348.
A W 169.

The causal body is known also as the Augoeides, the glorified man; it is not an image of any one of his past vehicles, but contains within itself the essence of all that was best in each of them. It thus indicates, more or less perfectly, as through experience it grows, what the Deity means that man shall be. For, as we have seen, by observation of the causal vehicle it is possible to see the stage of evolution which the man has reached. Not only can his past history be seen, but also to a considerable extent the future that lies before him.

The glorified form within the causal body is an approach to the archetype, and comes nearer to it as man develops. The human form appears to be the model for the highest evolution in this particular system. It is varied slightly in different planets, but is,

I L II 455.

broadly speaking, the same in general outline. In other solar systems forms may possibly be quite unlike it : on that point we have no information.

I L I 347. Prāna, or Vitality, exists in all planes, and therefore must play some part in the causal body, but concerning this no information is at present available.

S C 155. We may note, however, that after the formation of the causal body, the complexity of the prāna circulating in the nervous system of the physical body much increases, and it appears to become yet more enriched in the progress of human evolution. For, as the consciousness becomes active on the mental plane, the prāna of that plane mingles with the lower, as the activity of consciousness is carried on in higher regions.

I L I 447. In the causal body also, as in each of the other vehicles, there are Chakrams, or Force-Centres, which, in addition to other functions, serve as points of connection at which force flows from one vehicle to another. At the present time, however, no information is available regarding the Chakrams of the causal body.

CHAPTER XVII

CAUSAL THOUGHT

THE mental plane, as we know, is the sphere of action *M V I* 22.
of what we call mind, or manas, in man. As we have *T* 37.
already seen, the plane is divided into two parts, the higher, consisting of the three upper sub-planes, and the lower, consisting of the four lower sub-planes. The two divisions are known as arūpa, or formless, and rūpa, having form.

In man, Intellect has, as its vehicle, the causal body, with abstract thought as its function, whilst Mind has, as its vehicle, the mental body, with the function of concrete thinking.

The Mind acquires knowledge by utilising the senses for observations : it works on its percepts, and builds them into concepts. Its powers are attention, memory, reasoning by induction and deduction, imagination, and the like.

The names arūpa and rūpa are given in order to indicate a certain quality of the matter of the mental plane. In the lower part of it, the matter is very readily moulded by the action of human thought into definite forms ; in the higher division, this does not occur, the more abstract thought of that level expressing itself to the eye of the clairvoyant in flashes or streams.

On the arūpa levels, the difference in the effect of *D P* 24.
thought is very marked, especially as regards the ele- *M* 50.
mental essence. The disturbance set up in the mere *T P O* 774.
matter of the plane is similar, though greatly intensified in this much more refined form of matter. But, in the elemental essence, no form at all is now created, and the method of action is entirely changed.

On the lower sub-planes, an elemental or thought-form, which is there created, hovers about the person thought of, and awaits a favourable opportunity of expending its energy either upon his mental body, his astral body, or even his physical body. But, on the three higher sub-planes, the result is a kind of lightning flash of the essence from the causal body of the thinker, direct to the causal body of the object of his thought.

So that, while on the lower sub-planes the thought is always directed to the mere personality, on the higher sub-planes we influence the reincarnating ego, the real man himself. If the message has any reference to the personality, it will reach that personality only from above, through the instrumentality of the causal body.

T C 146–149. It is said to be a striking sight to observe the change from an abstract or arūpa idea to a concrete or rūpa thought, as the idea clothes itself in the matter of the four lower sub-planes.

The standard and simple example is that of a triangle. Difficult as it is to describe in words, which belong to the planes of form, the abstract idea of a triangle is a reality on the arūpa levels. It means a non-figure, which is yet a figure. The figure—which is yet no *particular* figure, is circumscribed by three lines, yet not by any particular lines: its three angles possess the property of making collectively two right angles; yet they are not particular angles.

On the arūpa levels, this abstract idea of a triangle has real existence. With the sense of the causal body it is seen, or apprehended. It is a fact of consciousness, external to the observer, even though it is not what we usually mean by a form.

If such an abstract triangle is thrown into contact with the matter of the rūpa sub-planes, instantly it becomes an indefinite number of triangles, each of which has a definite form. There will be triangles of every known shape—equilateral, isosceles, scalene, right-angled, acute-angled, obtuse-angled—all coming into visible existence.

If the abstract idea is brought down within the causal body, the observer becomes a fountain of triangles, which go off in all directions, much as a jet of water, which spurts up as a more or less coherent mass, comes down as a fountain, separating into innumerable drops and spray. That is perhaps the best physical analogy of the process that can be given.

As was fully explained in *The Mental Body*, concrete *D P* 15. thought naturally takes the shape of the objects which we thought about : abstract ideas, when thrown down into the rūpa levels, usually represent themselves by all kinds of perfect and most beautiful geometrical figures. It should, however, be remembered that many thoughts which down here are little more than mere abstractions, become on the mental plane concrete facts.

Causal consciousness thus deals with the *essence* of a *M* 50–51. *M P* 181–182. thing, whilst the lower mind studies its details. With the mind, we talk round a subject, or endeavour to explain it : with the causal consciousness, we take up the essence of the idea of the subject, and move it as a whole, as one moves a piece when playing chess. The causal plane is a world of realities : we no longer deal with emotions, ideas or conceptions, but with the thing in itself.

It may be well to describe rather more in detail the *A W* 285–287. process of arriving at causal thought. Whilst the lower mind dwells entirely on mental images, obtained from sensations, reasons on purely concrete objects, and is concerned with the attributes which differentiate one object from another, the ego, using the causal consciousness, having learned to discriminate clearly between objects, by dwelling upon their *unlikenesses*, now begins to group them together by some attribute which appears in a number of objects, otherwise dissimilar, and makes a link between them.

He draws out, abstracts, this common attribute, and sets all objects that possess it apart from the rest that are without it. In this way, he evolves the power of recognising identity amid diversity, a step towards the much later recognition of the One underlying the many.

He thus classifies all that is around him, developing

the synthetic faculty, and learning to construct as well as to analyse.

Presently, he takes another step, and conceives of the common property as an idea, apart from all the objects in which it appears, and thus constructs a kind of mental image higher than the image of a concrete object—the image of an idea that has no phenomenal existence in the world of form, but which exists on the higher levels of the mental plane, and affords material on which the ego, the Thinker himself, can work.

The lower mind reaches the abstract idea by reason, and, in so doing, accomplishes its loftiest flight, touching the threshold of the formless world, and dimly seeing that which lies beyond.

The Thinker, with his causal consciousness, sees these ideas, and lives among them habitually. As he exercises and develops the power of abstract reasoning, he becomes effective in his own world, and begins his life of active functioning in his own sphere.

Such a man would care little for the life of the senses, or for external observation, or for mental application to images of external objects. His powers are indrawn, no longer rushing outwards in the search for satisfaction. He dwells calmly within himself, engrossed with the problems of philosophy, with the deeper aspects of life and thought, seeking to understand causes, rather than troubling himself with effects, and approaching nearer and nearer to the recognition of the One that underlies all the diversities of external nature.

The method of passing from the lower mental to the causal consciousness, by means of an orderly process of concentration, meditation and contemplation, is described in detail in *The Mental Body*, and so need not be repeated here.

I L II 157. On the higher levels of the mental plane, thoughts act with much greater force than on the lower levels: one reason for this is, that, as comparatively few are as yet able to think on these higher levels, any thoughts, which are generated there, have the field practically to themselves : *i.e.*, there are not many other thoughts in that realm, with which they have to contend.

D P 94–95.

Most thoughts of the ordinary man begin in the mental body, on the lower mental levels, and clothe themselves, as they descend, with the appropriate astral elemental essence. But, when a man is active on the causal levels, his thought commences there, and clothes itself first in the elemental essence of the lower levels of the mental plane, and is consequently infinitely finer, more penetrating, and in every way more effective.

If the thought be directed exclusively to higher objects, its vibrations may be of too fine a character to find expression on the astral plane at all. But, if they do affect such lower matter, they will do so with much more far-reaching effect than those which are generated so much nearer to the level of that lower matter.

Following this principle a stage further, it is clear that the thought of the Initiate, taking its rise upon the Buddhic plane, above the mental world altogether, will clothe itself with the elemental essence of the causal sub-planes. Similarly, the thought of the Adept will pour down from the plane of ātmā, wielding the tremendous and wholly incalculable powers of regions beyond the ken of ordinary humanity.

Hence the truth of the saying that the work of one day, on levels such as these, may well surpass in efficiency the toil of a thousand years on the physical plane.

D P 15.
T C 147–152.

Students who are not accustomed to causal thought, to thinking in principles, should be careful that they do not, by their efforts to think abstractly, at first cause headaches, which mean, of course, in this instance, that the mechanism of the brain is being strained. Meditation, practised regularly for a number of years, should establish a certain tendency of the causal consciousness to be affected by the consciousness in the mental body. When that has been established, abstract thought at the causal levels should be possible, without risk of straining the thinking mechanism.

When the effort to form an abstract conception, say of a triangle, has been successful, the student may at first feel a little dazed in the attempt to grasp the abstract idea: later, the consciousness will suddenly change, and become clear. That means that the centre of consciousness has been transferred from the mental to the causal body, and the student becomes conscious, in his causal body, of a distinct existence outside himself.

That is the "intuition" of the causal body, which recognises the *outer*. The "intuition" of Buddhi, as we shall see in a later chapter, recognises the *inner*, enabling one to see things from the inside. With the intellectual intuition, one realises a thing which is outside oneself.

A W 174–175. Again the student may be reminded that, in spite of external differences of functioning between the higher and the lower mind, yet Manas, the Thinker, is one, the Self in the causal body. It is the source of innumerable energies, of vibrations of innumerable kinds. These it sends out, raying outwards from itself. The subtlest and finest of these are expressed in the matter of the causal body, which alone is fine enough to respond to them. They form what is sometimes called the Pure Reason, whose thoughts are abstract, whose method of gaining knowledge is intuition. Its very "nature is knowledge," and it recognises truth at sight as congruous with itself.

The less subtle vibrations pass outwards from the one Thinker, attracting the matter of the lower mental world, and becoming the activities of the lower mind, as has already been described.

A E P. It is, perhaps, somewhat unfortunate that Buddhi is also sometimes spoken of as Pure Reason, and its faculty is described as that of intuition. As psychology progresses, no doubt appropriate terms will be selected, and applied, specifically and solely, to the distinct functions of the causal consciousness, and to the Buddhic faculties.

T P 83–84: 25. *T P O* 210. It was said above, of Manas, that its very "nature is knowledge." That is so, because Manas is the reflection, in the atomic matter of the mental plane, of the cognitional aspect of the Self—of the Self as Knower. It is therefore possible to unfold a power of knowing truth at sight. This shows itself only when the lower mind, with its slow processes of reasoning, is transcended. For whenever the "I"—the expression of the Self whose "nature is knowledge"—comes into contact with a truth, he finds its vibrations regular, and therefore capable of producing a coherent image in himself: whereas the false causes a distorted image, out of proportion, by its very reflection announcing its nature.

As the lower mind assumes a more and more subordinate position, these powers of the ego assert their own predominance, and intuition—which is analogous to the direct vision of the physical plane—takes the place of reasoning, which may aptly be compared with the physical plane sense of touch.

Thus intuition develops out of reasoning in the same unbroken manner, and without change of essential nature, as the eye develops out of touch. The change of "manner" should not blind us to the orderly and sequential evolution of the faculty.

The student will, of course, be careful to distinguish genuine intuition from that pseudo-intuition of the unintelligent, which is merely impulse, born of desire, and is not higher, but lower than reasoning.

The act of thinking develops the spirillæ in the physical atoms: hence those who are definitely and carefully thinking day by day are not only improving their own powers of thought, but are also improving for others the amount of available material of a higher kind, thus facilitating high thinking. *T N P* 58.

In the etheric body of man, the brow chakram, or force-centre, which utilises the dark blue prāna, is associated with the principle of higher manas. *Ch.* 34.

CHAPTER XVIII

DEVELOPMENT AND FACULTIES OF THE CAUSAL BODY

In Chapter XV, we saw that only good elements are stored in the causal body, evil finding in that body no means of expression. We may now consider this matter a little further, and study the effects which are produced, more or less indirectly, on the causal body by the practice of evil.

M B 78. In a primitive man, the growth of the causal body is
M V I 74. necessarily exceedingly slow. As we have seen, it is
D 20.
A W 171. by the method of exciting sympathetic vibration that the higher qualities, developed by the life on lower planes, are gradually built into the causal body: but in the life of an undeveloped man there will be very few feelings or thoughts, belonging to the higher world, which can serve as food for the growth of the real man. Hence the growth is slow, for all the rest of the life does not aid it.

But even the worst of men can commonly show himself on the causal plane, though as an entirely undeveloped entity. His vices, even though continued through life after life, cannot soil the causal body. They can, however, make it more and more difficult to develop the opposite virtues.

T B 112–113. In every case, the existence of an evil quality in the
M 13. personality means a lack of the corresponding good quality in the causal body. For an ego cannot be evil, though he can be imperfect. The qualities which the ego develops cannot be other than good qualities, and, when they are well defined, they show themselves in each of all his numerous personalities: consequently, those personalities can never be guilty of the vices opposite to those good qualities.

A good quality which is lacking, may nevertheless be said to exist in the ego, although it has not yet been called into activity. As soon as it *is* called into activity, its intense vibrations will act upon the lower vehicles, and it will be impossible, as said, for the opposite evil ever again to find place in them.

Where there is a gap in the ego, indicating that there is a quality undeveloped, there need not necessarily be a definite vice in the personality; but there is also nothing *positive* in the personality to prevent the growth of the vice in question. Hence, since in all probability many other people around him already possess that vice, and since man is an imitative animal, it is more than likely that he will develop that vice. The vice, however, as we have seen, belongs only to the lower vehicles, and not to the real man in the causal body. In those lower vehicles its repetition may set up a momentum which it is hard to conquer: but, if the ego bestirs himself to create in himself the opposite virtue, the vice is cut off at the root, and can no longer exist, neither in this life nor in all the lives that are to come.

Thus the shortest way to get rid of evil, and prevent its reappearance, is to fill the gap in the ego, so that the good quality which is thus developed will show itself as an integral part of the man's character through all his future lives.

Whilst evil cannot be definitely stored in the causal *M V I* 72.
body, yet the practice of evil may affect the causal body; for every intensification of vice in the lower vehicles, every indulgence in it in the lower worlds, tends somewhat to dim the luminosity of the opposite virtues in the causal body.

The "I" cannot "assimilate anything that is evil," *T C* 50–52.
for it cannot touch the "I" level of consciousness. *A W* 172.
The ego is not conscious of evil; he knows nothing about it, so that it makes no impression upon him. The utmost result brought about in the causal body by very, very long continued lives of a low type, is what may be called a certain incapacity to receive the

opposite good impression for a very considerable period afterwards, a kind of numbness or paralysis of the matter of the causal body. This is not so much consciousness as unconsciousness; an unconsciousness which resists impressions of the good of the opposite kind. That is the limit of the harm that is done. Hence, when the life of evil has been very much prolonged, it will take many more lives in order to bring out the first response to the good side of activity.

This result was observed when, in studying past lives, an endeavour was made to understand how the causal body was not injured through a number of savage lives. In very prolonged cases, where there was an abnormal number of such lives, this effect of numbness was noted, brought about by the repeated beating upon it of evil, over a long period. A number of lives then had to be spent in restoring, so to say, the responsive vitality to that portion of the causal body. Such cases, however, are abnormal.

M B 79–80. We may pursue the study of the effects of evil still further. Where evil is subtle and persistent, it drags away, if the expression be permitted, something of the individual himself. If evil be continually followed, the mental body becomes so entangled with the astral body, that after death it cannot free itself entirely: some of its very substance is torn away from it, and, when the astral body in its turn dies and disintegrates, the matter of the mental body, which has been wrenched away, also goes back to the general stock of mental matter and is thus lost to the individual. In ordinary cases, the harm done to the causal body does not go further than this. We shall deal with this aspect of our subject in more technical detail in Chapter XXV.

M B 79. Where, however, the ego has become strong, both in intellect and in will, without at the same time increasing in unselfishness and love, it contracts itself round its own separated centre, instead of expanding, as it grows: it thus builds around it a wall of selfishness, and uses its developing powers for itself, instead of for others. In such cases, there arises the possibility, alluded to in so many of the world-scriptures, of the ego setting himself consciously against the "Good Law," of fighting deliberately against evolution. Then the causal body itself shows the dark hues, brought about by contraction, and loses the dazzling radiance which is its characteristic property. Harm such as this cannot be wrought by an ego who is poorly developed, nor by ordinary passional or mental faults. To effect injury so far-reaching, the ego must be highly evolved, and must have its energies awakened on the mental plane.

It is for this reason that ambition, pride and powers of the intellect, used for selfish aims, are so far more dangerous, and deadly in their effects, than the more palpable faults of the lower nature. So that the "Pharisee" is often further from the "kingdom of God" than the "publican and sinner." Along this line is developed the "black magician," the man who conquers passion and desire, develops will and the higher powers of the mind, not to offer them as forces to help forward the evolution of the whole, but in order to grasp all he can for himself as a unit, to hold, and not to share. Such men set themselves to maintain separation as against unity, striving to retard instead of to quicken evolution. They vibrate in discord with the whole, instead of in harmony, and are in danger of that rending of the ego himself, which means the loss of all the fruits of evolution.

Hitherto we have spoken mainly of the effects of evil on a man's growth: let us now look at the other side of the picture. All those, who are beginning to understand something of the causal body, can make its evolution a definite object in life. They can strive to think, feel and act unselfishly, and so contribute to its growth and activity. Life after life this evolution of the individual proceeds, and, in aiding its growth by conscious effort, we are working in harmony with the Divine will, and carrying out the purpose for which we are here. Nothing good, that is once woven into the causal body, can ever be lost or dissipated: *M B* 80–81.

for this is the man that lives, so long as he remains man.

Thus we see that by the law of evolution everything that is evil, however strong it may seem, has within itself the germ of its own destruction, while everything that is good has in it the seed of immortality. The secret of this lies in the fact that everything evil is inharmonious, because it sets itself against the cosmic law. Sooner or later, therefore, it is broken up by that law, dashed into pieces against it. Everything that is good, on the other hand, being in harmony with the law, is taken on by it and carried forward: it becomes part of the stream of evolution, of that "not ourselves which makes for righteousness," and therefore can never perish or be destroyed.

We may conceive of all the experiences of a man as passing through a fine sieve or mesh: only that which is good can pass through: that which is evil is left behind, rejected. In this, the very mechanism by which the causal body, the vehicle of the man that endures, is built up, lies not only the hope of man, but the certainty of his final triumph. However slow the growth, it is there: however long the way, it has its ending. The individual, which is our Self, is evolving, and cannot be utterly destroyed. Even though by our folly we may make the growth slower than it need be, none the less everything we contribute to it, however little, lasts in it for ever, and is our possession for all the ages that lie in front.

M V I 74–75. *I L I* 262. Whilst nothing evil can be stored in the causal body, it is, however, stored, if we may so use the term, in the lower vehicles to which it pertains. For, under the law of justice, every man must receive the results of his own actions, be they bad or good. But evil necessarily works itself out on the lower planes, because it is only in the matter of those planes that its vibrations can be expressed, and it has not even overtones capable of awakening a response in the causal body. Its force, therefore, is all expended at its own level, and it reacts in its entirety upon its creator in his astral and physical life, whether in this or in future incarnations.

More precisely, the result of evil is stored in the mental unit, and in the astral and physical permanent atoms; and so the man has to face it over and over again; but that, of course, is a very different matter from taking it into the ego and making it really a part of himself.

Good actions and thoughts also, of course, produce results on the lower planes, but, in addition to that, they have the immensely higher and permanent effect upon the causal body. Thus, all alike produce effects on the lower planes, and are manifested in the lower temporary vehicles, but good qualities alone are retained in the causal body as so much definite gain to the real man.

In this way, at first slowly, in the later stages with *T B* 50.
ever-increasing rapidity, a man's causal body is built. *D P* 81. *T* 37.
At each stage of his growth, a study of the colours and *M P* 180.
striations of the causal body reveals the progress the *I L I* 401.
ego has made since the causal body was first formed, when the entity emerged from the animal kingdom, and the exact stage of evolution at which he has now arrived.

As we have seen, in the later stages of evolution, both the causal and mental bodies expand enormously, exhibiting the most gorgeous radiance of many-coloured lights, glowing with intense splendour when comparatively at rest, and sending forth dazzling coruscations when in high activity.

As the causal body becomes able to express more and more of the ego, it extends further and further from its physical centre, until the man is able to enfold hundreds and even thousands of persons within himself, and so exercise a vast influence for good.

The pouring into the causal body of faculties *T P O* 844.
acquired by a personality is analogous to the pouring into the Group-Soul of the experiences acquired by the forms in which portions of the Group-Soul incarnate. Thus, for example, supposing that the quality of accuracy is developed in a personality: when that

quality goes back to the ego in the causal body, the same amount has to be spread over the whole causal body. The amount, which was quite sufficient to make one personality very accurate, when it goes into the ego, is only a fractional part of his requirements. He may consequently need many lives to develop enough of the quality to make it prominent in the next life, especially as the ego does not put into the next personality the same piece of himself, but simply a piece of the whole mass of himself.

M 12. The student must, all through his studies, recollect that the causal body is *not* the ego, but only such matter of the higher mental plane which has been vivified, and which expresses the *qualities* the ego has acquired.

M V I 140. The real man himself—the divine trinity within—we may not see: but the more our sight and knowledge increase, the more nearly we approach that which veils Itself in him. Thus we may think of the causal body as the nearest to a conception of the true man that our sight will at present give us.

T B 48. The student will recollect also, that it is by the size and shape of the causal body that are determined the

I L II 246. size and shape of the mental body. In fact, the aura of a man, which has a definite size, is the same as that of a section of the causal body, and, as the causal body grows, that section becomes larger, and the man has a larger aura.

M V I 123. Furthermore, in the case of a developed man, the mental body becomes a reflection of the causal body, since the man learns to follow solely the promptings of the higher self, and to guide his reason exclusively by them.

T P 85. In the process of meditation (*vide The Mental Body*, p. 160), as the mental body is stilled, the consciousness escapes from it, and passes into and out of the "laya centre," the neutral points of contact between the mental body and the causal body. The passage is accompanied by a momentary swoon, or loss of consciousness—the inevitable result of the disappearance of objects of consciousness—followed by consciousness in the higher. The dropping out of objects of consciousness, belonging to the lower worlds, is thus followed by the appearance of objects of consciousness in the higher world. Then the ego can shape the mental body according to his own lofty thoughts, and permeate it with his own vibrations. He can mould it after the high visions of the planes beyond his own, of which he has caught a glimpse in his highest moments, and can thus convey downwards and outwards ideas to which the mental body would otherwise be unable to respond.

Such ideas are the inspirations of genius, that flash down into the mind with dazzling light, and illuminate a world.

We may here usefully repeat the substance of what *S P* 54–56. was said in *The Mental Body*, p. 160, etc., directing our attention now, not so much to the lower brain consciousness, as to that of the ego working in the causal body. Genius, which is of the ego, *sees* instead of arguing. True intuition is one of its faculties. The lower manas or mind, working in the brain apparatus, arranges facts, gathered by observation, balances them one against the other, and draws conclusions from them. By the process of ratiocination it operates, using the methods of induction and deduction.

Intuition, on the other hand, as etymology indicates, is in-sight, looking within—a process as direct and swift as physical sight. It is the exercise of the eyes of the intelligence, the unerring recognition of a truth presented on the mental plane. Proof is unnecessary, because it is above and beyond reason. Great care must, of course, be taken to distinguish mere kāmic impulse from true intuition. It is only when the desires and appetites of the lower kāmic self are stilled and at rest that the voice of the higher mind can make itself heard in the lower personality.

In *Isis Unveiled*, pp. 305–306, H. P. Blavatsky explains the matter with force and lucidity. Allied to the physical half of man's nature, she says, is reason : allied to his spiritual part is his conscience, which is that instantaneous perception between right and wrong which can be exercised by the spirit which, being a portion of the divine wisdom and purity, is itself absolutely pure and wise. Its promptings are independent of reason, and can manifest themselves clearly only when they are unhampered by the baser attractions of the lower nature. Reason, she points out, being wholly dependent on the evidence of other senses, cannot be a quality pertaining directly to the divine spirit. For spirit *knows*—hence reasoning is useless. Hence the ancient Theurgists maintained that the rational part of man's soul (spirit) never entered wholly into the man's body, but only overshadowed him, more or less through the irrational or astral soul, which serves as an intermediary agent or medium between spirit and body. The man who has conquered matter sufficiently to receive the direct light from his shining *Augoeides* (see p. 101), feels truth intuitionally. He could not err in his judgment, notwithstanding all the sophisms suggested by reason, for he is *illuminated*. Hence, prophecy, vaticination, and so-called divine inspiration, are simply the effects of this illumination from above, by our own immortal spirit.

S P 30–32. As with a flame we may light a wick, and the colour of the flame of the burning wick will depend on the nature of the wick, and of the liquid in which it is soaked, so in each human being the flame of manas sets alight the brain and kāmic wick, and the colour of the light from the wick will depend upon the kāmic nature, and the development of the brain-apparatus.

In her article on "Genius," H. P. Blavatsky explained this matter clearly: what we call the manifestations of genius in a person are only the more or less successful efforts of the ego to assert itself through its outer objective form. The *egos* of a Newton, an Æschylus, a Shakespeare, are of the same essence and substance as the *egos* of a yokel, an ignoramus, a fool, or even an idiot. The self-assertion of their informing *genii* depends on the physiological and material construction of the physical man. No *ego* differs from another *ego* in its primordial or original essence and nature. That which makes of one mortal a great man and of another a vulgar, silly person is, as said, the quality and make-up of the shell or casing, the adequacy or inadequacy of brain and body to transmit and give expression to the light of the real *inner* man—the *ego.*

To use a familiar simile, physical man is the instrument, the ego the performing artist. The potentiality of perfect melody rests in the instrument, and no skill of the artist can awaken faultless harmony out of a broken or badly constructed instrument. This harmony depends upon the fidelity of transmission, by word and act, to the objective plane, of the unspoken divine thought in the very depths of man's subjective or inner nature: in a word, of his ego.

Mental ability, intellectual strength, acuteness, subtlety, are manifestations of lower manas in man: they may reach as far as what H. P. Blavatsky spoke of as "artificial genius," the outcome of culture and purely intellectual acuteness. Often its nature is demonstrated by the presence of kāmic elements in it, *i.e.*, of passion, vanity, arrogance.

At the present stage of human evolution, higher manas can but rarely manifest itself. Occasional flashes of it are what we call true genius. "Behold in every manifestation of genius, *when combined with virtue*, the undeniable presence of the celestial exile, the divine ego whose jailer thou art, O man of matter." Such manifestations depend upon an accumulation of individual antecedent experiences of the ego in its preceding life or lives. For, although it is omniscient in its essence and nature, yet it still requires experience, through its *personalities*, of the things of earth, in order to apply the fruition of its abstract experience to them. And the cultivation of certain aptitudes, throughout a long series of incarnations, must finally culminate, in some one life, as *genius*, in one direction or another. It is clear from the above that, for the manifestation of true genius, purity of life is essential.

D 21–23. It is important to recognise the part which the ego in the causal body plays in the formation of our conceptions of external objects. The vibrations of nerve-threads present to the brain merely impressions: it is the work of the ego to classify, combine, and arrange them. The discrimination of the ego, acting through the mind, is brought to bear upon everything that the senses transmit to the brain. Furthermore, this discrimination is not an inherent instinct of the mind, perfect from the first, but is the result of the comparison of a number of previous experiences.

D P 31. Before considering the possibility of functioning consciously on the causal plane, we may remind ourselves that, for a man still attached to a physical body to move in *full* consciousness on the mental plane—*i.e.*, either the lower or the higher mental—he must be either an Adept or one of Their Initiated pupils, for until a student has been taught by his Master how to use his mental body he will be unable to move with freedom even upon its lower levels.

To function consciously during physical life upon the higher levels denotes, of course, still greater advancement, for it means the unification of the man, so that down here he is no longer a mere personality, more or less influenced by the individuality above, but is himself that individuality or ego. He is certainly still trammelled and confined by a body, but nevertheless he has within him the power and knowledge of a highly developed ego.

L I 401. At present, most people are not more than just conscious in the causal body: they can work only in the matter of the third sub-plane, *i.e.*, the lowest part of the causal body, and in fact only the lowest matter even of that is usually in operation. When they are on the Path, the second sub-plane opens up. The Adept, of course, uses the whole causal body, while his consciousness is on the physical plane. These details will be considered a little more fully in a later chapter.

D P 4. Passing now to more specific and detailed powers of the causal body, it will be recollected, as explained in the two preceding volumes of this series, that it is not possible for a man to pass to another planet of our chain either in his astral or his mental body. In the causal body, however, when very highly developed, this achievement is possible, though even then by no means with the ease or the rapidity with which it can be done on the Buddhic plane, by those who have succeeded in raising their consciousness to that level.

It appears, however, that a causal body would not *I L II* 266–
normally be able to move in interstellar space. In 268.
that space it seems that atoms lie far apart and equidistant, and this is probably their normal condition when undisturbed. That is what is meant by speaking of the atoms as "free." Within the atmosphere of a planet they are never found at all in that state, for even when they are not grouped in forms, they are at any rate enormously compressed by the force of attraction.

In interplanetary space, the conditions are probably not exactly the same as in interstellar space, for there may be a great deal of disturbance due to cometic and meteoric matter, and also the tremendous attraction of the sun produces a considerable compression within the limits of this system.

Hence the atomic matter of a man's causal body is crushed together by attraction into a definite and quite dense shape, even though the atoms are in no way altered in themselves, and are not grouped into molecules. While such a body can exist comfortably on its own atomic plane, in the neighbourhood of a planet, where the atomic matter is compressed, it would not be able to move or function in far-away space where the atoms are "free" and uncompressed.

The power of magnification belongs to the causal *I L II* 203–
body, and is associated with the brow chakram, the 204.
force-centre between the eyebrows. From the central portion of this chakram what may be called a tiny microscope is projected, having for its lens only one atom. In this way an organ is produced, commensurate in size with the minute objects to be observed.

The atom employed may be either physical, astral or mental, but, whichever it is, it needs a special preparation. All its spirillæ must be opened up, so that it is just as it will be in the seventh round of our chain of worlds.

If an atom of a level lower than the causal be used as an eye-piece, a system of reflecting counterparts must be introduced. The atom can be adjusted to any sub-plane, so that any required degree of magnification can be applied, in order to suit the object which is being examined. A further extension of the same power enables the operator to focus his own consciousness in the lens through which he is looking, and then to project it to distant points.

The same power, by a different arrangement, can be used for diminishing purposes, when one wishes to view as a whole something far too large to be taken in at once by ordinary vision.

I L II 236. The sight of the causal body enables one to foresee the future to some extent. Even with physical senses one may sometimes foretell certain things. Thus, for example, if we see a man leading a life of debauchery, we may safely predict that, unless he changes, he will presently lose health and fortune. What we cannot tell, by physical means, is whether the man will change or not.

But a man who has the sight of a causal body could often tell this, because to him the reserve forces of the other would be visible. He could see what the ego thought of it all, and whether he was strong enough to interfere. No merely physical prediction is certain, because so many of the causes which influence life cannot be seen on this lower plane. But, when the consciousness is raised to higher planes, we can see more of the causes, and so can come nearer to calculating the effects.

I L II 237. It is, of course, easier to foresee the future of an undeveloped man than of one more advanced. For the ordinary man has little will-power ; karma assigns him certain surroundings, and he is the creature of those surroundings; he accepts the fate marked out for him, because he does not know that he can alter it.

A more developed man, however, takes hold of his destiny, and moulds it; he makes his future what he wills it to be, counteracting the karma of the past by setting fresh forces in motion. Hence his future is not so easily predicable. But no doubt even in this case an Adept, who could see the latent will, could also calculate how he would use it.

Students of *The Mental Body* will recollect that there *M* 80. is there given a description of the Ākāshic Records, or the Memory of Nature, as it is sometimes called. In reading these Records, the work is done through the causal body, the mental body vibrating only in response to the activity of the causal body. For that reason, no satisfactory or reliable reading of the Records can be done without definite development of the causal body.

Bishop Leadbeater describes an interesting and *M* 76–82. unusual case where, through reckless mental overwork, a man so aroused the faculties of his causal body that he was able, spasmodically, to read the Records with great clarity of detail. In addition, he was able to exercise the power of magnification to some extent, particularly in regard to perfumes. The result, which is characteristic of this faculty, was a *roughening* of a smell, the smell losing its smoothness, and becoming like woollen cloth, so to say, or a basin of sand. The reason for this is that the faculty of magnification, which belongs to the causal body, causes the tiny physical particles which arouse in us the sense of smell to become separately appreciable, like the grains on sandpaper, and so the sense of roughness is produced.

Needless to say, this method of arousing the powers of the causal body by overwork is strongly to be deprecated, as it is far more likely to result in breakdown of the brain or nervous system than, as happened in this rare instance, to arouse causal faculties.

If a man raises his consciousness to the highest sub- *I L I* 146–149. division of his causal body, and focusses it exclusively *T P O* 59–60: 689. in the atomic matter of the mental plane, he has before him three possibilities of moving his consciousness, which correspond to some extent with the three dimensions of space.

Obviously, (1) a way is open to him to move it downwards into the second sub-plane of the mental, or upward into the lowest sub-plane of the Buddhic, provided, of course, that he has developed his Buddhic body sufficiently to be able to utilise it as a vehicle.

(2) A second line of movement is the short cut from the atomic sub-division of one plane to the corresponding atomic sub-division of the planes above or below, without touching any of the intermediate sub-planes.

(3) A third possibility is not so much a *movement* along another line, at right angles to both of these others, but rather a possibility of looking up such a line, the line that joins the ego and the Monad, much as a man at the bottom of a well might look up at a star in the sky above him.

For there is a direct line of communication between the atomic sub-plane of the mental in this lowest *cosmic* plane and the corresponding atomic mental in the *cosmic* mental plane. Although we are as yet infinitely far from being able to climb upwards by that line, yet Bishop Leadbeater states that once at least the experience came of being able to look up it for a moment. What is seen, he says, it is hopeless to try to describe, for no human words can give the least idea of it. But at least this much emerges, with a certitude that can never be shaken, that what we have hitherto supposed to be our consciousness, our intellect, is simply not ours at all, but His. Not even a reflection of His, but literally and truly a part of His consciousness, a part of His intellect. Some little help in understanding this may be derived from the knowledge that the human ego itself is a manifestation of the Third Outpouring which comes from His First Aspect, the eternal and all-loving Father.

I L I 34. The growth and development of the causal body is greatly assisted by the work of the Masters, for They deal more with egos in their causal bodies than with the lower vehicles of men. They devote themselves to pouring spiritual influence upon men, raying out, as the sunlight radiates upon flowers, thereby evoking from them all that is noblest and best in them, and so promoting their growth. Many people are sometimes conscious of helpful influences of this description, but are quite unable to trace them to their source. This work will be explained somewhat more fully in a later chapter.

CHAPTER XIX

LIFE AFTER DEATH: THE FIFTH HEAVEN

In *The Astral Body* and *The Mental Body* we have dealt with the life of a man after death on the astral plane, and also on the lower mental plane, in his mental body, in the First, Second, Third and Fourth Heaven-worlds, on the Seventh, Sixth, Fifth and Fourth Sub-Planes respectively. We now have to describe the life after death in the causal body, on the three higher levels of the mental plane.

D P 19–20. The distinction between the two great divisions of the mental plane—the lower or rūpa (form) and the higher or arūpa (formless)—is very marked: so different, indeed, are the two worlds, that different vehicles of consciousness are necessary for functioning in them.

In *The Mental Body*, pp. 202–204, the general rationale and purpose of the life in devachan has already been explained, and so need not be repeated here. It was also explained in that book why devachan is a necessity for the great majority of people. In certain exceptional cases, however, we saw that a man sufficiently advanced, with the permission of a very high authority, may "renounce devachan," and take a series of rapid incarnations, without any appreciable intervals between them.

T P O 384. In the lower mental plane, matter is dominant: it is the first thing that strikes the eye; and consciousness shines with difficulty through the forms. But in the higher planes life is the most prominent thing, and forms are there only for its purposes. The difficulty in the lower planes is to give the life expression in the forms: in the higher, it is the reverse—to hold and give form to the flood of life. It is only above the

dividing line between the lower and higher mental planes that the light of consciousness is subject to no wind, and shines with its own power. The symbol of a spiritual fire is very fitting for consciousness at those levels, as distinguished from the lower planes, where the symbol of fire burning fuel is more appropriate.

In the arūpa levels, matter is subordinated to life, *T P O* 771.
altering at every moment. An entity changes form with every change of thought. Matter is an instrument of his life and is no expression of himself. The form is made momentarily, and it changes with every change of his life. This is true not only of the arūpa levels of manas, but also in a subtle way of the plane of Buddhi, and it is true also of the spiritual ego.

Glorious as has been the life in the heaven-worlds of *T B* 95.
the lower mental plane, it eventually comes to an end. *D P* 39 : 50. *O S D* 434–
The mental body in its turn drops away, as have done 435.
the other bodies, and the man's life in his causal body *L A D* 36. *A W* 182 :
begins. All through the heaven-life, the personality 191.
of the last physical life is distinctly preserved, and it is only when the consciousness is finally withdrawn into the causal body that this feeling of personality is merged in the individuality, and the man for the first time since his descent into incarnation realises himself as the true and comparatively permanent ego.

In the causal body the man needs no "windows"—which, as the student will recollect, were formed by his own thoughts in the lower heavens—for this, the causal plane, is his true home, and all his walls have fallen away.

The majority of men have as yet very little consciousness at this height; they rest dreamily unobservant and scarcely awake. Such vision, however, as they have is true, however limited it may be for lack of development.

The higher heaven-world life plays a very small part in the life of the ordinary man, for in his case the ego is not sufficiently developed to be awake in the causal body. Backward egos, in fact, never *consciously* attain the heaven-world at all, while a still larger number obtain only a comparatively slight touch of some of the lower sub-planes.

But in the case of a man who is spiritually developed, his life, as an ego in his own world, is glorious and fully satisfying.

D P 36. *O S D* 435. *L A D* 36. Nevertheless, consciously or unconsciously, every human being must touch the higher levels of the mental plane, before reincarnation can take place. As his evolution proceeds, this touch, of course, becomes more and more definite and real to him. Not only is he more conscious there as he progresses, but the period he passes in that world of reality becomes longer, for his consciousness is slowly but steadily rising through the different planes of the system.

I L II 435–436. The time spent in the higher mental world may vary, according to the stage of development, from two or three days of unconsciousness, in the case of an ordinary undeveloped man, to a long period of years of conscious and glorious life, in the case of exceptionally advanced people.

I L II 461–462. The length of time spent in the heaven-worlds between incarnations is dependent upon three principal factors: (1) the class to which an ego belongs; (2) the mode in which he attained individualisation; and (3) the length and nature of his last life. As this matter has been treated in detail in *The Mental Body*, Chapter XXI, it is unnecessary to repeat here what was said there.

O S D 45–46. Even when we have fully realised how small a part of each life-cycle is spent on the physical plane, in order fairly to estimate its true proportion to the whole, we must also bear thoroughly in mind the far greater reality of the life in the higher worlds. This is a point which it is impossible to emphasise too strongly, for the vast majority of people are as yet so entirely under the dominion of their physical senses, that the unrealities of the lower world seem to them the only reality, whilst the nearer anything approaches to true reality, the more unreal and incomprehensible it appears to them.

For reasons which are sufficiently comprehensible, the astral world has been called the world of illusion: but it is nevertheless at least one step nearer to reality: far indeed as is astral sight from the clear, all-embracing vision of the man on his own plane, it is at least keener and more reliable than physical sense. And as is the astral to the physical, so is the mental to the astral, except that the proportion is raised to a higher power. Hence not only is the time spent on these higher planes far longer than the physical life, but every moment of it may, if properly used, be enormously more fruitful than the same amount of time on the physical plane could possibly be.

As evolution proceeds, the principle governing the *D P* 36–37.
life after death is that life on the lower levels, both of *T B* 95.
the astral and the mental planes, gradually shortens, while the higher life becomes steadily longer and fuller. Eventually the time arrives when the consciousness is unified, *i.e.*, when the higher and the lower selves are indissolubly united, and the man is no longer capable of wrapping himself up in his own cloud of thought, and mistaking the little that he can see through for the whole of the great heaven-world around him; then he realises the possibilities of his life, and so for the first time truly begins to live. But, by the time that he attains these heights, he will already have entered upon the Path, and taken his future progress definitely into his own hands.

It is only when the consciousness has withdrawn *D P* 79.
from the lower bodies, and is once more centred in the *I L II* 67–68.
ego, that the final result of the incarnation just con- *I L I* 374–375.
cluded is known. Then it is seen what new qualities *A W* 193–
he has acquired in that particular little cycle of his 194: 201–202.
evolution. At that time also, a glimpse of the life as a whole is obtained; the ego has for a moment a flash of clearer consciousness, in which he sees the results of the life just completed, and something of what will follow from it in his next birth.

This glimpse can hardly be said to involve a knowledge of the nature of the next incarnation, except in the vaguest and most general sense. No doubt the main object of the coming life would be seen, and the specific progress which he is intended to make in it, but the vision would be chiefly valuable as a lesson in the karmic result of his action in the past. It offers him an opportunity, of which he takes more or less advantage, according to the stage of development to which he has attained.

At first he makes little use of it, since he is but very dimly conscious, and very poorly fitted to apprehend facts, and their varied interrelations; but gradually his power to appreciate what he sees increases, and later comes the ability to remember such flashes at the end of previous lives, and to compare them, and so to estimate the progress which he is making along the road which he has to traverse: in addition, he will devote some time to his plans for the life which lies before him. His consciousness gradually increases, until he comes to have an appreciable life on the higher levels of the mental plane, each time that he touches them.

THE FIFTH HEAVEN: THE THIRD SUB-PLANE

D P 79–83. *A W* 202–203.

This is, of course, the lowest of the arūpa or formless mental sub-planes: it is also the most populous of all the regions with which we are acquainted, because here are present almost all the sixty thousand million souls who are said to be engaged in the present human evolution—all, in fact, except the comparatively small number who are capable of functioning on the second and first sub-planes.

As we have already seen, each soul is represented by an ovoid form, which at first is a mere colourless film, but which later, as the ego develops, begins to show a shimmering iridescence like a soap-bubble, colours playing over its surface like the changing hues made by sunlight on the spray of a waterfall.

Those who are connected with a physical body are distinguishable from those in the disembodied state by a difference in the types of vibrations set up on the surface of their causal bodies, and it is therefore easy, on this plane, to see at a glance whether an individual is or is not in incarnation at the time.

The immense majority, whether in or out of the body, are but dreamily semi-conscious, though few are now in the condition of mere colourless films. Those who are fully awake are marked and brilliant exceptions, standing out amid the less radiant crowds like stars of the first magnitude. Between these and the least-developed are ranged every variety of size and beauty, each thus representing the exact stage of evolution at which he has arrived.

The majority are not yet sufficiently definite, even in such consciousness as they possess, to understand the purpose of the laws of the evolution in which they are engaged. They seek incarnation in obedience to the impulse of the Cosmic Will, and also to *Tanhā*, the blind thirst for manifested life, the desire to find some region in which they can feel and be conscious of living. In their earlier stages, such entities cannot feel the intensely rapid and piercing vibrations of the highly refined matter of their own plane; the strong and coarse, but comparatively slow, movements of the heavier matter of the physical plane are the only ones that can evoke any response from them. Hence it is only on the physical plane that they feel themselves to be alive at all, and this explains their strong craving for re-birth into earth-life.

Thus for a time their desire agrees exactly with the law of evolution. They can develop only by means of these impacts from without, to which they are gradually aroused to respond, and in this early stage they can receive them only in earth-life. By slow degrees their power of response increases, and is awakened, first to the higher and finer physical vibrations, and still more slowly to those of the astral plane. Next, their astral bodies, which until now have been merely bridges to convey sensations to the ego, gradually become definite vehicles which they can use, and their consciousness begins to be centred rather in their emotions, than in mere physical sensation.

At a later stage, but always by the same process of learning to respond to impacts from without, the egos learn to centre their consciousness in the mental body, to live in and according to the mental images which they have formed for themselves, and so to govern their emotions by the mind.

Yet further along the long road of evolution, the centre moves up to the causal body, and the egos realise their true life. When that stage is reached, however, they will be found upon a higher sub-plane than this (the third), and the lower earthly existence will be no longer necessary for them. But for the present we are dealing with the less evolved majority, who still put forth, as groping, waving tentacles into the ocean of existence, the personalities which are themselves on the lower planes of life. But they are as yet in no sense aware that these personalities are the means whereby they are to be nourished and to grow. They see nothing of their past or future, not being yet conscious on their own plane. Nevertheless, as they are slowly drawing in experience, and assimilating it, there develops a sense that certain things are good to do, and others bad, and that expresses itself imperfectly in the connected personality as the beginning of a conscience, a feeling of right and wrong. Gradually, as they evolve, the sense more and more clearly formulates itself in the lower nature, and becomes a less inefficient guide to conduct.

By means of the opportunities given by the flash of consciousness, to which we have previously referred, the most advanced egos of this sub-plane develop to a point at which they are engaged in studying their past, tracing out the causes set going in it, and learning much from the retrospection, so that the impulses sent downwards become clearer and more definite, and translate themselves, in the lower consciousness, as firm convictions and imperative intuitions.

It should be unnecessary to point out that the

thought-images of the rūpa or form levels are not carried into the higher heaven-world. All illusion now is past, and each ego knows his real kindred, sees them, and is seen, in his own royal nature, as the true immortal man that passes on from life to life, with all the ties intact that are knit to his real being.

On this third sub-plane are also to be found the causal bodies of the comparatively few members of the animal kingdom who are individualised. Strictly speaking, as we have previously seen, these are not animals any longer. They are practically the only examples now to be seen of the quite primitive causal body, undeveloped in size, and as yet coloured only very faintly by the first vibrations of newly born qualities. *D P* 95–96.

When the individualised animal retires into his causal body, to await the turn of the wheel of evolution, which shall give him the opportunity of a primitive human incarnation, he seems to lose almost all consciousness of outer things, and to spend the time in a sort of delightful trance of the deepest peace and contentment. Even then, interior development of some sort is surely taking place, though its nature is difficult for us to comprehend. In any event, he is enjoying the highest bliss of which, at his level, he is capable.

CHAPTER XX

THE SIXTH HEAVEN: SECOND SUB-PLANE

D P 83–85. *A W* 203–205. FROM the densely thronged Fifth Heaven, we pass now into a more thinly populated world, as out of a great city into a peaceful countryside. For, at the present stage of human evolution, only a small minority of individuals have risen to this loftier level, where even the least advanced is definitely self-conscious, and also conscious of his surroundings.

He is able, at least to some extent, to review the past through which he has come, and is aware of the purpose and method of evolution. He knows that he is engaged in a work of self-development, and recognises the stages of physical and *post-mortem* life, through which he passes in his lower vehicles.

The personality, with which he is connected, is seen by him as part of himself, and he endeavours to guide it, using his knowledge of the past as a store of experience from which he formulates principles of conduct, clear and immutable convictions of right and wrong. These he sends down into the lower mind, superintending and directing its activities.

In the earlier part of his life on this sub-plane, he may continually fail to make the lower mind understand logically the foundations of the principles he impresses upon it: yet, nevertheless, he succeeds in making the impression, so that such abstract ideas as truth, justice and honour, become unchallenged and ruling conceptions in the lower mental life.

So firmly are such principles wrought into the very fibres of his being that, no matter what may be the strain of circumstance or the torment of temptation, to act against them becomes an impossibility. For these principles are of the life of the ego.

While, however, he thus succeeds in guiding his lower vehicle, his knowledge of that vehicle and its doings is often far from precise and clear. He sees the lower planes but dimly, understanding their principles rather than their details, and part of his evolution on this sub-plane consists in coming more and more consciously into direct touch with the personality, which so imperfectly represents him below.

Only such persons as are deliberately aiming at spiritual growth live on this sub-plane, and they have, in consequence, become largely receptive of influences from the planes above them. The communication grows and enlarges, and a fuller flood pours through. Under this influence, the thought takes on a singularly clear and piercing quality, even in the less developed: the effect shows itself in the lower mind as a tendency to philosophic and abstract thinking.

In the more highly evolved, the vision is far-reaching: it ranges with clear insight over the past, recognising the causes set up, their working out, and what remains of their effects still unexhausted.

Egos, living on this plane, have wide opportunities for growth when freed from the physical body, for here they may receive instruction from more advanced entities, coming into direct touch with their teachers. No longer by thought-pictures, but by a flashing luminousness impossible to describe, the very essence of the idea flies like a star from one ego to another, its correlations expressing themselves as light waves pouring out from the central star, and needing no separate enunciation. A thought here is like a light placed in a room: it shows all things round it, but requires no words to describe them.

In this, the Sixth Heaven, a man sees also the *A W* 204.
vast treasures of the Divine Mind in creative activity, and can study the archetypes of all the forms that are being gradually evolved in the lower worlds. He may unravel the problems connected with the working out of those archetypes, the partial good that seems as

evil to the limited vision of men encased in flesh. In the wider outlook of this level, phenomena assume their due relative proportions, and a man sees the justification of the divine ways, so far as they are concerned with the evolution of the lower worlds.

CHAPTER XXI

THE SEVENTH HEAVEN: FIRST SUB-PLANE

THIS, the most glorious level of the heaven-world, has but few denizens as yet from our humanity, for on its heights dwell none but the Masters of Wisdom and Compassion, and Their Initiated pupils. *D P* 85–88. *I L II* 335. *A W* 155–156: 205–206.

In one of the earlier letters, received from a Master, it was stated that to comprehend the condition of the First and Second Elemental Kingdoms—*i.e.*, those on the causal and lower mental planes—was impossible except to an Initiate: hence we cannot expect success in attempting to describe them on the physical plane.

Of the beauty of form, and colour, and sound, on the causal plane, no words can speak, for mortal language has no terms in which those radiant splendours may find expression.

In touching the seventh heaven, we come in contact for the first time with a plane which is cosmic in its extent: for this, the atomic part of our mental plane, is the lowest sub-plane of the mental body of the Planetary Logos. On this level, therefore, may be met many an entity which mere human language has no words to portray. For our present purposes, however, it will be best to put aside altogether those vast hosts of beings whose range is cosmic, and confine ourselves strictly to the inhabitants peculiar to the mental plane of our own Chain of worlds.

Those who are on this sub-plane have accomplished the mental evolution, so that in them the higher shines out ever through the lower. From their eyes the illusion-veil of personality has been lifted, and they know and realise that they are *not* the lower nature, but use it only as a vehicle of experience.

In the less evolved of them, it may yet have power to shackle and to hamper, but they can never fall into the blunder of confusing the vehicle with the self behind it. From this they are saved, because they carry their consciousness, not only from day to day, but from one incarnation to another, so that past lives are not so much looked back upon, as always present in the consciousness, the man feeling them as one life, rather than as many lives.

On this sub-plane, the ego is conscious of the lower heaven-world, as well as of his own. If he has there any manifestations, as a thought-form, in the heaven-life of his friends, he can make the fullest use of them.

On the third sub-plane, and even in the lower part of the second, his consciousness of the sub-planes below him was still dim, and his action in the thought-form largely instinctive and automatic. But as soon as he got well into the second sub-plane, his vision rapidly became clearer, and he recognised the thought-forms, with pleasure, as vehicles through which he was able to express more of himself, in certain ways, than he could do through his personality.

Now that he is functioning in the causal body, amidst the magnificent light and splendour of the highest heaven, his consciousness is instantaneously and perfectly active at any point in the lower divisions to which he wills to direct it, and he can, therefore, intentionally project additional energy into such a thought-form, when he wishes to use it for the purpose of teaching.

From this highest level of the mental plane come down most of the influences poured out by the Masters of Wisdom, as They work for the evolution of the human race, acting directly on the souls, or egos, of men, shedding upon them the inspiring energies which stimulate spiritual growth, which enlighten the intellect, and purify the emotions.

From here genius receives its illumination : here all upward efforts find their guidance. As the sun-rays fall everywhere from one centre, and each body that receives them uses them after its nature, so from the Elder Brothers of the race fall on all men the light and life which it is Their function to dispense. Each uses as much as he can assimilate, and thereby grows and evolves. Thus, as everywhere else, the highest glory of the heaven-world is found in the glory of service, and they who have accomplished the mental evolution are the fountains, from which flows strength for those who are still climbing.

On the three higher levels of the mental plane are to *D P* 98.
be found the hosts of arūpa or formless devas, who possess no body denser than the causal. The nature of their life appears to be so essentially different from the life we lead as to make it impossible to describe in physical words.

Arūpa devas are connected with the guidance of the *T C* 170.
worlds, of races, of nations.

There is also a very limited class of men, conscious *T C* 188.
on the arūpa levels of the mental plane, who have been "sorcerers" in the past. In them the higher intellect is awakened, and with it the intellectual recognition of unity. They now perceive that they have been on the wrong path, that it is not possible to hold back the world, and prevent it from climbing on the upward arc. Being still tied by the karma they have made, they have to work on the wrong side, that is, on the side of disintegration. But they work with a changed motive, and endeavour to turn their forces against those men who are in need of being strengthened by having to struggle against resistance in their spiritual life. This truth appears to have been perceived by Marie Corelli, who dealt with the point in her book *The Sorrows of Satan*. The *Satan* there described is always glad when he is defeated: he exerts himself to oppose, but rejoices when the man proves himself spiritual enough to resist.

This side of life is recognised also in the Hindu Purānas. There are cases in which a man has evolved to a very high point of knowledge, and then incarnates, to expiate some of his past karma, in the form of an opponent of good, like Rāvana. By his past karma he is compelled to gather up in himself the evil forces of the world, in order that they may be destroyed. Other religions have the same idea in different forms.

CHAPTER XXII

TRISHNĀ: THE CAUSE OF REINCARNATION

WE have now practically completed our study of the nature, functions, growth and development of the causal body. Having thus studied what we may call the form-side of the ego, it is now necessary that we endeavour to obtain some further understanding of the ego himself, as a conscious, functioning entity.

In the present chapter we shall commence the study of the ego in his relation to his personalities: this practically amounts to the life-side of reincarnation. The first part of our subject will be Trishnā—that "thirst" which is the primary reason why the ego seeks reincarnation. In the next chapter we will deal more specifically with the form-side of reincarnation, *i.e.*, its mechanism.

Then we shall deal with other aspects of the attitude of the ego towards the personality. After that, we shall pass to a study of the life of the ego on his own plane. Finally, we must study, so far as our materials permit, the relation of the ego to the Monad.

The primary and essential reason for reincarnation is *D P* 78 : 81.
the Cosmic Will, which impresses itself upon the ego, *M V I* 68. *O S D* 90.
appearing in him as a desire for manifestation. In *R* 36–37.
obedience to this, the ego copies the action of the Logos *T P O* 260: 425.
by pouring himself forth into the lower planes.

More specifically, this desire is known in Samskrit as Trishnā, or thirst, in Pali as Tanhā. It is the blind thirst for manifested life, the desire to find some region where the ego can (1) express himself, and (2) receive those impressions and impacts from without which alone enable him to be conscious of living, to feel himself alive.

This is not desire for life in the ordinary sense of the *I L I* 375.

word, but rather for a more perfect manifestation, a desire to feel himself more thoroughly alive and active, a desire for that complete consciousness which involves the power to respond to all possible vibrations from the surroundings on every plane, so that the ego may attain the perfection of sympathy, *i.e.*, of *feeling-with*.

T P O 425. As we shall see more fully later on, the ego on his own plane is far from being fully conscious, but what consciousness he has gives him a feeling of great pleasure, and arouses a kind of hunger for a fuller realisation of life. It is this hunger of the ego, in fact, which lies behind the world's great clamour for a fuller life.

T C 59. It is not an outside pressure which drives a man back into incarnation : he comes because he wants to come. If the ego did not want to come back, he would not return : but so long as any desire remains for anything that the world can give him, he will want to come back. Thus an ego is *not* driven, against his will, back to this world of troubles, but his own intense hunger for it brings him back.

T C 60 : 114. We may take an analogy from the physical body. When food has been taken, and completely assimilated, the body wants more food, becomes hungry. No one has to drive the man to eat : he gets food, and eats it, because he wants it. Similarly, so long as man is imperfect, so long as he has not assimilated everything this world can give, and utilised it to the full, so that he does not want anything more from this world, so long will he return to re-birth.

R 37–38 : 41. Trishnā may be conceived as one of the many ways in which the universal law of periodicity manifests itself. In the Esoteric Philosophy, this law is recognised as extending to the emanation and reabsorption of the universe, the Night and Day of Brahmā, the outbreathing and the inbreathing of the Great Breath.

Hence the Hindus have pictured the God of Desire as the impulse to manifestation. " Kāma . . . is in the *Rig Veda* (x. 129) the personification of that feeling which leads and propels to creation. He was the *first movement* that stirred the ONE, after its manifestation from the purely abstract Principle, to create. 'Desire first arose in It, which was the primal germ of mind; and which sages, searching with their intellect, have discovered to be the bond which connects Entity with Non-Entity.'" (*The Secret Doctrine*, II. 185.) Kāma (Desire) is, essentially, the longing for active sentient existence, existence of vivid sensation, the tossing turbulence of passionate life.

When spiritual Intelligence comes into contact with this thirst for sensation, its first action is to intensify it. As the Stanza says: "From their own essence they filled (*i.e.*, intensified) the Kāma." (*Ibid.* 170.) Thus Kāma, for the individual as for the Kosmos, becomes the primary cause of reincarnation, and, as Desire differentiates into desires, these chain down the Thinker to earth, and bring him back, time after time, to re-birth. The Hindu and Buddhist scriptures are, of course, filled with this statement of truth.

Until the realisation of Brahman is reached, there *T C* 121–122.
must always be Trishnā. When a man has assimilated all that he has acquired, and made it part of himself, then Trishnā will arise and drive him out to seek new experiences.

At first, this is a thirst for *external* experiences, and this is the sense in which Trishnā is usually employed. There is, however, another and a keener thirst, well expressed in the phrase: "My soul is athirst for God; yea, even for the living God." This is the thirst of the part to find the whole to which it belongs. If we think of the part coming forth from, but never losing the link with, the whole, then there is always a certain retractive force, trying to bring the part back. The Spirit, which is divine, can find no permanent satisfaction outside divinity: it is this dissatisfaction, this desire to search, which is the root of Trishnā, and which brings a man out of devachan, or, in fact, out of any condition, until the end of the search is reached.

It is quite possible for a man to obtain a certain *T C* 60: 94–95. *T P O* 262.
lower kind of Moksha—a temporary liberation from

re-birth. Thus certain of the less developed *yogis* in India deliberately kill out all desires belonging to this particular world. Realising that the world is transitory, that it is hardly worth while to take very much trouble to remain in it, especially if there has been much suffering or disappointment, the man reaches that form of *vairāgya* (non-attachment) which is called technically " burning-ground *vairāgya* "; this does not lead to full Liberation, but it does result in a partial liberation.

As one of the Upanishats states, a man is born in the world to which his desires lead him. Hence, having killed all desire for anything in *this* world, the man passes away from it, and is not reborn in it. He will then pass into a *loka* (world) which is not permanent, but in which he may remain for long ages. There are a number of such worlds, connected very often with the worship of a particular Divine form, connected with special kinds of meditation, and so on, and a man may pass into one of these, and remain there for a quite indefinite time. In the case of those who have given themselves very largely to meditation, their desire is entirely towards the Objects of meditation: consequently they stay in the mental world, whither their own desires have led them.

Whilst such people have taken themselves out of the troubles of this world, they will ultimately come back to a world, either this world, if it is still going on, or a world similar to this, where they can take up their evolution at the point at which it was dropped. Hence the troubles are only postponed, and it does not, therefore, seem to be worth while to adopt the plan described.

T C 61. It is because it is possible to " kill out " desire that occult teachers prescribe instead transmutation of desire. That which is killed will rise again: that which is transmuted is changed for ever. A person, in a very imperfect condition of evolution, who kills out desire, kills at the same time all possibility of the higher evolution, because he has nothing to transmute.

Desire is dead for the present life, which means that all the higher life of the emotions and of the mind is for the time killed.

The false *vairāgya* is a *repulsion* from the lower, brought about by disappointment, trouble, or weariness of some kind: the true *indifference* to the lower things results from desire for the higher life, and brings about a quite different result.

In *The Voice of the Silence* it is said that the soul wants " points that draw it upwards " ; by killing out desire a man gets rid of the taste for life only temporarily: the taste is still there latent, and will in due time revive.

If a man, who has killed out desire in the manner described, is quite an average person, with no special intellectual or moral qualities, he will remain, as said, away from this world, in a condition in which he is quite happy, but in which he is of no particular use, either to himself or to anybody else. *T C* 96–98.

If, on the other hand, the man is one who has gone a considerable way along the Path, he may have reached a stage of meditation in which his mental powers are of very great value. He may be able, even though unconsciously, to influence the world, and so help in that great stream of mental and spiritual energy which is drawn upon by the Masters for Their work in the world. This is the reservoir which is filled with spiritual energy by the Nirmānakayas (*vide The Mental Body*, p. 193).

A man of this kind, who is filled with the spirit of service, would pass to a world where he could work along that particular line. It would be a world about the level of the causal body. Here he would live, literally for ages, pouring out his stream of concentrated thought, for the helping of others, and so helping to supply this reservoir of spiritual power.

CHAPTER XXIII

THE PERMANENT ATOMS AND THE MECHANISM OF REINCARNATION

In this chapter we shall deal with the part played by the permanent atoms in re-birth, and also with certain further details of the mechanism of re-birth.

I L II 436. *S C* 106 : 242–243 : 92–93. *T C* 145. *T* 36.

It has already been explained, in this series of books, that, after the death of the physical body, the ego steadily withdraws through plane after plane, until eventually he is clothed only in his causal vehicle. At physical death, the life-web, together with prāna, is withdrawn into the heart, round the physical permanent atom. The physical permanent atom then rises along the Sushumna-nādī—a canal running from the heart to the third ventricle—into the head, to the third ventricle of the brain. Then the whole of the life-web, collected round the permanent atom, rises slowly to the point of junction of the parietal and occipital sutures, and leaves the physical body—now dead.

As the ego vacates each of his bodies, the permanent atoms of those bodies pass into a dormant condition, and are retained in the causal body in that quiescent state. While the man is in his causal body only, he thus has within that body the physical permanent atom, the astral permanent atom, and the mental permanent molecule, or unit, as it is more usually called. These three, wrapped in the buddhic life-web, appear as a brilliant nucleus-like particle in the causal body. They are, of course, all that now remains to the ego of the physical, astral and mental bodies of his previous incarnation.

These various stages are illustrated by the left-hand portion of Diagram XXV. Whilst the man is in possession of all his vehicles, the permanent atoms are shown with rays projecting from them, indicating that they are actively functioning. As each body dies, and is left behind, the permanent atom concerned becomes dormant, as is shown by the plain ring without rays, and retreats within the causal body. As the permanent atoms thus "go to sleep," the normal flow of life in the spirillæ is lessened, and, during the whole period of repose, the flow is small and slow. In the diagram, the causal body is shown, on the causal level, with the three permanent particles within it, all dormant.

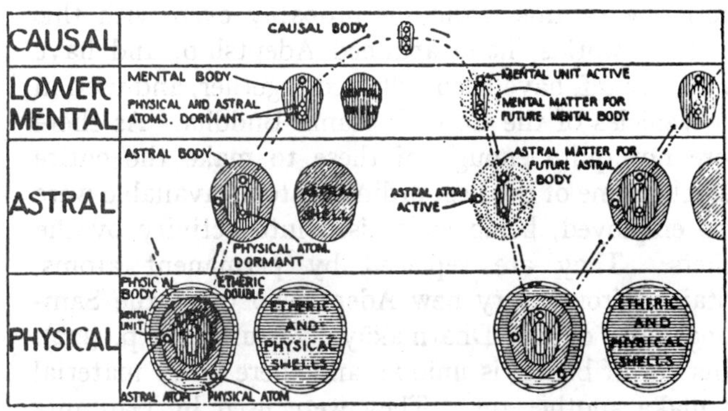

DIAGRAM XXV.—The Cycle of Re-birth.

The student should realise that it is necessary for *M* 16.
evolution that these permanent atoms should be *S C* 162.
carried over, the reason being that the developed man must be master of *all* the planes or worlds, and the permanent atoms form the only direct channel, imperfect though it be, between the spiritual triad, or ego, and the forms he is connected with. If it were conceivable that he could develop without permanent atoms, he might possibly become a glorious archangel upon higher planes, but he would be entirely useless in these lower worlds, having cut off from himself the power of feeling and of thinking. We must not, therefore, drop the permanent atoms: our business is to purify and develop them.

T P O 600. *I L I* 159–160. We may note here that permanent atoms are much more evolved than are other atoms, being at the fullest development of seventh round atoms in men who are about to become Adepts. They are thus as highly developed as atoms can possibly be, and, as we have seen, are charged with all the qualities which they have brought over from previous births.

When a person reaches the level of a Buddha, it is quite impossible for him to find atoms useful to him, except those which have been used as permanent atoms by human beings.

All the permanent atoms of all those who, in connection with this world, or probably even with this chain of worlds, have attained Adeptship, and have cast them off, have been collected together, and used in the vehicles of the Lord Gautama Buddha. As there were not quite enough of these to make the entire vehicle, some of the best ordinary atoms available were also employed, being galvanised into activity by the others. They are replaced by permanent atoms, obtained from every new Adept who takes the Sambhogakāya or the Dharmakāya vesture (see p. 322). This set of bodies is unique, and there is no material to make another set. They were used by Gautama Buddha, and afterwards preserved.

The causal, mental and astral bodies of the Buddha were used also by the Christ, along with the physical body of Jesus, and by Shankarāchārya, and are now again being used by the Lord Maitreya.

S C 106–107 : 243. *I L II* 436–437. *K* 43. *A W* 208. Returning from this digression on permanent atoms, to the time when the life on the higher mental subplanes comes to an end, we perceive that Trishnā, *i.e.*, desire for further experience, reasserts itself, and the ego once more turns his attention outwards, stepping over the threshold of devachan into what has been called the plane of reincarnation, bringing with him the results, small or great, of his devachanic work.

With his attention turned outwards, as said, the ego ends forth a thrill of life, which arouses the mental unit. The flow in the spirillæ of this unit, and in the other permanent atoms in their turn, which during the period of repose, has been small and slow, is now increased, and the mental unit, thus stimulated, begins to vibrate strongly. This is shown in the diagram, on the right-hand side, by a reappearance of the rays round the mental unit.

The life-web then begins to unfold again, and the vibrating mental unit, acting as a magnet, draws around itself mental matter, with vibratory powers resembling, or accordant with, its own.

The devas of the Second Elemental Kingdom bring this material within reach of the mental unit, and, in the earlier stages of evolution, they also shape the matter into a loose cloud around the permanent unit: but, as evolution proceeds, the ego himself exercises an ever-increasing influence over the shaping of the material. This cloud of matter—which is not yet of course a vehicle, properly so-called—is indicated in the diagram by the dotted outline.

When the mental body is partially formed, the life-thrill from the ego awakens the astral permanent atom, and a similar procedure takes place, a cloud of astral matter being drawn round the astral permanent atom.

In his descent to incarnation, we thus see that the ego does not receive ready-made mental and astral bodies: instead, he receives material out of which these bodies will be built, in the course of the life that is to follow. Moreover, the matter which he receives is capable of providing him with mental and astral bodies, of exactly the same type as those he had at the end of his last mental and astral lives, respectively.

The method whereby the ego obtains a new etheric body, into which, as into a mould, the new physical body is built, has been fully described in *The Etheric Double*, p. 67, and so need not be repeated here. We *S C* 91–93.
may add, however, that during human antenatal life the prolongation of the Sūtrātmā is formed, consisting of a single thread, which weaves a network, a shimmer-

ing web of inconceivable fineness and delicate beauty, with minute meshes, reminding one of the closely woven cocoon of the silk-worm.

Within the meshes of this web the coarser particles of the bodies are built together. Thus, if the bodies are looked at with buddhic vision, they all disappear, and in their places is seen this web of life, as it is called, which supports and vivifies all the bodies.

During the antenatal life, the thread grows out from the physical permanent atom and branches out in every direction, the growth continuing until the physical body is full grown. During physical life the prāna, or vitality, courses along the branches and meshes.

S C 99. It appears that it is usually the presence of the permanent atom which renders possible the fertilisation of the ovum, from which the new body is to grow.
I L II 449–450. Nevertheless, when a child is still-born, there has usually been no ego behind it (and presumably, therefore, no permanent atom), and of course no etheric elemental (*vide The Etheric Double*, p. 67). Although there are vast hosts of egos seeking incarnation, many of them still at so early a stage that almost any ordinary surroundings would be equally suitable for them, yet it does sometimes happen that, at a given time, there is no ego able to take advantage of a particular opportunity ; in that case, though the body may be formed, to a certain extent, by the thought of the mother, yet, as there is no ego, it is never really alive.

I L II 429–430. *S C* 99. The ordinary ego is, of course, by no means in a position to choose a body for himself. The place of his birth is usually determined by the combined action of three forces : these are : (1) the law of evolution, which causes an ego to be born under conditions which will give him an opportunity of developing exactly those qualities, of which he stands most in need ; (2) the law of karma. The ego may not have deserved the best possible opportunity, and so he has to put up with the second or third best. He may not even have deserved any great opportunity at all, and so a tumultuous life of small progress may be his fate. We shall return a little later to this question of the karma of an ego; (3) the force of any personal ties of love or hate, that the ego may have previously formed. Sometimes a man may be drawn into a position, which he cannot be said to have deserved in any other way than by the strong personal love, which he has felt for some one higher in evolution than himself.

A more advanced man, who is already on the Path, may be able to exercise a certain amount of choice as to the country and family of his birth. But such a man would be the first to put aside entirely any personal wish in the matter, and resign himself wholly into the hands of the eternal law, confident that whatever it brings to him must be far better for him than any selection of his own.

Parents cannot choose the ego who shall inhabit the body to which they give birth, but by so living as to offer an unusually good opportunity for the progress of an advanced ego, they can make it exceedingly probable that such an ego will come to them.

We have seen that as the ego descends to a fresh incarnation, he has to take up the burden of his past, much of which has been stored as vibratory tendencies in his permanent atoms. These germs or seeds are known to Buddhists as Skandhas, a convenient word for which there seems to be as yet no exact equivalent in English. They consist of material qualities, sensations, abstract ideas, tendencies of mind, mental powers, the pure aroma of all these having been built into the causal body, the remainder being stored, as stated, in the permanent atoms and mental unit. *T C* 123: 145. *D A* 62–63.

H. P. Blavatsky, in her vivid, forceful and inimitable language, gives the following description of the ego coming to re-birth, and being met by his Skandhas: "Karma, with its arm of Skandhas, waits at the threshold of Devachan, whence the Ego re-emerges to assume a new incarnation. It is at this moment that the future destiny of the now-rested Ego trembles in the scales of just retribution, as it now falls once again *R* 44.

under this sway of active Karmic law. It is in this re-birth which is ready for it, a re-birth selected and prepared by this mysterious, inexorable, but in the equity and wisdom of its decrees, infallible LAW, that the sins of the previous life of the Ego are punished. Only it is into no imaginary Hell, with theatrical flames and ridiculous tailed and horned devils, that the Ego is cast, but verily on to this earth, the plane and region of his sins, where he will have to atone for every bad thought and deed. As he has sown, so will he reap. Reincarnation will gather around him all those other Egos who have suffered, whether directly or indirectly, at the hands, or even through the unconscious instrumentality, of the past personality. They will be thrown by Nemesis in the way of the *new* man, concealing the *old*, the eternal Ego. . . . The new 'personality' is no better than a fresh suit of clothes with its specific characteristics, colour, form and qualities; but the *real* man who wears it is the same culprit as of old." (*Key to Theosophy*, pp. 141–2.)

Hence it is the law of Karma which guides the man unerringly towards the race and the nation wherein are to be found the general characteristics that will produce a body, and provide a social environment, fitted for the manifestation of the general character, built up by the Ego in previous earth-lives, and for the reaping of the harvest he has sown.

R 47. Karma thus traces the line, which forms the Ego's path to the new incarnation, this Karma being the collectivity of causes set going by the Ego himself.

In considering this play of karmic forces, however, there is one factor to which due weight should be given: *viz.*, the ready acceptance by the ego, in his clear-sighted vision, of conditions for his personality, far other than those the personality might be willing to choose for itself. The schooling of experience is not always pleasant, and, to the limited knowledge of the personality, there must be much of earth-experience which seems needlessly painful, unjust and useless. But the Ego, ere he plunges into the "Lethe of the body," sees the causes which result in the conditions of the incarnation, on which he is to enter, and the opportunities which will be afforded for growth : hence it is easy to see how lightly will weigh in the balance all passing griefs and pains, how trivial, to that piercing, far-seeing gaze, the joys and woes of earth.

For what is each life but a step in the " Perpetual progress for each incarnating Ego, or divine soul, in an evolution from the outward to the inward, from the material to the Spiritual, arriving at the end of each stage of absolute unity with the Divine Principle. From strength to strength, from the beauty and perfection of one plane to the greater beauty and perfection of another, with accessions of new glory, of fresh knowledge and power in each cycle, such is the destiny of every Ego." (*Key to Theosophy*, p. 155.)

And, as Dr. Besant graphically puts it, " with such a destiny, what boots the passing suffering of a moment, or even the anguish of a darkened life ? "

Continuing with our brief examination of the *I L II* 499.
question of the karma of an ego, it is possible to see the great mass of the accumulated karma—known as the *sanchita* or piled-up karma—hovering over the ego. Usually it is not a pleasant sight, because, by the nature of things, it contains more evil than good. The reason for this is as follows.

In the earlier stages of their development, most men have, through ignorance, done many things that they should not have done, and consequently have laid up for themselves, as a physical result, a good deal of suffering on the physical plane. The average civilised man, on the other hand, is trying to do good rather than harm, and therefore, on the whole, is likely to be making more good karma than bad. But by no means all of the good karma goes into the accumulated mass, and so we get the impression, in that mass, of a preponderance of evil over good.

This again needs a little further explanation. The *I L II* 500.
natural result of good thoughts, or good actions, is to improve the man himself, to improve the quality of his

vehicles, to bring out in him qualities of courage, affection, devotion, and so forth. These effects thus show themselves in the man himself, and in his vehicles, but *not* in the mass of piled-up karma which is waiting for him.

If, however, he performs a good action, with the thought of its reward in his mind, then good karma for that action will come to him, and it will be stored up, with the rest of the accumulation, until such time as it can be brought forward and materialised into activity.

Such good karma naturally binds the man to earth just as effectually as evil karma: consequently, the man who is aiming at real progress learns to do all actions entirely without thought of self, or of the result of his action. This is not to say that any man can avoid the result of his actions, be they good or bad:
I L II 501. but he can change the character of the result. If he forgets himself entirely, and does good actions out of the fulness of his heart, then the whole force of the result is spent in the building of his own character, and nothing of it remains to bind him to the lower planes. The fact is that in each case the man gets what he wants: in the words of the Christ: "Verily I say unto you, they have their reward."

I L II 510–511. An ego may sometimes choose whether he will take certain karma in the present life, though often the brain-consciousness may know nothing of the choice: the very adverse circumstances, at which a man is grumbling, may thus be exactly what he has deliberately chosen for himself, in order to forward his evolution.

A pupil of a Master may often dominate and largely change his karma, setting in motion new forces in many directions, which naturally modify the working out of the old ones.

L II 512. All of us have more or less of evil karma behind us, and, until that is disposed of, it will be a perpetual hindrance to us in our higher work. Hence one of the earliest steps, in the direction of serious progress, is to work out whatever of this evil still remains to us. This results in the Agents of Karma giving us the opportunity of paying off more of this debt, in order that the way may be cleared for our future work; this, of course, may, and often does, involve a considerable increase of suffering in various directions.

The portion of karma selected for discharge in a particular life is known as "ripe," or *prārabda* karma. With this in view, the mental, astral and physical bodies are constructed for a particular length of life. That is one reason why suicide is such a grievous mistake: it constitutes a direct refusal to work out the karma, selected for that particular incarnation, and merely postpones the trouble, as well as generating new karma of an unpleasant nature. *T C* 101–102. *O S D* 48. *K* 47–48.

Another reason against suicide is that each incarnation costs the ego no inconsiderable trouble in its preparation, and also in the wearisome period of early childhood, during which he is gradually, and with much effort, gaining some control over his new vehicles. It is obviously, therefore, alike his duty, and his interest, to make the most of his vehicles, and to preserve them as carefully as possible. Certainly he ought by no means to yield them up, until the Great Law compels him to do so, except at the bidding of some higher and overmastering duty from outside, such as the duty of the soldier to his country.

The selection of "ripe" karma for a particular incarnation is, of course, a highly complicated process: it has, for example, to be sufficiently *congruous* to be worked out at a particular age of the world, in a particular family, a particular environment of people and circumstances.

As a man's will is free, it may happen that the karma selected for him, for a particular life, is worked through sooner than the Administrators of Karma had expected, if one may put it that way. In such a case, They give him more, that being the explanation of the otherwise perplexing statement that "Whom the Lord loveth He chasteneth." *T P O* 227. *S G O* 361–362.

The prārabda karma of an individual divides itself *I L II* 497–499.

into two parts. That which is to express itself in the physical body is made by the Devarājas into the elemental which builds the body, as described in *The Etheric Double*, Chapter XV.

The other and far larger block, which is to indicate his fate through life, the good or evil fortune which is to come to him, is made into another thought-form which does not descend. Hovering over the embryo, it remains upon the mental plane. From that level it broods over the man, and takes or makes opportunities to discharge itself by sections, sending down from itself a flash like lightning to strike, or a finger to touch, sometimes far down on the physical plane, sometimes a sort of extension which reaches only the astral plane, and sometimes what we may call a horizontal flash or finger upon the mental plane.

This thought-form goes on discharging itself until it is quite empty, and then returns to the matter of the plane. The man can, of course, modify its action by the new karma which he is constantly making. The ordinary man has usually scarcely will enough to create any strong new causes, and so the elemental empties itself of its contents according to what may be described as its original programme, taking advantage of convenient astrological periods and surrounding circumstances, which make its work easier or more effective. And so the horoscope of the man may work out with considerable exactitude.

But if the man be sufficiently developed to possess a strong will, the elemental's action is likely to be much modified, and the life will by no means follow the lines laid down in the horoscope.

Sometimes the modifications introduced are such that the elemental is unable fully to discharge itself before the time of the man's death. In that case, whatever is left of it is again absorbed into the great mass of the sanchita or accumulated karma, and out of that another and more or less similar elemental is made, ready for the next physical life.

S C 100. The time and place of the physical birth are determined by the " temperament," sometimes called the " colour " or the " key-note " of the person, this again being determined, to some extent, by the permanent atom. The physical body *must* be born into the world, at a time when the physical planetary influences are suitable to the " temperament " : hence it is born " under " its astrological " Star." Needless to say, it is not the Star that imposes the temperament, but the temperament that fixes the epoch of birth under that Star. Hence arise the correspondences between Stars and characters, and the usefulness, for educational purposes, of a skilfully drawn horoscope, as a guide to the personal temperament of a child.

It seems probable that, in the majority of cases, the exact time and manner of a man's death are *not* decided before or at his birth. Astrologers often assert that they cannot foretell the death of a subject, though they can calculate that, at a certain time, malefic influences will be strong, so that the man *may* die then : if, however, he does not die then, his life will continue, until a certain other occasion, when evil aspects again threaten him, and so on. *I L II* 508-509.

It is likely that these uncertainties represent points, which are left open for later decision, depending largely upon the modifications introduced by the action of the man, during his life, and by the use which he makes of his opportunities.

In any event, we should avoid the error of attaching an exaggerated importance to the time and manner of death. We may be assured that Those, who are in charge of such matters, possess a much truer appreciation of relative values, and have regard to the progress of the ego concerned, as the one matter of importance. *I L II* 505.

Whilst we are dealing with the subject of death, it may be mentioned that the fundamental objection to killing is that it interferes with the course of evolution. To kill a man is to cut him off from the opportunity of evolution which he would otherwise have had in that body. He will, of course, have another opportunity in another body later on, but he has been delayed, and *T P O* 309.

additional trouble has been given to the agents of karma in finding another place for his evolution.

It is obviously much more serious to kill a man than an animal, because the man has to develop an entirely new personality, whereas the animal goes back to the group-soul, from which another incarnation is a comparatively easy matter, but even this lesser amount of karma should not be generated thoughtlessly or needlessly.

I L II 452. To an advanced ego, all the earlier stages of childhood are exceedingly wearisome. Sometimes a really advanced person avoids all this, by asking some one else to give him an adult body, a sacrifice which any of his disciples would always be delighted to make for him.

This method, however, also has its drawbacks. Every body has its own little peculiarities and habits, which cannot readily be changed, so that it must to some extent be a misfit to another ego. In the case under consideration, the man would have retained his old mental and astral bodies, which are, of course, counterparts of his previous physical body. To adapt these to the new physical body, grown by some one else, may obviously often be a very difficult business. Further, if the new physical body be a baby, this adaptation can be done gradually, but, if it is an adult body, it has to be done immediately, which means an amount of strain that is distinctly unpleasant.

I L II 442. In *The Etheric Double*, p. 67, it was explained how the new physical body is gradually built into the mould provided by the etheric double, this etheric double being built in advance for the incoming ego by an elemental, which is a joint thought-form of the four Devarājas.

I L II 448–449. *M P* 47. This elemental takes charge of the body from the first, but, some time before physical birth takes place, the ego also comes into contact with his future habitation, and from that time onwards the two forces are working side by side. Sometimes the characteristics, which the elemental is directed to impose, are but few in number, and consequently it is able to retire at a comparatively early age, and to leave the ego in full control of the body. In other cases, where the limitations are of such a character that a good deal of time is necessary for their development, it may retain its position until the body is seven years old.

In the majority of cases, however, the actual work done by the ego, upon the new vehicles, up to the point at which the elemental withdraws, is inconsiderable. He is certainly in connection with the body, but generally pays but little attention to it, preferring to wait until it has reached a stage where it is more responsive to his efforts.

During the embryonic period, whilst the physical body is being built, out of the substance of the mother, the ego broods over the mother, but can do little towards the shaping of the body. The embryo is unconscious of its future, dimly conscious only of the flow of the maternal life, impressed by maternal hopes and fears, thoughts and desires. Nothing from the ego can affect it, save a feeble influence coming through the physical permanent atom, and it does not share, because it cannot answer to, the wide-reaching thoughts, the aspiring emotions of the ego, as expressed by him in his causal body. *S C* 47–48.

During the years whilst the ego is slowly coming into full touch with the new vehicles, he is, on his own plane, carrying on his own wider, richer life. His touch with the new physical body is manifested as the growth of the *brain*-consciousness.

Egos differ greatly in the interest which they take in their physical vehicles: some hover over them anxiously from the first, and take a good deal of trouble about them, while others are almost entirely careless with regard to the whole matter.

The case of an Adept is very different. As there is no evil karma to be worked out, no artificial elemental is at work, and the ego himself is in sole charge of the development of the body from the beginning, finding himself limited only by heredity. *M P* 47–48.

This enables a far more refined and delicate instrument to be produced: but it also involves more trouble for the ego, and engages for some years a considerable amount of his time and energy. Consequently, for this, and no doubt for other reasons also, an Adept does not wish to repeat the process more often than is strictly necessary, and He therefore makes His physical body last as long as possible.

Whilst our bodies grow old and die, for various reasons, from inherited weakness, disease, accident, self-indulgence, worry and overwork, in the case of the Adept none of these causes is present, though we must, of course, remember that His body is fit for work, and capable of endurance, immeasurably beyond those of ordinary men.

I L II 454-455. In the case of the ordinary man, there seems to be but little continuity of personal appearance life after life, though cases of strong similarity have been found. As the physical body is to some extent an expression of the ego, and the ego remains the same, there must be some cases where it expresses itself in similar forms. But as a rule racial, family and other characteristics over-ride this tendency.

When an individual is so advanced that the personality and ego are unified, the personality tends to have impressed upon it the characteristics of the glorified form in the causal body, which, of course, is relatively permanent.

When the man is an Adept, all his karma is worked out; the physical body is the nearest possible presentment of that glorified form. The Masters therefore will remain recognisable through any number of incarnations, so that one would not expect to see much difference in Their bodies, even though They might be of another race.

Prototypes of what bodies are to be like in the seventh Race have been seen, and they are described as transcendently beautiful.

T C 124-127. Emphasis has often been laid on the period of seven years, in connection with the coming down of the ego to take full possession of the physical body. For this there is a physical reason. In the human embryo, there is a certain set of cells which do not, like the other cells, go through the process of sub-division. This set of cells works its way up to the upper part of the embryo, but does not sub-divide: when the child is born, they are still separate, and remain separate for a considerable period in post-natal life. Changes, however, do occur within the cells, and they send out branches. These branches, after a time, meet, the intervening dividing walls being absorbed, so that the cells are completely inter-communicating: thus is built a channel. The process occupies some seven years, until a fair network is formed, becoming more and more complicated later on.

Physiologists and psychologists point out that, until this complex network is made, the child cannot reason to any great extent, and he should not be given any mental process of complicated reasoning, which puts too great a strain upon him. Materialistic science affirms that, with the growth of this network, the power of reasoning grows. The occultist would explain the phenomenon, by saying, that as the physical mechanism is perfected, the power of reasoning which already exists in the ego, is able to manifest itself. The ego has to wait until the brain is ready for him to come into close touch with and permeate it.

I L II 438–439. *T C* 127. *T P O* 195.

It was stated above that during the descent of the ego to re-birth, there are drawn, round the permanent atoms, materials for the building of the new mental and astral bodies. If the young child is left entirely to himself, the automatic action of the astral permanent atom will tend to produce for him an astral body, precisely similar to that which he had in the last life. There is, however, no reason whatever why all these materials should be used, and, if the child is wisely treated, and reasonably guided, he will be encouraged to develop to the fullest all the germs of good which he has brought over from his previous life, while the evil germs will be allowed to slumber. If that is done, these evil germs will gradually atrophy, and drop away from him, and the ego will unfold within himself the opposite virtues, and then he will be free, for all his future lives, from the evil qualities which these germs indicated.

Parents and teachers may help him towards this desirable consummation, not so much by any definite facts which they teach him, as by the encouragement which they give to him, by the rational and kindly treatment uniformly accorded to him, and, above all, by the amount of affection lavished upon him.

In *The Astral Body* and *The Mental Body*, in the chapters on *Re-Birth*, we have already laid great stress on the immense services which may—and should—be rendered to an ego, by those who are responsible for his upbringing and training, so that it is unnecessary to repeat here what was said in those books.

T P O 295–296. We may, however, add that one who, instead of arousing love and good qualities in his charges, awakens in them evil qualities, such as fear, deceit, and the like, is hampering the progress of the egos concerned, and thus doing them serious positive harm. Misuse of such an opportunity involves a terrible fall for the man. In some cases, for example, cruelty of this nature may result in insanity, hysteria or neurasthenia. In other cases, it results in a cataclysmic descent in the social scale, such as a brahman being reborn as a pariah, as a result of cruelty to children.

On the same principle, a man who, having wealth and power, uses his position to oppress his employees, generates very bad karma. The only aspect of the matter, which concerns the agents of karma, is that the man in such a position has in his hands an opportunity of being a helpful influence in the life of a number of people. He neglects or abuses such an opportunity at his own peril.

CHAPTER XXIV

THE EGO AND REINCARNATION

We come now to deal more specifically with the attitude which the ego takes up towards his incarnation in a personality.

M V I 67–68. *O S D* 90.

Since the appointed method for the evolution of the latent qualities of the ego is by means of impacts from without, it is clearly necessary that the ego should descend far enough to enable him to meet such impacts as can affect him. The method of achieving this result is, as we know, that of reincarnation, the ego putting forth part of himself into the lower planes for the sake of the experience to be gained there, and then withdrawing back again into himself, bearing with him the results of his endeavour.

It must not be thought, however, that the ego makes any movement in space. It is rather that he endeavours to focus his consciousness at a lower level, to obtain an expression through a denser variety of matter.

This putting forth of part of himself into incarnation has often been compared with an investment. The ego expects, if all goes well, to reclaim not only the whole of his capital invested, but also a considerable amount of interest, and he usually obtains this. But, as with other investments, there is occasionally loss instead of gain ; for it is possible that some portion of that which he puts down may become so entangled with the lower matter that it may be impossible wholly to reclaim it. With this "investment" aspect of reincarnation we shall deal in full detail in our next chapter.

M V I 70–71.

The student will by now have fully realised that each stage of the descent of the ego into incarnation means submission to limitation : consequently no expression of the ego upon any of the lower planes can ever be a perfect expression. It is merely an indication of its qualities, just as a picture is a representation, on a two-dimensional surface, of a three-dimensional scene. In exactly the same way the true quality, as it exists in the ego, cannot be expressed in matter of any lower level. The vibrations of the lower matter are altogether too dull and sluggish to represent it, the string is not sufficiently taut to enable it to respond to the note which resounds from above. It can, however, be tuned to correspond with it in a lower octave, like a man's voice singing in unison with a boy's, expressing the same sound, as nearly as the capabilities of the inferior organism permit.

O S D 91. It is not possible in physical language to express exactly this matter of the descent of the ego ; but, until we are able to raise our own consciousness to those levels, and see exactly what takes place, the best impression we can have of it is perhaps the idea of the ego putting down part of himself, like a tongue of fire, into planes of matter grosser than his own.

L A D 32–34. *O S D* 90–91 : 430–431. *M P* 179. The ego, belonging as he does to a higher plane, is a much greater and grander thing than any manifestation of him can be. His relation to his personalities is that of one dimension to another—that of a square to a line, or a cube to a square. No number of squares could ever make a cube, because the square has only two dimensions, while the cube has three. So no number of expressions on any lower plane can ever exhaust the fulness of the ego. Even if he could take a thousand personalities, he could still not sufficiently express all that he is. The most for which he can hope is that the personality will contain nothing which is not intended by the ego—that the personality will express as much of the ego as *can* be expressed in this lower world.

Whilst the ego may have but one physical body, for that is the law, he can ensoul any number of thought-forms which friends who love him may make of him, and he is only too pleased to have these additional opportunities of manifesting himself, as he is able, through those thought-forms, to develop qualities in himself.

Just as in physical consciousness a man may be simultaneously conscious of many physical contacts, as well as of emotions, and of thoughts, without any confusion, so may the ego be simultaneously conscious and active through both his own personality, and also through any number of thought-forms which his friends may make of him.

The wise man thus recognises that the true man is the ego, not the personality, or the physical body, and he sees that it is the life of the ego only which is really of moment, and that everything connected with the body must unhesitatingly be subordinated to those higher interests. He recognises that this earth-life is given to him for the purposes of progress, and that that progress is the one important thing. The real purpose of his life is the unfoldment of his powers as an ego, the development of his character. He recognises that this development is in his own hands, and that the sooner it is perfected the happier and more useful will he be. *T B* 142–143 : 109.

Furthermore, he soon learns by experience that nothing can be really good for him, as an ego, or for any one, which is not good for all: in due time he thus learns to forget himself altogether, and to ask only what will be best for humanity as a whole.

The development of the ego is thus the object of the whole process of descent into matter: the ego assumes veils of matter precisely because through them he is able to receive vibrations to which he can respond, so that his latent faculties may thereby be unfolded. *T B* 45.

The whole object of the ego in putting himself down is that he may become more definite, that all his vaguely beautiful feelings may crystallise into a definite resolution to act. All his incarnations form a process by means of which he may gain precision and definiteness. *T P O* 751.

Hence specialisation is his way of advancement. He comes down into each race or sub-race in order that he may acquire the qualities for the perfection of which that sub-race is working. The fragment of the ego which is put down is highly specialised. When a certain quality is developed, the ego absorbs it into himself in due course, and he does that over and over again. The personality scatters something of its special achievement over the whole, when it is withdrawn into the ego, so that the ego becomes a little less vague than before.

S P 25–26. In *The Key to Theosophy*, pp. 183–4, H. P. Blavatsky describes the objective of reincarnation in vivid language: "Try to imagine a 'Spirit,' a celestial being, whether we call it by one name or another, divine in its essential nature, yet not pure enough to be one with the ALL, and having, in order to achieve this, so to purify its nature as finally to gain that goal. It can do so only by passing *individually* and *personally*, *i.e.*, spiritually and physically, through every experience and feeling that exists in the manifold or differentiated universe. It has, therefore, after having gained such experience in the lower kingdoms, and having ascended higher and still higher with every rung on the ladder of being, to pass through every experience on the human planes. In its very essence it is Thought, and is, therefore, called in its plurality *Mānasaputra*, 'the Sons of (universal) Mind.' This *individualised* 'Thought' is what we Theosophists call the *real* human Ego, the thinking entity imprisoned in a case of flesh and bones. This is surely a spiritual entity, not *matter* [that is, not matter as we know it on the plane of the objective universe], and such entities are the incarnating Egos that inform the bundle of animal matter called mankind, and whose names are *Mānasa* or minds."

S P 26. *R* 10–11. *P M* 97–100. The student should note that the term Mānasaputra, which means literally the "Sons of Mind," is used in the above quotation in a special sense. The term is a wide one, and covers many grades of intelligences, from the "Sons of the Flame" Themselves, down to the entities who individualised in the Moon

Chain, and took their first purely human incarnation in the Earth Chain.

Many similes and metaphors have from time to time been employed, to illustrate the relation between the ego and his personalities, or incarnations. Thus, each incarnation has been compared to a day at school. In the morning of each new life the ego takes up his lessons again, at the point where he left it the night before. The time taken by the pupil in qualifying himself is left entirely to his own discretion and energy. The wise pupil perceives that school-life is not an end in itself, but merely a preparation for a more glorious and far wider future. He co-operates intelligently with his Teachers, and sets himself to do the maximum of work which is possible for him, in order that as soon as he can he may come of age and enter into his kingdom as a glorified ego. *T B* 98–99.

The dipping down of the ego into the physical world, for brief snatches of mortal life, has been likened to the diving of a bird into the sea after fish. Personalities are also like the leaves put forth by a tree; they draw in material from outside, transform it into useful substance, and send it into the tree as sap, by which the tree is nourished. Then the leaves, having served for their season, wither and drop off, to be in due time succeeded by a fresh crop of leaves. *T* 35–36. *R* 60. *A W* 21

As a diver may plunge into the depths of the ocean to seek a pearl, so the ego plunges into the depths of the ocean of life to seek the pearl of experience: but he does not stay there long, for it is not his own element. He rises up again, into his own atmosphere, and shakes off the heavier element, which he leaves behind. Therefore it is truly said that the Soul that has escaped from earth has returned to its own place, for its home is the "land of the Gods," and on earth it is an exile and a prisoner. *D A* 45.

The ego may be regarded as a labourer who goes out into a field, toiling in rain and sunshine, in cold and heat, returning home at night. But the labourer is also the proprietor, and all the results of his labour fill *K* 32–33.

his own granaries, and enrich his own store. Each personality is the immediately effective part of the individuality, representing it in the lower world. There is no injustice in the lot that falls to the personality, because the ego sowed the karma in the past, and the ego must reap it. The labourer that sowed the seed must harvest it, though the clothes in which he worked as sower may have worn out during the interval between the sowing and the reaping. He who reaps is the same as he who sows, and, if he sowed but little seed, or seed badly chosen, it is he who will find but a poor harvest when, as reaper, he goes again into the field.

D A 49–50. *T P O* 358. The ego has been described as moving in eternity like a pendulum between the periods of life terrestrial and life posthumous. The hours of the posthumous life, to one who really understands, are the only reality. So, very often, the *ego* really begins his personal life-cycle with the entry into the heaven-world, and pays a minimum of attention to the personality during its period of collecting materials.

As we have seen, in the cycle of incarnation, the period spent in devachan, which, for all except for the very primitive, is of enormous duration compared with the breaks in it spent on earth, may fairly be called the normal state. A further reason for regarding this as the normal, the earth-life as the abnormal, is that in devachan the man is much nearer the source of his Divine life.

The ego may be regarded as the actor, his numerous and different incarnations being the actor's parts. Like an actor, the ego is bound to play many such parts, which often are disagreeable to him : but, like a bee, collecting honey from every flower, the ego collects only the nectar of moral qualities and consciousness, from every terrestrial personality in which he has to clothe himself, until at last he unites all these qualities in one, and becomes a perfect being, sometimes termed Dhyān Chohan.

S P 25. In *The Voice of the Silence* the personalities are spoken of as " shadows " : the candidate for initiation is exhorted thus: "Have perseverance as one who doth for evermore endure. Thy shadows live and vanish; that which in thee shall live for ever, that which in thee *knows*, for it is knowledge, is not of fleeting life; it is the man that was, that is, and will be, for whom the hour shall never strike."

Thus through the ages the ego, the Immortal *R* 30–31.
Thinker, patiently toils at his work of leading the animal-man upwards, till he is fit to become one with the Divine. Out of any one life he may win but a mere fragment for his work, yet on that slightly improved model will be moulded the next man, each incarnation showing some advance, though in the early stages it may be almost imperceptible. Slowly is accomplished the task of lessening the animal, of increasing the human. At a certain stage in this progress, the personalities begin to become translucent, to answer to the vibrations from the Thinker, and dimly to sense that they are something more than isolated lives, are attached to something permanent and immortal. They may not quite recognise their goal: but they begin to thrill and quiver, under the touch of the ego. Thereafter progress becomes more swift, the rate of development increasing enormously in the later stages.

The above are but analogies, useful perhaps, but *M* 11–12. *O S D* 92.
crude, for it is a matter of exceeding difficulty to express the relation of the ego to the personality. On the whole, perhaps the best way to put it is to say that the personality is a fragment of the ego, a tiny part of him expressing itself under serious difficulties. When we meet another person on the physical plane, it would be somewhere near the truth to say that we know a thousandth part of the real man: moreover, the part that we see is the worst part. Even if we are able to look at the causal body of another man, we see but a manifestation of the ego on his own plane, and are still far from seeing the true man.

Regarding the ego as the real man, and looking at *M* 13–14.
him on his own plane, we see him to be indeed a glorious being. The only way in which down here we

can form a conception of what he really is, is to think of him as some splendid angel. But the expression of this beautiful being on the physical plane may fall far short of all this: in fact, it must do so: first, because it is only a tiny fragment; secondly, because it is so cramped by its conditions.

If a man puts his finger into a hole in a wall, or into a small metal pipe, so that he cannot even bend the finger, it is obvious that he could express but very little of himself through that finger. Much like this is the fate of that fragment of the ego which is put down into this dense body.

We may carry the analogy a little further, by supposing that the finger has a considerable amount of consciousness of its own, so that, shut off as it is from the rest of the body, it temporarily forgets that it is merely a part of the whole body. Forgetting the freedom of the wider life, it tries to adapt itself to the hole, it gilds its sides and makes it an enjoyable hole by acquiring money, property, fame and so forth, not realising that it only begins really to live when it withdraws itself from the hole altogether, and recognises itself as a part of the body. Clumsy as is the image, it may yet give some sort of idea of the relation of the personality to the ego.

I L I 121. *S G O* 63. Other, and more picturesque analogies are to be found in certain ancient myths. Thus Narcissus was a youth of great beauty, who fell in love with his own image reflected in the water, and was so attracted by it that he fell in and was drowned, and was afterwards changed by the gods into a flower and bound to earth. This, of course, refers to the ego looking down upon the waters of the astral plane and the lower world, reflecting itself in the personality, identifying itself with that personality, falling in love with its image, and being bound to earth.

So also Prosperine, while picking the narcissus, was seized and carried off by Desire to the underworld; and, although she was rescued from complete captivity by the efforts of her mother, yet after that she had to spend her life half in the lower world and half in that above: that is to say, partly in material incarnation, and partly out of it.

Another old mystery-teaching was that of the minotaur, which signified the lower nature in man—the personality which is half man and half animal. This was eventually slain by Theseus, who typifies the higher self, or the individuality, which has been gradually growing and gathering strength, until at last it can wield the sword of its Divine Father, the Spirit. *I L I* 122.

Guided through the labyrinth of illusion, which constitutes these lower planes, by the thread of occult knowledge given him by Ariadne (who represents intuition), the higher self is enabled to slay the lower, and to escape safely from the web of illusion. Yet there still remains for him the danger that, developing intellectual pride, he may neglect intuition, even as Theseus neglected Ariadne, and so fail for this time to realise his highest possibilities.

It is abundantly clear that a view of reincarnation can be obtained, in proper perspective, only if we regard it from the point of view of the ego. Each movement of the ego towards the lower planes is a vast circular sweep. The limited vision of the personality is apt to take a small fragment of the lower arc of the circle, and regard it as a straight line, attaching quite undue importance to its beginning and ending, while the real turning-point of the circle entirely escapes it. *D P* 77–78. *O S D* 40–42.

From the point of view of the ego, during the earlier part of that little fragment of existence on the physical plane, which we call life, the outward force of the ego is still strong: at the middle of it, in ordinary cases, that force becomes exhausted, and the great inward sweep begins.

Nevertheless, there is no sudden or violent change, for this is not an angle, but still part of the curve of the same circle—exactly corresponding to the moment of aphelion in a planet's course round its orbit. Yet it is the real turning-point of that little cycle of evolution, though with us it is not marked in any way. In the old Indian scheme of life it *was* marked as the end of the *grihastha* or " householder " period of the man's earthly existence.

In that ancient system, a man spent the first twenty-one years of his life in education, and the next twenty-one in doing his duty as householder and head of the family. But then, having attained middle life, he gave up altogether his worldly cares, resigned his house and property into the hands of his son, and retired with his wife into a little hut near by, where he devoted the next twenty-one years to rest and spiritual converse and meditation. After that came the fourth stage, of perfect isolation and contemplation in the jungle, if he wished it. In all this, the middle of life was the real turning-point, and it is evident that it is a much more important point than either physical birth or death, for it marks the limit of the out-going energy of the ego, the change, as it were, from his out-breathing to his in-breathing.

From this point, there should be nothing but a steady drawing inward of the whole force of the man, and his attention should be more and more withdrawn from mere earthly things, and concentrated on those of higher planes. Such considerations cannot fail to impress upon us how exceedingly ill-adapted to real progress are the conditions of modern European life.

In this arc of evolution, the point at which the man drops his physical body is not a specially important one : by no means so important, in fact, as the next change, his death on the astral plane, and his birth into the heaven-world, or, otherwise expressed, the transfer of his consciousness from astral to mental matter, in the course of the steady withdrawal mentioned.

T P O 260. As was mentioned in Chapter XIII., the whole course of the movement down into matter is called in India the *pravitti mārga*, literally the path of pursuit, of forthgoing ; the *nivritti mārga* is the path of return, of retirement, of renunciation. These terms are relative, and can be applied to the whole course of the evolution of the ego, to an individual incarnation in a personality, etc.

On the pravritti mārga, on which are the vast majority of men, desires are necessary and useful, these being the motives that prompt him to activity. On the nivritti mārga desire must cease. What was *desire* on the pravritti mārga becomes *will* on the nivritti mārga : similarly *thought*, alert, flighty, changing becomes *reason :* work, activity, restless *action*, becomes in its turn *sacrifice*, its binding force thus being broken. *I Y* 117-120.

CHAPTER XXV

THE EGO AND HIS "INVESTMENT"

WE come now to study the subject of reincarnation, regarding the putting forth by the ego of a personality as an "investment" made by the ego.

I L I 419. This "investment" analogy is not a mere figure of speech, but has a definite and material side to it. When the ego, in his causal body, takes to himself in addition a mental and an astral body, the operation involves the actual entangling of a portion of the matter of his causal body with matter of those lower astral and mental types. This "putting-down" of a portion of himself is, therefore, closely analogous to an investment.

As in all investments, the ego hopes to get back more than he puts out: there is, however, a risk of disappointment, a possibility that he may lose something of what he invests: in fact, under very exceptional circumstances there may even be a total loss which leaves him, not absolutely bankrupt, but without available capital.

I L I 401: 419–420. *T P O* 530. Elaborating this analogy, we may remind ourselves that the causal body consists of matter of the first, second and third sub-planes of the mental plane. By far the greater portion of it belongs to the first subplane: a lesser portion belongs to the second subplane, and still less to the third.

For the vast majority of men, there is as yet no activity beyond the lowest of these three types, and even that is usually very partial. It is, therefore, only some of the lowest type of causal matter that can be put down to lower levels, and only a small fraction even of that part can be entangled with mental and astral matter. Hence, only a very small portion of the ego is in activity with reference to the personality.

In fact, with people who are unevolved, probably not more than one-hundredth part of the matter of the third sub-plane is active. With occult students, a little of the second sub-plane matter is generally in activity also. More advanced students have a great deal of that sub-plane in activity, and in the stage below that of the Arhat, about one-half of the ego is active.

The ego, being as yet half asleep, has but a very weak and imperfect control of that which he puts down. But, as his physical body grows up, and his astral and mental bodies also develop, the causal matter entangled with them is awakened, by the vigorous vibrations which reach it through them. The fraction-of-a-fraction, which is fully entangled, gives life and vigour, and a sense of individuality, to these vehicles, and they in turn react strongly upon it, and arouse it to a keen realisation of life.

This keen realisation of life is, of course, exactly what it needs, the very object for which it is put down ; and it is the longing for this keen realisation which is *trishnā*, with which we have already dealt in a previous chapter.

But just because this small fraction has had these experiences, and is therefore so much more awake than the rest of the ego, it may often be so far intensified as to think itself the whole, and forget for the time its relation to its " Father which is in heaven." It may temporarily identify itself with the matter through which it should be working, and may resist the influence of that other portion which has been put down, but not *entangled*—that which forms the link with the great mass of the ego on his own plane. *I L I* 420–422.

Diagram XXVI may serve to make this matter a little more clear. The causal body is here shown as roughly the shape of a chalice in section. That portion of the ego which is awakened on the third causal sub-plane is itself divided into three parts, which we will call (a), (b) and (c). (a) is a very small part of the ego, and remains on its one plane ; (b) is a small part of (a), is put down, but remains unentangled with the matter of the lower planes: it acts as a link between (a) and (c); (c) in turn is a small part of (b), and is thoroughly entangled with lower matter of the mental and astral bodies.

(a) we may think of as the body of a man; (b) as his arm stretched out; (c) as the hand which grasps, or perhaps rather the tips of the fingers which are dipped in matter.

We have here a very delicately balanced arrangement, which may be affected in various ways. The intention is that the hand (c) should grasp firmly and guide the matter with which *it* is entangled, being fully directed all the time by the body (a) through the arm (b). Under favourable circumstances, additional strength, and even additional matter, may be poured from the body (a) through the arm (b) into the hand (c), so that the control may become more and more perfect.

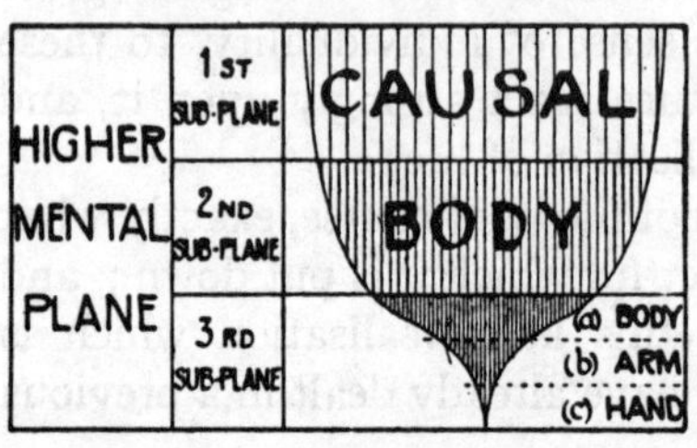

DIAGRAM XXVI.—The Causal Body as a Chalice.

The hand (c) may grow in size as well as in strength, and the more it does so the better, so long as the communication through the arm (b) is kept open freely, and the body (a) retains control. For the very entanglement of the causal matter, which constitutes the hand (c), awakens it to a keen activity, and an accuracy of response to fine shades of vibration, which it could gain in no other way, and this, when transmitted through the arm (b), to the body (a), means the development of the ego himself.

I L I 422–423. Unfortunately the course of events does not always follow the ideal plan of working indicated above. When the control of the body (a) is feeble, it sometimes happens that the hand (c) becomes so thoroughly immeshed in lower matter that, as said, it actually identifies itself with that lower matter, forgets for the time its high estate, and thinks of itself as the whole ego.

If the matter be of the lower *mental* plane, then we shall have a man who is wholly materialistic. He may perhaps be keenly intellectual, but not spiritual; he may very likely be intolerant of spirituality, and quite unable to comprehend or appreciate it. He may probably call himself practical, matter-of-fact, unsentimental, while in reality he is hard as the nether millstone; and, because of that hardness, his life, from the point of view of the ego, is a failure, and he is making no spiritual progress.

If, on the other hand, the matter in which he is so fatally entangled be *astral*, he will, on the physical plane, be one who thinks only of his own gratification, who is utterly ruthless when in pursuit of some object which he strongly desires, a man quite unprincipled, and of brutal selfishness. Such a man lives in his passions, just as the man immeshed in mental matter lives in his mind. Cases such as these have been spoken of as "lost souls," though they are not irretrievably lost.

H. P. Blavatsky says of such men: "There is, however, still hope for a person who has lost his Higher Soul through his vices, while he is yet in the body. He may still be redeemed and made to turn on his material nature. For either an intense feeling of repentance, or one single earnest appeal to the Ego that has fled, or, best of all, an active effort to amend one's ways, may bring the Higher Ego back again. The thread of connection is not altogether broken" (*Secret Doctrine*, III 527). *I L I* 423 424.

In returning to our analogy of the investment, we note that, in making his investment, the ego expects not only to recover the hand (c), but he expects also that it will be improved both in quality and quantity. Its *quality* should be better, because it should be much more awake, and capable of instant and accurate response to a far more varied gamut of vibrations than *I L I* 427–428.

before. This capacity the hand (c), when reabsorbed, necessarily communicates to the body (a), though, of course, the store of energy which made such a powerful wave in the hand (c) will be able to create only a ripple, when distributed throughout the whole substance of the body (a).

We should remind ourselves here that although the *vehicles* can respond to, and express, evil thoughts and emotions, and although their excitement under such vibrations can produce perturbation in the entangled causal matter (c), yet it is quite impossible for (c) to reproduce those vibrations itself, or to communicate them to the arm (b) or the body (a), simply because matter of the three higher mental levels can no more vibrate at the rate of the lowest plane than the string of a violin tuned to a certain pitch can be made to produce a note lower than that pitch.

I L I 428–429. The hand (c) should also be increased in *quantity*, because the causal body, like all other vehicles, is constantly changing its matter, and, when special exercise is given to a certain part of it, that part grows in size, and becomes stronger, precisely as a physical muscle does, when it is used.

Every earth-life is an opportunity, carefully calculated, for such development in quality and quantity as is most needed by the ego; a failure to use that opportunity means the trouble and delay of another similar incarnation, and sufferings probably aggravated by the additional karma incurred.

I L I 429–430. Against the increment, which the ego has a right to expect from each incarnation, we must offset a certain amount of loss which, in the earlier stages, is scarcely avoidable. In order to be effective, the entanglement with lower matter must be very intimate, and it is found that when this is so, it is scarcely ever possible to recover every particle, especially from the connection with the *astral* body.

When the time comes for separation from the astral body, it is almost always a shade and not a mere shell (*vide The Astral Body*, pp. 170–1) that is left behind on the astral plane; and that very distinction means that some of the causal material is lost. Except in the case of an unusually bad life, however, this amount should be much smaller than that gained by growth, so that there should be, on the whole, a profit on the transaction.

Diagram XXVIIA illustrates this case, which may be regarded as the normal state of affairs.

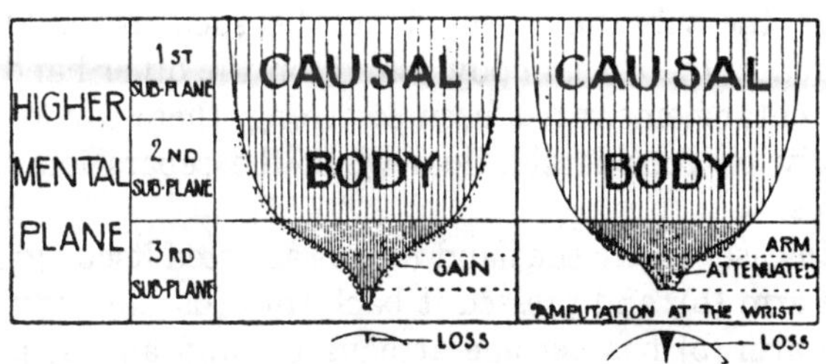

A. Normal Case. B. Abnormal Case.

DIAGRAM XXVII.—The Ego and His Investment (I)

The student should not allow the analogy of the *I L I* 430–431.
arm and hand to mislead him into thinking of the arm (b) and the hand (c) as permanent appanages of the ego. During a life-period they may certainly be considered as separate, but at the end of each life-period they withdraw into the body (a), and the result of the experience is distributed, as it were, through the whole mass of its substance. When, therefore, the time comes for the ego again to put part of himself into incarnation, he does not, nor can he, stretch out again the old arm (b), and the old hand (c), for they have become absorbed in him and become part of him, just as a cupful of water emptied into a bucket becomes part of the water in the bucket, and cannot be separated from it.

Any colouring matter—symbolising the qualities developed by experience—which was present in the cup is distributed, though in paler tint, through the whole bucketful of water. The plan is, therefore, exactly parallel to that we have already studied in the case of group-souls, except that a group-soul may put down many tentacles simultaneously, while the ego puts forth one only at a time. In each incarnation, therefore, the personality is obviously quite a different one from those preceding it, though, of course, the ego behind it remains the same.

I L I 429-430. In the case of men, such as those described above, men living entirely in their passions or their minds, there would be no gain, either in quality or quantity, since the vibrations would not be such as could be stored in the causal body. And, on the other hand, as the entanglement has been so strong, there would certainly be considerable loss when the separation took place.

I L I 424-425. In cases where the hand (c) has asserted itself against the arm (b), and pressed it back towards the body (a), the arm (b) has become attenuated, and almost paralysed, its strength and substance being withdrawn into the body, while the hand (c) has set up for itself, and makes on its own account jerky and spasmodic movements, which are not controlled by the brain. If the separation could become perfect, it would correspond to an amputation at the wrist; but this very rarely takes place during physical existence, although only so much of communication remains as is necessary to keep the personality alive. Diagram XXVIIB illustrates the case we have been describing.

Such a case is not hopeless, for even at the last moment fresh life may be poured through the paralysed arm, if a sufficiently strong effort be made, and thus the ego may be enabled to recover some proportion of the hand (c), just as he has already recovered most of the arm (b). Nevertheless, such a life has been wasted, for, even if the man just contrived to escape serious loss, at any rate nothing has been gained, and much time has been frittered away.

I L I 431-432. The most disastrous catastrophe which can occur to an ego is that in which the personality captures the part of the ego which is put down, and actually causes it to break away. Such cases are exceedingly rare, but they have happened. This time, the hand (c), instead of *repelling* the arm (b), and driving it gradually back into the body (a), by degrees *absorbs* the arm (b) and detaches it from the body (a). Diagram XXVIIIc illustrates such a case. This could be accomplished only by determined persistence in deliberate evil, in short, by black magic. Continuing the analogy, this is equivalent to amputation at the shoulder, or to the loss by the ego of nearly all his available capital. Fortunately for him, he cannot lose everything, because the arm (b) and the hand (c) together are only a small proportion of the body (a), and behind (a) is the great undeveloped portion of the ego, on the first and

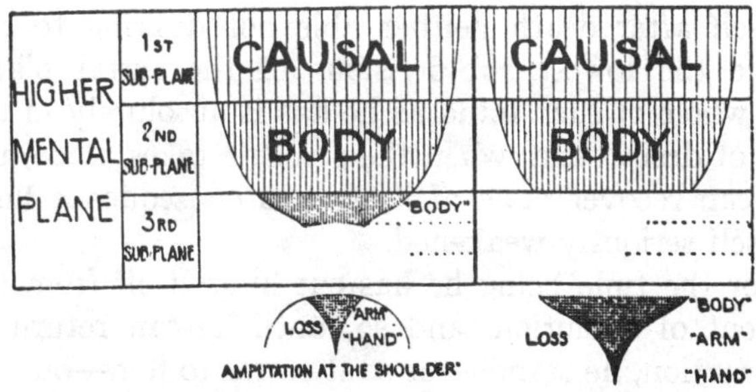

C. Result of Black Magic. D. Extreme Case.

DIAGRAM XXVIII.—The Ego and His Investment (II)

second mental sub-planes. Mercifully a man, however incredibly foolish or wicked, cannot completely wreck himself, for he cannot bring that higher part of the causal body into activity, until he has reached a level at which such evil is unthinkable.

There are certain men, who deliberately set themselves in opposition to nature and, instead of working for unity, towards which the whole force of the universe is pressing, they debase every faculty they possess for purely selfish ends. They spend their lives in striving for separateness, and for a long time they attain it: it is said that the sensation of being utterly alone in space is the most awful fate that can ever befall a man.

This extraordinary development of selfishness is, of *I L I* 433.

course, the characteristic of the black magician, and it is among their ranks only that men can be found who are in danger of this terrible fate. Many and loathsome as are their varieties, they may all be classed in one or other of two great divisions. Both classes use such occult arts as they possess for selfish purposes, but these purposes differ.

In the commoner and less formidable type, the object pursued is the gratification of sensual desire of some sort : naturally, the result of such a life is to centre the man's energy in his astral body. Having succeeded in killing out from himself every unselfish or affectionate feeling, every spark of higher impulse, nothing is left but a remorseless, ruthless monster of lust, who finds himself after death neither able nor desiring to rise above the lowest sub-divisions of the astral plane. The whole of such mind as he has is absolutely in the grip of desire, and, when the struggle takes place, the ego can recover none of it, and in consequence finds himself seriously weakened.

I L I 434. For the time being he has cut himself off from the current of evolution, and so, until he can return to incarnation, he stands—or so it seems to him—outside that evolution, in the condition of *avīchi*, the waveless. Even when he does return to incarnation, it cannot be among those whom he has known before, for he has not enough available capital left, to provide ensoulment for a mind and body at his previous level. He must now be content, therefore, to occupy vehicles of a far less evolved type, belonging to some earlier race. He has thus thrown himself far back in evolution, and must climb over again many rungs of the ladder.

He will probably be born as a savage, but will most likely be a chief among them, as he will still have some intellect. It has been said that he may even throw himself so far back that he may be unable to find in the world, in its present condition, any type of human body low enough for the manifestation which he now requires, so that he may be incapacitated from taking any further part in this Scheme of evolution, and may

therefore have to wait, in a kind of condition of *I L I* 435.
suspended animation, for the commencement of *S P* 45-46.
another.

Meanwhile, the amputated personality, having broken the "silver thread that binds it to the Master," is, of course, no longer a permanent evolving entity, but remains full of vigorous and wholly evil life, entirely without remorse or responsibility. As it is destined to disintegrate amidst the unpleasant surroundings of the "eighth sphere," it tries to maintain some sort of existence on the physical plane as long as possible. The sole means of prolonging its baneful existence is vampirism of some sort: when that fails, it has been known to seize upon any available body, driving out the lawful owner. The body chosen might very probably be that of a child, both because it might be expected to last longer, and because an ego, which had not yet really taken hold, could be more easily dispossessed.

In spite of its frenzied efforts, its power seems soon to fail, and it is said there is no instance on record of its successfully stealing a second body, after its first theft is worn out. The creature is a demon of the most terrible type, a monster for whom there is no permanent place in the Scheme of evolution to which we *I L I* 436.
belong.

Its natural tendency, therefore, is to drift out of this evolution and to be drawn into that astral cesspool known as the "eighth sphere," because what passes into it stands outside the ring of our seven worlds, or globes, and cannot return into their evolution. There, surrounded by loathsome relics of all the concentrated vileness of the ages that are past, burning ever with desire, yet without possibility of satisfaction, this monstrosity slowly decays, its mental and causal matter being thus at last set free. Such matter will never rejoin the ego from which it has torn itself, but will be distributed among the other matter of the plane, to enter gradually into fresh combinations, and so be put to better uses. Such entities are, as already stated, exceedingly rare: and, moreover, they have power to seize only those who have in their nature pronounced defects of a kindred type.

The other type of black magician, in outward appearance more respectable, is yet really even more dangerous, because more powerful. This is the man who, instead of giving himself up altogether to sensuality, sets before himself the goal of a more refined but not less unscrupulous selfishness. His object is the acquisition of an occult power higher and wider, but still to be used always for his own gratification and advancement, to further his own ambition, or satisfy his own revenge.

In order to gain this, he adopts the most rigid asceticism as regards mere fleshly desires, and starves out the grosser particles of his astral body, as perseveringly as does the pupil of the Great White Brotherhood. But, though it is only a less material kind of desire, with which he will allow his mind to become entangled, the centre of his energy is none the less entirely in his personality. When, therefore, the separation, at the end of the astral life, takes place, the ego is unable to recover any of his investment. For this man the result is, therefore, much the same as in the former case, except that he will remain in touch with the personality much longer, and will to some extent share its experiences, so far as it is possible for an ego to share them.

I L I 438. *S D* 45. The fate of that personality, however, is very different. The comparatively tenuous astral integument is not strong enough to hold it for any length of time on the astral plane, and yet it has entirely lost touch with the heaven-world, which should have been its habitat. For the whole effort of the man's life has been to kill out such thoughts as naturally find their result at that level. His one endeavour has been to oppose natural evolution, to separate himself from the great whole, and to war against it; and, as far as the personality is concerned, he has succeeded. It is cut off from the light and life of the solar system: all that is left to it is the sense of absolute isolation, of being alone in the universe.

Thus, in this rare case, the lost personality practically shares the fate of the ego from which it is in process of detaching itself. But, in the case of the ego, such an experience is only temporary, although it may last for what we should call a very long time, and the end of it will be reincarnation, and a fresh opportunity.

For the personality, however, the end is disintegration—the invariable end, of course, of that which has cut itself off from its source.

In a case of this kind, involving the loss of an entire *T P O* 875.
personality, the ego does no evil intentionally. He has let the personality get out of hand, and for that he is responsible. He is therefore responsible for weakness, rather than for direct evil. Whilst the ego has fallen back terribly, yet he does go on: probably not immediately, because he seems to be stunned at first.

After such an experience, an ego would always be peculiar. He would be dissatisfied, and would have recollections of something higher and greater than now he could reach. It is a fearful condition, but still the ego has to take the karma of it, and realise that he has brought it upon himself.

It is reported that there is another even more *I L I* 439.
remote possibility. Just as the hand (c) may absorb the arm (b) and revolt against the body (a), setting up on its own account and breaking away altogether, it is (or at any rate has been in the past) just possible that the disease of separateness and selfishness may infect the body (a) also. Even it is then absorbed into the monstrous growth of evil, and may be torn away from the undeveloped portion of the ego, so that the causal body itself may be hardened and carried away, instead of only the personality. Diagram XXVIIID illustrates this case.

This class of case would correspond, not to an amputation, but to an entire destruction of the body. Such an ego could not reincarnate in the human race; ego though it be, it would fall into the depths of animal life, *I L I* 440. and would need at least a whole Chain period to regain the status which it had lost. This, though theoretically possible, is practically scarcely conceivable. It will be noted, however, that even in this case the undeveloped part of the ego remains as the vehicle of the monad.

T P O 877. Whilst some ancient scriptures speak of men sinking back into the animal kingdom, there is no direct evidence of any such cases. There are other cases in which man may come into touch with animal consciousness, and suffer terribly through it (*vide The Astral Body*, p. 142), but to reincarnate as an animal is not possible now, whatever may have been possible in the distant past.

I L I 425–427: 262–264. We may here make a slight digression, in order to explain how it is that even in cases such as those described above a really serious loss is no easy matter.

Owing to the fact that good thoughts and emotions work in the higher types of matter, and that finer matter is far more easily moved than coarser matter, it follows that a given amount of force spent in good thought or feeling produces perhaps a hundred times as much effect as precisely the same amount of force sent out into coarser matter. If this were not so, it is obvious that the ordinary man would make no progress at all.

If a man throws a certain amount of energy into some evil quality, it has to express itself through the lower and heavier astral matter; and, whilst any kind of astral matter is exceedingly subtle as compared with anything on the physical plane, yet, as compared with the higher matter of its own plane, it is just as gross as lead is on the physical plane, when compared with the finest ether.

If, therefore, a man should exert exactly the same amount of force in the direction of good, it would have to move through the much finer matter of the higher sub-planes, and would produce, as said, at least a hundred times as much effect, or, if we compare the lowest with the highest, probably more than a thousand times as much.

Whilst we are probably entitled to assume that 90 per cent. of the thought and feeling of the undeveloped man is self-centred, even if not actually selfish, yet, if 10 per cent. of it is spiritual and unselfish, the man must already be rising somewhat above the average. In fact, if these proportions did produce commensurate results, the vast majority of humanity would take nine steps backwards for every one forwards, and we should have retrogression so rapid that a few incarnations would deposit us in the animal kingdom, out of which we evolved.

Happily for us, however, the effect of 10 per cent. of force, directed to good ends, enormously outweighs that of 90 per cent. devoted to selfish purposes, and so, on the whole, such a man makes an appreciable advance from life to life.

A man who can show even 1 per cent. of good makes a slight advance, so it will be readily understood that a man whose account balances exactly, so that there is neither advance nor retrogression, must have been living a distinctly evil life; while to obtain an actual descent in evolution, a person must be an unusually consistent villain.

Apart from these considerations, we have also to bear in mind that the Logos Himself is, by His resistless power, steadily pressing the whole system onwards and upwards, and that, however slow this cyclic progression may seem to us, it is a fact which cannot be neglected, for its effect is, that a man who accurately balances his good and evil, comes back, not to the same *actual* position, but to the same *relative* position, and therefore even he has made some slight advance, and is, as it were, in a position just a little better than that which he has actually deserved and made for himself.

It is thus clear, that if any one is so foolish as to want to go really backwards against the stream, he will have to work hard and definitely towards evil. There is no fear of "sliding" back. That is one of the old delusions, which remains from the times of the belief in the orthodox " devil," who was so much stronger than the Deity that everything in the world was working in his favour. The fact is that the exact opposite is the case, and everything round a man is calculated to assist him, if only he understands it.

CHAPTER XXVI

THE EGO AND THE PERSONALITY

In *The Mental Body* we examined the relationship between the personality and the ego, principally from the point of view of the personality. It is now necessary to study more deeply the relationship between the ego and the personality, this time from the point of view of the ego.

Let us first recapitulate the main facts regarding the constitution of man as Monad, Ego and Personality.

The fragment of the Divine Life, which we know as *I L II* 371–
the Monad, manifests itself upon the plane of ātmā as 372. *M* 64.
the triple spirit (*vide* Diagram XII p. 36).

Of these three aspects, one, the spirit itself, remains upon its own plane, that of ātmā. The second, that of intuition, or pure reason, as it is sometimes called, puts itself down one stage, and expresses itself through the matter of the plane of buddhi. The third aspect, that of intelligence, puts itself down two planes, and expresses itself through the matter of the higher mental plane.

This expression of the Monad, on the planes of ātmā, buddhi and manas, is the ego, or individuality.

The ego expresses itself on the lower planes as a personality, which is also triple in its manifestation, and is, moreover, an accurate reflection of the arrangement of the ego. But, like other reflections, it reverses itself.

Intelligence, or higher manas, reflects itself in lower manas. Pure reason, or buddhi, reflects itself in the astral body: and, in some way much more difficult to comprehend, the spirit of ātmā reflects itself upon the physical plane.

There is always a link or line of communication *M P* 178. *T P O* 357: 531: 438.

between the higher self, or ego, and the lower self, or personality. This link is known as the *antahkarana.* This Samskrit word means the inner organ, or inner instrument. H. P. Blavatsky spoke of it as the link, channel or bridge between higher manas and kāma-manas during incarnation. Speaking of one who can unite kāma-manas with higher manas, through the lower manas, she speaks of lower manas, *when pure and free from kāma,* as the antahkarana.

The antahkarana may be regarded as the arm stretched out, between the little piece of the ego that is awakened, and the part put down, the hand. When the two are perfectly joined, *i.e.,* when the ego and the personality are perfectly in tune, and united, then the attenuated thread of antahkarana ceases to exist. Its destruction implies that the ego no longer needs an *instrument,* but works directly on the personality: when one will operates the ego and the personality, then there is no longer any need for the antahkarana.

T P O 356. The term antahkarana, or internal agency, is used also in another sense, to denote the whole of the triple higher self or ego, because this is the channel or bridge between the Monad and the lower self.

M P 178–179. *T P O* 371. In its earlier stages, man's evolution consists in the opening of this antahkarana, or line of communication, so that the ego may be increasingly able to assert himself through it, and finally entirely to dominate the personality, so that it may have no separate thought or will, but may be merely, as it should be, an expression of the ego on the lower planes, so far, of course, as the limitations of the lower planes permit.

The link that binds the lower to the higher self is often spoken of as a thread—a thread of silver, as befits an emblem of purity.

T P O 438. The heart is the centre in the body for the higher triad, ātmā-buddhi-manas, so that when the consciousness is centred in the heart, during meditation, it is most susceptible to the influence of the higher self or ego. The head is the seat of the psycho-intellectual man; it has its various functions in seven cavities, including the pituitary body and the pineal gland. He who in concentration can take his consciousness from the brain to the heart should be able to unite kāma-manas to the higher manas, through the lower manas, which, when pure and free from kāma, is the antahkarana. He will then be in a position to catch some of the promptings of the higher triad.

The man who is absolutely untrained has practically no communication with the ego: the Initiate, on the other hand, has full communication. Consequently we find, as is to be expected, that there are men at all stages between these two extremes.

The student will by this time have appreciated the enormous importance of realising the existence of this connection between the higher and the lower self, and of doing everything that he can to strengthen that link so that the ego and the personality may gradually come to function as one entity. To help him in this task may, perhaps, be regarded as the *grand motif* of this series of four books, explanatory of man's constitution, and the various bodies through which he functions. *A E P.*

Whilst thus endeavouring, in many ways and by many devices, to appreciate and realise the great difference between the view-points of the personality and the ego, we must ever bear in mind, as has been repeatedly said, that there is only *one* consciousness; *I L I* 371. yet often we clearly feel two, and are led to wonder *T P O* 16. whether the ego is entirely dissociated from the physical body. We must, however, realise that there *is* only one consciousness, the apparent difference being caused only by the limitations of the various vehicles.

We should not, therefore, imagine that there are two entities in man. There never is any lower self as a separate being, but, as we have seen, the ego puts down a tiny portion of himself into the personality, in order to experience the vibrations of the lower planes.

The fundamental identity between higher and lower *K* 30–31. manas must be kept constantly in mind. For convenience' sake, we distinguish between them; but the difference is one of functioning activity, not of nature.

Lower manas is one with higher manas, in the same way that the ray is one with the sun.

M P 177-178. The tiny fragment of the ego, which is put down into the personality, is the point of consciousness which clairvoyants can see moving about in the man. According to one system of symbology, it is seen as "the golden man the size of a thumb," who dwells in the heart. Others, however, see it rather in the form of a star, a brilliant star of light.

A man may keep this Star of Consciousness where he will; that is to say, in any one of the seven principal chakrams or centres of the body. Which of these is most natural to a man depends largely upon his type or "ray," and probably also upon his race and sub-race.

Men of the Fifth Root Race nearly always keep this consciousness in the brain, in the centre dependent upon the pituitary body. There are, however, men of other races to whom it comes more natural to keep it habitually in the heart, the throat or the solar plexus.

The Star of Consciousness is thus the representative of the ego in the lower planes, and, as it manifests through the lower vehicles, we call it the personality, the man as he is known to his friends down here.

M P 179. Although, as we have seen, the ego is but a fragment of the Monad, yet he is complete as an ego in his causal body, even when his powers are undeveloped; whereas in the personality there is but a touch of his life.

I L I 372: 389. *M* 18. *T P O* 119: 190: 242: 751. Furthermore, whilst in the case of the ordinary man, the consciousness of the ego on his own plane is only partial and vague, yet, so far as it is active, it is always on the side of good, because it desires that which is favourable to its own evolution as a soul.

In fact, the never-changing desire of the ego is for progress, for the unfoldment of the higher self, and for the bringing of the lower vehicles into tune as its instruments.

Any of those thoughts that we call evil are for the ego impossible; for, in the ego, so far as any quality is developed, it is pure. If, for example, affection is there, it is utterly untainted by jealousy, envy or selfishness. It is a mirror of the divine love, in so far as the ego can reproduce it at his level.

Furthermore, the ego is never likely to be wrong. He is, apparently, not deceived about anything; but that he is ignorant of certain matters is quite clear, for indeed the very purpose of incarnation is to remove that ignorance.

But, as we have seen, the fragment of the ego, which has been put down into lower matter, becomes so keenly and vividly conscious in that matter, that it thinks and acts as though it were a separate being; it forgets that it belongs to the less developed, but far wider consciousness of the ego, and sets up in the business of life on its own account, and tries to go as it wants, rather than as the ego wishes.

Furthermore, the ego, with all his mighty powers, is very much less accurate than the lower mind, and the personality, valuing above all the discriminating powers of the lower mind which it is intended to develop, often comes in consequence to despise the far higher but vaguer self, and acquires a habit of thinking of itself as independent of the ego. *T P O* 751.

We may note here that all through the course of our evolution there is always a danger that a man should identify himself with that point at which, or that vehicle in which, he is most fully conscious.

Hence, as we have seen, sometimes it seems as though the fragment worked against the whole; but the man who is instructed declines to be deluded, and reaches back through the keen, alert consciousness of the fragment, to the true consciousness behind, which is as yet so little developed. That is what Mr. Sinnett called "giving allegiance to the higher self."

We have already seen that, in the nature of things, there can be no evil in the causal body, or in the ego. But wherever there is a gap in the causal body there is a possibility that the lower vehicles may run into some sort of evil action. Thus, for example, the astral elemental may take possession of the man and rush him *T P O* 752.

into the commission of a crime. In such a case the ego is not sufficiently awake to step in and prevent the action, or perhaps he does not understand that the passion or greed of the astral body may force the lower self into the commission of a crime. Evil, therefore, does not come from the Higher Self: it comes from a *lack* in the Higher Self: because, if the ego were more developed, he would check the man on the brink of the evil thought, and the crime would not be committed.

I L I 380–381. *M P* 178. In ordinary men, the ego has not much grasp of the personality, nor a clear conception of his purpose in sending it forth; and, as we have seen, the small piece which meets us in the personality grows to have ways and opinions of its own. It is developing by the experience it gains, and this is passed on to the ego; but, together with this real development, it usually gathers a good deal which is hardly worthy of that name. It acquires knowledge, but also prejudices, which are not really knowledge at all. It does not become quite free of those prejudices—prejudices, be it noted, of knowledge, of feeling and of action—until the man reaches Adeptship. Gradually it discovers these things to be prejudices, and progresses through them; but it has always a great deal of limitation, from which the ego is entirely free.

H S II 294–296. In order to assist the ego in controlling his vehicles, and to help him to utilise them for his own purposes, a very great deal can be done by parents and teachers during infancy and early childhood. For it makes a vast difference when the good, rather then the evil, germs in the child's bodies are aroused first. If, by exceeding care before birth, and for several years after it, the parents are able to excite only the good tendencies, then the ego will naturally find it easy to express himself along those lines, and a decided habit is set up in that direction. Then, when an evil excitation comes, it finds a strong momentum in the direction of good, which it strives in vain to overcome.

Similarly, if the evil tendencies have been aroused

first, then excitations towards what is good have to struggle against the predisposition towards evil. In this case, there is in the personality a taste for evil, a readiness to receive and indulge in it. In the other case, however, there is a strong natural distaste for evil, which makes the work of the ego much easier.

In the average man there is a perpetual strain going on between the astral and mental bodies, and also neither of these bodies is in the least in tune with the ego, or prepared to act as his vehicle. What is needed is the purification of the personality, and also the channel between it and the ego must be opened and widened. *T P O* 366.

Until this is done, the personality sees everything and everybody from its own very limited point of view. The ego cannot see what is really going on ; he perceives only the distorted picture of the personality, which is like a camera with a defective lens, that distorts the light rays, and a faulty plate, which makes the result blurred, indistinct and unequal.

Hence, in the case of most people, the ego cannot derive any satisfaction from the personality, until it is in the heaven-world. The ego himself knows the true from the false : he recognises the truth when he sees it, and rejects the false. But, generally, when he casts an eye downwards into the personality, he finds so crazy a confusion of inconsequent thought-forms, that he can distinguish nothing definite. He turns away in despair, and decides to wait for the quietude of the heaven-world, before attempting to pick up the fragments of truth out of this unseemly chaos.

Under the more peaceful conditions of devachan, as the emotions and thoughts of the recent physical life come up one by one, and envisage themselves in the vivid light of that world, they are examined with clear vision, the dross is thrown away, and the treasure is kept.

The disciple should, of course, try to bring about this condition, while still in the physical body, by purifying the personality, and harmonising it with the ego or soul.

I L I 372–373. Although the ego is undoubtedly only very partially expressed by his physical body, yet it would be inaccurate to speak of him as dissociated from that body. If we imagine the ego as a solid body, and the physical plane as a surface, then, if the solid is laid on the surface, obviously the plane figure, representing the contact of the solid with the surface, would be an exceedingly partial expression of the solid. Further, if the various sides of the solid were laid on the surface successively, we might obtain impressions which differed considerably from one another. All of them would be imperfect and partial, because in all cases the solid would have an extension in an entirely different direction, which could in no way be expressed on the flat surface.

In the case of an ordinary man, we shall obtain a nearly accurate symbolism of the facts if we suppose the solid to be conscious, only so far as it is in contact with the surface. Nevertheless, the results gained, through the expression of such consciousness, would inhere in the solid considered as a whole, and would be present in any later expression of it, even though that might differ considerably from previous expressions.

I L I 375–376. When the ego is still undeveloped, he cannot respond to more than very few of the extremely fine vibrations of the higher mental plane, so that they pass through him practically without affecting him. At first it needs powerful and comparatively coarse vibrations to affect him : as these do not exist on his own plane, he has to put himself down to lower levels in order to find them.

Hence full consciousness comes to him at first only in the lowest and densest of his vehicles, his attention being focussed for a long time in the physical plane ; so that, although that plane is so much lower than his own, and offers so much less scope for activity, yet in those early stages he feels himself much more alive when he is working there.

As his consciousness increases, and widens its scope, he gradually begins to work more and more in matter one stage higher, *i.e.*, in astral matter. At a much later stage, when he has attained to clear working in astral matter, he begins to be able also to express himself through the matter of his mental body. Still later, the end of his present effort is achieved when he works as fully and clearly in the matter of the causal body on the higher mental plane as he does now on the physical plane.

When an ego becomes sufficiently developed to come *I L I* 380. under the direct influence of a Master, the amount of that influence, which can be passed on to the personality, depends upon the connection between that personality and the ego, which is very different in different cases: there is, in fact, an infinite variety in human life.

As the spiritual force rays upon the ego, something *I L I* 381–382. of it must flow through to the personality always, because the lower is attached to the higher, just as the hand is attached to the body by the arm. But the personality can receive only what it has made itself able to receive.

There is also another important factor which comes into operation. The Master often plays upon qualities in the ego which are much obscured in the personality, so that, in such a case, very little comes down to the personality. Just as only those experiences of the personality can be handed on to the ego, which are compatible with the nature and interests of the ego, so only those impulses, to which the personality can respond, can express themselves in it. We must also bear in mind that whilst the ego tends to exclude the material, and receive the spiritual, so the general tendency of the personality—at least in the earlier stages—is to exclude the spiritual, and receive the material.

A clairvoyant may sometimes see these influences at work. Thus, on a certain day, he may notice a characteristic of the personality much intensified, with no outward reason. The cause is often to be found in what is taking place at some higher level—the stimulation of that quality in the ego. A man may find himself, for example, overflowing with affection or devotion, and quite unable on the physical plane to explain why. The cause is usually the stimulation of the ego, or, on the other hand, it may be that the ego is taking some special interest in the personality for the time being.

T P O 99. The relationship between a pupil and his Master is not at all unlike that of the personality to the ego. Just as the ego may be considered to put down a small fragment of himself into the personality, and express himself—however imperfectly—through that personality, so in the same sort of way the pupil not merely represents the Master, but *is* the Master in a very real sense, but the Master under tremendous limitations; those limitations consist, not only of the conditions of the lower planes themselves, but also, of course, of the personality of the pupil, which is by no means transcended.

Furthermore, even if the pupil's ego had gained perfect control of his lower vehicles, there would still be the difference between the *size* of the ego of the pupil, and of the ego of the Master, because the pupil is naturally a smaller ego than the Master whom he follows, and therefore can be only an incomplete representative of Him.

I L I 382–383. Meditation is a method of drawing the attention of the ego: it should, however, be borne in mind that, in the practice of meditation, instead of trying to interrupt the ego, and draw him down to the personality, we should strive to reach up to him in his higher activity. Higher influence is certainly invited by meditation, which is *always* effective, even though on the physical plane things may seem to be very dull, and quite without zest. The feeling of dullness in the personality may, in fact, be due to the reaching upwards of the ego, and his consequent neglect to send energy down to the personality.

L I 383: 330–331. Meditation and the study of spiritual subjects in this earthly life undoubtedly make a very great difference in the life of the ego: for meditation, conscientiously done, opens the channel between personality and ego, and keeps it open. It should, however, be borne in mind that physical meditaton is not directly for the ego, but for the training of the various vehicles to be a channel for the ego. In fact, during physical meditation, the ego regards the personality much as at any other time—he is usually slightly contemptuous. Nevertheless, the force which comes down is always that of the ego, but, as it is only a small part, it tends to give a one-sided conception of things.

The ordinary person, who has not taken up spiritual matters seriously, has only a thread of connection between the personality and ego: in fact this channel is often so narrow that sometimes it appears to be almost choked up. On some special occasion—as, for example, that of "conversion"—the force may break through again. For more developed persons, there is a constant flow, in some measure, between ego and personality. *I L I* 383: 387.

These considerations should bring home to us that it is by no means always accurate to judge the ego by his manifestation in the personality. Thus, for example, an ego of an intensely practical type may make much more show, on the physical plane, than another of far higher development, whose energy happens to be concentrated almost exclusively upon the causal or buddhic levels. Hence people who judge merely by physical plane appearances are frequently entirely wrong, in their estimation of the relative development of others. *I L I* 384.

Each of the successive descents of the ego into the lower planes is a limitation so indescribable that the man, whom we meet down here on the physical plane, is at the best a fragment of a fragment, and as an expression of the real man is so inadequate as to furnish us with nothing even remotely resembling a conception of what that man will be at the end of his evolution. *T P O* 259.

Until one can see the ego, one has no conception of how great he really is, how infinitely wiser and stronger than the incarnate entity. Every one, in reality, is *T P O* 843.

very much better than he ever seems to be. The greatest saint can never fully express his ego ; on that higher plane he is a still greater saint than he can ever be down here. But, magnificent as he is, he is still, if we may say so, vague in his magnificence.

T P O 895–896. There are really three ways in which the ego may be developed, and may influence the life. (1) The way of the scientist and the philosopher : these develop not only the lower mind, but also the higher, so that a great deal of its more abstract and comprehensive kind of thought comes down into their consciousness. For such as these, the development of buddhic consciousness will come later.

(2) The method of using the higher emotions, such as affection, devotion or sympathy, and so awakening the buddhic principle to a great extent, without developing especially the intermediate causal body. Nevertheless, the causal body will be affected, since all buddhic development reacts very powerfully on the causal body. These people are not necessarily developing a buddhic vehicle in which they can permanently live : but the use of the higher emotions unquestionably evokes vibrations in the buddhic matter. Hence there is a stir in the as yet unformed buddhic vehicle, so that many of its vibrations come down and brood over the astral body. Thus the man may receive a considerable amount of influence from the buddhic plane before the vehicle is at all fully developed.

(3) The more obscure method in which the will is called into activity, the physical body in some way reacting on the ātmic matter. Very little is known as to how this operates.

The method of most students is through devotion, and keen sympathy with their fellow-men.

I L I 383–385. A fairly advanced ego may sometimes be rather inconsiderate of his body, because whatever is put down into the personality means so much taken from the ego, and he may therefore grudge such expenditure of force. An ego may be somewhat impatient, and withdraw himself somewhat from the personality : in such cases, however, there would always be a flow between ego and personality, which is not possible with the ordinary man. In the ordinary man the fragment of the ego is, as it were, put down, and left to fend for itself, though it is not completely cut off. At the more advanced stage mentioned, however, there is a constant communication between the two along the channel. The ego can, therefore, withdraw himself whenever he chooses, and leave a very poor representation of the real man behind. So we see that the relations between the lower and the higher self vary much in different people, and at different stages of development.

An ego, busy with his own occupations on his own plane, may forget for a time to pay his personality proper attention, just as even a good and thoughtful man may occasionally, under some special pressure of business, forget his horse or his dog. Sometimes, when that happens, the personality reminds him of its existence by blundering into some foolishness, which causes serious suffering. *I L I* 385–386.

One may notice that sometimes, after the completion of a special piece of work, that has needed the co-operation of the ego to a large extent—as, for example, lecturing to a large audience—the ego takes away his energy, and leaves the personality with only enough to feel rather dispirited. For a time, he admitted that there was some importance in the work, and therefore poured down a little more of himself, but afterwards he leaves the unfortunate personality feeling rather depressed.

We must ever recollect that the ego puts down into the personality only a very small part of himself: and as that part constantly becomes entangled in interests which, because they are so partial, are often along lines different from the general activities of the ego himself, the ego does not pay any particular attention to the lower life of the personality, unless something rather unusual happens to it. *I L I* 379.

In the physical life of the ordinary man or the *M P* 183.

world there is little of interest to the ego, and it is only now and then that something of real importance occurs, that may for a moment attract his attention, so that from it he draws whatever is worth taking.

The ordinary man lives in patches ; more than half the time he is not awake to the real and higher life at all. If a man complains that his ego takes very little notice of him, let him ask himself how much notice he has taken of his ego. How often, for example, in any given day, has he even thought of the ego ?

If he wishes to attract the attention of the ego, he must make the personality useful to him. As soon as he begins to devote the greater part of his thought to higher things—in other words, as soon as he really begins to live—the ego will be likely to take somewhat more notice of him.

M P 184. The ego is well aware that certain necessary parts of his evolution can be achieved only through his personality, in its mental, astral and physical bodies. He knows, therefore, that he must some time attend to it, must take it in hand, and bring it under his control.

But we can well understand that the task may often seem uninviting, that a given personality may appear anything but attractive or hopeful. If we look at many of the personalities around us, their physical bodies full of drugs and poisons, their astral bodies reeking with greed and sensuality, and their mental bodies having no interests beyond money-making, and perhaps " sport " of the cruder varieties, it is not difficult to see why an ego, surveying them from his lofty height, might decide to postpone his serious effort to another incarnation, in the hope that the next set of vehicles might be more amenable to influence than those upon which his horrified gaze now rests. We can imagine that he might say to himself : " I can do nothing with that ; I will take my chance of getting something better next time ; it can hardly be worse, and meantime I have much more important business to do up here."

M P 184–185. A similar state of affairs not infrequently happens in the early stages of a new incarnation. As we have already seen, from the birth of the child the ego hovers over it, and, in some cases, begins to try to influence its development while it is still very young. But, as a general rule, he pays little attention to it until about the age of seven, by which time the work of the karmic elemental should be practically finished.

But children differ so widely, that it is not surprising to find that the relation between the egos, and the personalities involved, differs widely also. Some child-personalities are quick and responsive, some are dull and wayward. When dullness and unresponsiveness are prominent, the ego often withdraws his active interest for the time, hoping that, as the childish body grows, it may become cleverer or more responsive.

To us such a decision may seem unwise, because, if the ego neglects his present personality, it is unlikely that the next will be an improvement upon it ; and, if he allows the child-body to develop without his influence, the undesirable qualities which have been manifested may quite possibly grow stronger, instead of dying out. But we are hardly in a position to judge, since our knowledge of the problem is so imperfect, and we can see nothing of the higher business, to which the ego is devoting himself.

From this it will be seen how impossible it is to judge, with any precision, the position in evolution of any one whom we see on the physical plane. In one case, karmic causes may have produced a very fair personality, having an ego of only moderate advancement behind it. In another case, those causes may have *M P* 186.
given rise to an inferior or defective personality, belonging to a comparatively advanced ego.

When the ego decides to turn the full force of his energy upon the personality, the change which he can produce is very great. No one who has not personally investigated the matter cannot imagine how wonderful, how rapid, how radical, such a change may be, when conditions are favourable—that is, when the ego is reasonably strong, and the personality not incurably vicious—more especially when a determined effort is made by the personality, on its side, to become a perfect expression of the ego, and make itself attractive to him.

To understand how this can be, it is, of course, necessary to look at the matter simultaneously from two points of view. Most of us down here are very emphatically personalities, and think and act exclusively as
M P 187. such ; yet we know all the time that in reality we are egos, and those of us who, by many years of meditation, have rendered ourselves more sensitive to finer influences, are often conscious of the intervention of the higher self.

The more we can make a habit of identifying ourselves with the ego, the more clearly and sanely shall we view the problems of life. But, in so far as we feel ourselves to be personalities, it is obviously our duty, and our interest, to open ourselves to the ego, to reach up towards him, and persistently to set up within ourselves such vibrations as will be of use to him. At least we should be sure that we do not stand in the way of the ego, that we always do our best for him, according to our lights.

Since selfishness is the intensification of the personality, the first step should be to rid ourselves of that vice. Next, the mind should be kept filled with high thoughts ; for, if it is continually occupied with lower matters—even though those lower matters may be quite estimable in their way—the ego cannot readily use it as a channel of expression.

When the ego makes a tentative effort, when he puts down, as we might say, an explanatory finger, he should be received with enthusiasm, and his behests should be instantly obeyed, that he may more and more take possession of the mind, and so come into his inheritance, so far as these lower planes are concerned.
T P O 844. The personality should, so to speak, stand aside, and let the ego, the "warrior," fight in him.
T P O 846. In so doing, however, the personality must take care

that he is devoted to the *work*, not to his *personal* share or part in it. He must take care that, in a rush of personality, he remembers all the time that it is the ego that is working in him.

Although the vagueness of the ego, unless he were developed, may perhaps preclude him from indicating a particular line of work, yet when the personality, being more definite, has found the work, the ego can and does pour himself down into it, and enables him to do it in a much better manner and in an altogether grander frame of mind than the personality could attain unaided.

" But if thou [the personality] look not for him [the ego], if thou pass him by, then there is no safeguard for thee. Thy brain will reel, thy heart grow uncertain, and in the dust of the battlefield thy sight and senses will fail, and thou wilt not know thy friends from thy enemies." (*Light on the Path.*) This is what happens when the personality does not look for the higher guidance of the ego.

This is a step necessary to be taken, by a man who intends to set his feet upon the Path which leads to Initiation, for, at Initiation, the lower and the higher become one, or rather the lesser is absorbed by the greater, so that there should be nothing left in the personality, which is not a representation of the ego, the lower being merely an expression of the higher. With this, however, we shall deal more fully in Chapter XXXI, which deals specifically with Initiation. *M P* 188.

It is obvious, therefore, that the personality should endeavour to ascertain what the ego desires, and provide him with the opportunities he wants. The study of inner things, as mentioned, and living the spiritual life, wakes up the ego, and attracts his attention. To take an example: suppose you have an ego whose principal method of manifesting himself is by affection. That quality is what he wants to exhibit by his personality: consequently, if the personality tries to feel strong affection, and makes a speciality of that, the ego will promptly throw more of himself into the *I L I* 388. *I L II* 142 personality, because he finds in it exactly what he desires.

T P O 15–16. In the savage, the self expresses itself in all kinds of emotions and passions, of which the ego could not possibly approve, but, in the developed man, there are no emotions but such as he chooses to have. Instead of being swayed by emotions, and carried off his feet, he simply selects them. He would say, for example: "Love is a good thing: I will allow myself to feel love. Devotion is a good thing: I will allow myself to feel devotion. Sympathy is beautiful: I will allow myself to feel sympathy." This he does with his eyes open, intentionally. The emotions are thus under the dominion of the mind, and that mind is an expression of the causal body, so that the man is coming very near to the condition of complete unity of the higher and lower self.

I L II 141. The connection between the ego and the mental body is of the greatest importance, and every effort should be made to keep it active and alive. For the ego is the force behind, which makes use of the qualities and powers of the personality. In order that we may think of anything we must first remember it; in order that we may remember it, we must have paid attention to it; and *the paying of attention is the descent of the ego into his vehicles* in order to look through them.

Many a man with a fine mental body and a good brain makes little use of them, because he pays little attention to life—that is to say, because the ego is putting but little of himself down into these lower planes, and so the vehicles are left to run riot at their own will. The remedy for this has already been stated: it is to give the ego the conditions he requires, when there will be no reason to complain of his response.

I L I 388–389. It appears that the actual experiences of the personality cannot be transmitted to the ego: but the essence of them may be passed to him. The ego cares little for details, but he does want the essence of experiences. This being so, it is evident that the ordinary man has in his life very little that appeals to the ego.

The system of yielding up the results of the lower work, but not the detailed experiences, proceeds all the time until Adeptship is attained. *T P O* 769.

The student will do well to follow the advice given in *Light on the Path*: watch for the ego, and let him fight through you: but at the same time remember always that you *are* the ego. Therefore identify yourself with him, and make the lower give way to the higher. Even if you fall many times, there is no reason to be disheartened, for even failure is to a certain extent success, since by failure we learn, and so are wiser to meet the next problem. It is not expected that we should invariably succeed, but only that we shall always do our best. *I L I* 390.

Moreover, we must recollect that the ego has associated himself with the personality because he has a hunger, or thirst (Trishnā), for vivid experience. As he develops, the hunger abates little by little, and sometimes, when he is advanced, and has become more sensitive to the delights and activities of his own plane, he goes to the other extreme of neglecting his personality, caught as it is in the grip of karma, sunk in conditions which are now full of sorrow or of boredom to the ego, because he feels that he has outgrown them. *T P O* 260–261.

This diminution of the thirst has taken place as he developed his personality. When he gained full consciousness on the astral plane, the physical began to appear dull by comparison; reaching the lower mental world, he found the astral dark and dismal; and all four of the lower levels lost their attraction when he began to enjoy the still more vivid and luminous life of the causal body.

As has already been pointed out, it is necessary ever to bear in mind that consciousness is *one*: it is, therefore, quite mistaken to conceive of the ego, or higher self, as something "above," something essentially foreign to ourselves, and consequently hard to reach. *G E* 22–24.

Often we speak of the "tremendous effort" required to reach the higher self: at other times of the inspiration, etc., which comes from the higher self to us down below. In all these cases, we make the fundamental mistake of identifying ourselves with that which we are not, instead of that which we fundamentally are. The first condition of spiritual achievement is the certainty, beyond any doubt, that we are the ego or higher self: the second condition is that we have full confidence in our own powers as the ego, and the courage to use them freely.

Instead, therefore, of looking upon the consciousness of the personality as usual and normal, we should accustom ourselves to look upon the consciousness of the personality as abnormal and unnatural, and the life of the ego as our own true life, from which by continuous effort we keep ourselves estranged.

G E 37–40. This attitude to the various bodies should be adopted in practical life. Thus, the physical body should not be permitted to work of its own accord, but should be deliberately and consciously trained to obey the behests of the ego. In this way will be brought about what the Hermetic philosophers called the "regeneration" of the body. This is a real change which, when accomplished, for ever breaks the dominion of the physical body over the consciousness, making it instead an instrument for the use of the ego.

G E 40–47. A similar change should be brought about with regard to the astral body. Instead of permitting the world of emotion to influence it and determine its activity, the ego should himself decide and determine what emotions he will entertain, what feelings he permits himself to radiate from his astral body. Thus the consciousness of the ego becomes disentangled from the astral body, and that body becomes subservient to the wishes of the ego.

G E 47–50. Perhaps most essential of all is control of the mental body, because thought is the manifestation of the supreme Creative Energy. We should never allow thought-images to be incited from without: instead, when thought-images are made, they should be created by the deliberate, self-conscious action of the ego himself.

Great danger lies in an undisciplined imagination. Were it not for the imagination, external objects of desire would have no power over us. The ego should therefore acquire full control over the imagination, and permit it to exercise its function only in such directions as he determines. *G E* 50–55.

Uncontrolled imagination acts also as a powerful factor in undermining and weakening the will. Only too often, after some resolution has been made, the imagination is allowed to play with the unpleasant aspects of what it has been decided to do, until eventually it is made to appear so unpleasant that the idea of doing it is given up altogether. Shakespeare uttered deep psychological truth when he made Hamlet say: "the native hue of resolution is sicklied o'er with the pale cast of thought." *G E* 90–94.

The remedy for this unfortunate habit is obvious: the will and the attention should be irrevocably concentrated, not on the difficulties or unpleasantnesses which we imagine confront us, but on the task which is to be done. "Nerve us with constant affirmatives," said Emerson.

Pursuing the analysis a little further, we should abandon the widespread idea that the will *does* things, that we carry through something by an effort of the will. To do and carry out is *not* the function of the will, but of a quite different aspect of the ego, the creative activity. *G E* 88–89.

The will is the Ruler, the King who says "this shall be done," but who does not go and do things Himself. Psychologically speaking, the will is the power to hold the consciousness focussed on one thing and exclude everything else. In itself, it is perfectly serene, quiet, and unmoving, being, as said, just the power to hold one thing and exclude all else.

It is scarcely possible to fix the limits of the power of the human will when properly directed. It is so *S G O* 201.

much more far-reaching than the ordinary man ever supposes, that the results gained by its means appear to him astounding and supernatural. A study of its powers brings one gradually to realise what was meant by the statement that if faith were only sufficient it could remove mountains, and cast them into the sea; and even that oriental description seems scarcely exaggerated when one examines authenticated instances of what has been achieved by this marvellous power Perhaps the most important factor in a successful use of the will is perfect confidence, which, of course, may be gained in various ways, according to the type of person concerned.

T P O 7. As soon as a man realises that there is the inner and spiritual world of the ego, which is of enormously more importance in every way than that which is external, he may well adopt the attitude of an actor, who plays his part in the world, only because of the true life inside. An actor takes various parts at different times, just as we come back in other incarnations and wear other kinds of bodies. But all the time the actor has his real life as a man and as an artist as well, and, because he has that life of his own, he wants to play his part well, in the temporary life of the stage. Similarly, we should wish to do well, in our temporary physical life here, because of the great reality behind, of which it is but a very small fragment.

If this is clearly realised, we shall see what is the relative importance of this outer life: that its only value to us is that we shall play our part well, whatever that part may be. What kind of part it is, and what happens to us in this mimic existence—these things matter little. It may be an actor's business to go through all sorts of pretended sorrows and difficulties;
T P O 8. but these do not trouble him in the least. He may, for example, have to be killed every night in a duel; what does the feigned death matter to him? The only thing that concerns him is that he should acquit himself well.

Hence, it should not be difficult to realise that the

world about us is a mimic world, and that it really does not matter what experiences may come to us. All the things that happen to people from the outside are the result of their karma. The causes were set going long ago in other lives, and cannot now be altered. Therefore it is useless to worry about the things that happen: they should be borne philosophically. The way in which they are borne moulds the character for the future, and that is the only important thing. One should use karma to develop courage, endurance and various other good qualities, and then dismiss it from the mind.

Thus the groping, striving, struggling divine Self becomes, as evolution proceeds, the true Ruler, the inner Ruler Immortal. A man who grasps that he is himself that Immortal Ruler, seated within his Self-created vehicles of expression, gains a sense of dignity and power which grows ever stronger, and more compelling on the lower nature. The knowledge of the truth makes us free. *S C* 303–304.

The Inner Ruler may still be hampered by the very forms he has shaped for self-expression, but, knowing himself as the Ruler, he can work steadfastly to bring his realm into complete subjection. He knows that he has come into the world for a certain purpose, to make himself fit to be a co-worker with the Supreme Will, and he can do and suffer all which is necessary to that end.

He knows himself divine, and that his Self-realisation is only a matter of time. Inwardly, the divinity is felt, though outwardly it is not yet expressed; his task is to become in manifestation what he is in essence. He is king *de jure*, not yet *de facto*.

As a Prince, born to a crown, patiently submits to the discipline which is fitting him to wear it, so the sovereign Will in us is evolving to the age when royal powers will pass into its grasp, and may therefore patiently submit to the necessary discipline of life. *T P O* 339–340.

A correct view of the relationship, between the ego and his successive personalities, should suffice to clear *S G O* 112–115. *I L I* 161–166.

up the misunderstandings which have arisen regarding the teachings of the Lord Buddha. The Buddha preached constantly against the idea, which was evidently prevalent in His time, of the continuation of the *personality*. But, while He taught that nothing of all that, with which men generally identify themselves, lasts for ever, He made most unequivocal statements about the successive lives of men. He gave examples of preceding lives, and compared successive incarnations to days that one may have spent in this village or in that.

Nevertheless, the Southern Church of Buddhism now teaches that only karma persists, not an ego; as though man in one life made a certain amount of karma, and then died, and nothing was left of him, but another person was born, and had to bear the karma which that person did not make.

With curious illogicality, however, in spite of the formal teaching to the contrary, a *practical* belief in the continued existence of the individual persists, because, for example, Buddhist monks speak of attaining nirvāna, and recognise that this will take many lives.

The real significance of this teaching of the Buddha lies in the great emphasis He laid on the external temporary part of man which does *not* endure, and the implication that the parts of man which are not temporary or external, do survive as the enduring ego, the real man.

T P O 383. His teaching, however, went still deeper than this. There is a passage in the Shrī Vakya Sudhā which warns the aspirant that when he repeats the great formula "I am That," he must take care what he means by "I." It explains that the separate individual should be understood as threefold, and that it is the union with Brahman *only of the highest of these three* that is proclaimed by "Thou art That," and such sayings. We have already abundantly seen that the personality is not "I": and even the "you" in me is not "I": the "I" is something indistinguishable from the universal Self, in which the many and the One are one. The Lord Buddha's teaching denies the permanency of the " you " that men call " I."

Much wisdom is often wrapped up in etymology. *M V I* 30. Thus the very word " person " is compounded of the two Latin words *per* and *sona*, and therefore signifies " that through which the sound comes "—*i.e.*, the mask worn by the Roman actor to indicate the part which he happened at the moment to be playing. Thus we very appropriately speak of the group of temporary lower vehicles, which an ego assumes when he descends into incarnation, as his " personality."

Almost equally instructive are the words *individual* and *individuality* which are highly appropriate when applied to the ego. *A E P.* For *individual* means that which *is not divisible without loss of identity ; subsisting as one ;* and *individuality* is defined as *separate and distinct existence.* Going a stage further still, the word *exist* derives from *ex*, out, and *sistere*, to make to stand. Thus the ego or individuality is *made to stand out* (from the Monad), and manifests itself *through* the mask of the personality.

MONAD

EGO

PERSONALITIES

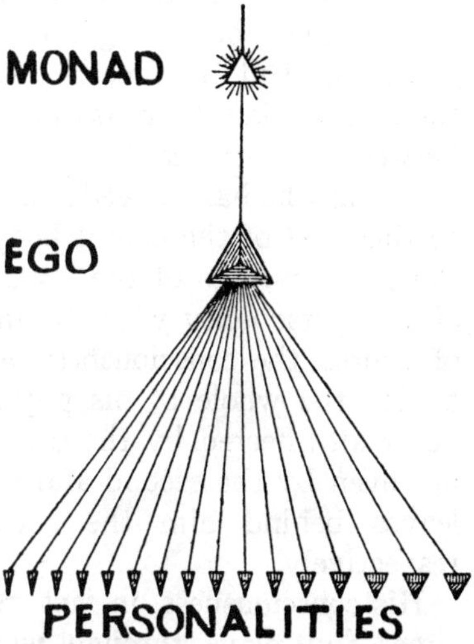

DIAGRAM XXIX.—The Ego and His Personalities.

Diagram XXIX is an attempt to illustrate one aspect of the relationship between the ego and his successive personalities. We see in the diagram, first, the Monad, deriving his life from the Unmanifest, and projecting below himself his ego, with his threefold characteristics or aspects The ego in turn projects from himself into the lower planes a series of successive personalities. These are shown in the drawing as gradually widening out, as they develop, until eventually the last personality is equilateral, being fully and symmetrically developed, thereby expressing, as fully as its inherent limitations permit, the nature and powers of the ego.

I L I 384. As people develop, the personal consciousness may be unified with the life of the ego—as far as that is possible—and then there is only the one consciousness: even in the personal consciousness there will be the consciousness of the ego, who will know all that is going on. But, as already said, with many people, at the present day, there is often considerable opposition between the personality and the ego.

I L II 66–69. A man who has succeeded in raising his consciousness to the level of the causal body, and thereby unifying the consciousness of the lower and the higher selves, of the personality with the individuality or ego has, of course, the consciousness of the ego at his disposal during the whole of his physical life. This will not be at all affected by the death of the physical body, nor even by the second and third deaths in which he leaves behind him the astral and mental bodies respectively.

His consciousness, in fact, resides in the ego all the time, and plays through whatever vehicle he may happen at any given moment to be using.

For him the whole series of his incarnations is only one long life: what we call an incarnation is to him a day in that life. All through his human evolution, his consciousness is fully active. Incidentally, we may note that he is generating karma just as much at one period as at another; and while his condition at any given moment is the result of the causes he has set in motion in the past, yet there is no instant at which he is not modifying his conditions by the exercise of thought and will. Whilst this consideration applies to all men, yet it is clear that one who possesses the ego-consciousness is in a position to modify his karma more deliberately, and with more calculated effect, than one who has not achieved continuous ego-consciousness.

H. P. Blavatsky speaks of the Higher Self as the "great Master," though she is here using the term Master in an unusual sense, different from that in which it is mostly employed to-day. It is, she says, the equivalent of Avalokiteshvara, and the same as Ādi-Buddha with the Buddhist occultists, Ātmā with the Brahmanas, and Christos with the ancient Gnostics. *T P O* 372.

CHAPTER XXVII

THE EGO *IN* THE PERSONALITY

THERE are a number of ways in which the activity of the ego may be more specifically observed as operating through the consciousness of the personality. In the

I L I 388–389. first place, as has been pointed out more than once, anything evil or selfish cannot, by the very mechanism of the higher planes, affect the ego, and we may therefore say that he has nothing to do with it. Unselfish thoughts and feelings alone can affect the ego : all the lower thoughts and feelings affect the permanent atoms, not the ego : and, as we have seen, corresponding to them we find gaps in the causal body, not " bad " colours. The ego is concerned solely with purely unselfish feelings and thoughts.

I L I 268–269. Most people are conscious of times when they are filled with splendid inspiration and exaltation, with glowing devotion and joy. These moments, of course, are precisely those when the ego succeeds in impressing himself upon the lower consciousness; but that which is then felt is, in reality, there all the time, though the personality is not always conscious of it. The aspirant should endeavour to realise, both by reason and by faith, that it is *always* there, and it will then appear as though he actually felt it, even at times when the link is imperfect, and when he does not feel it in the personal consciousness.

T P O 352–353. Moreover, it is obvious that while the mind is responding to the appeals of the physical, astral and lower mental planes, it is not likely to hear the message that the ego is trying to transmit to the personality from his own higher planes.

T P O 800–801. An emotional impulse, belonging to the astral plane, is sometimes mistaken for real spiritual aspiration, because what happens in the buddhic vehicle, if brought down to the personality, is reflected in the astral body. A standard example of this phenomenon is to be found in religious revivalist meetings. Such great emotional upheavals, whilst sometimes beneficial, are in many instances harmful, tending to throw people off their mental balance.

Two simple but excellent rules may be given for *T P O* 798.
differentiating between a true intuition and mere impulse. First: if the matter be laid aside for a while, and "slept on," an impulse will probably die away: a genuine intuition will remain as strong as ever. Second: true intuition is always connected with something unselfish; if there is any touch of selfishness it may be taken as certain that it is only an astral impulse, and not a true buddhic intuition.

The influence of the ego is often felt on occasions *T P O* 213–
when one seems to *know* by inner conviction that a 214.
thing is true, without being able to reason it out. The ego knows, and has good reason for his knowledge; but sometimes he cannot impress his reasons on the physical brain, though the bare fact that he knows manages to come through. Hence, when a new truth is presented to us, we know at once whether we can accept it or not.

That is not superstition, but an intense inner conviction. Superficially, it may appear to be abandoning reason in favour of intuition; but then it must be remembered that *buddhi*, which we translate as "intuition," is known in India as "*pure reason.*" It is the reason of the ego, which is a type higher than that which we have on the lower planes.

More specifically, we may say that manas gives *T P O* 412.
inspiration: buddhi gives intuition as to right and wrong: ātmā is the directing conscience, *commanding* that the man should follow that which he knows to be best, often when the mind is trying to invent some excuse to do otherwise.

Again, the manifestations of genius are but the *T N P* 27.
momentary grasping of the brain by the large con- *A W* 177.

sciousness of the ego, forcing it into an insight, a strength of grip, and a width of outlook, that causes its noble reach. This large consciousness *is* the real Self, the real man. Many things that we see around us, or that happen to us, are hints of this larger consciousness, whisperings, scarcely articulate as yet, but with all the promise of the future, that come from the land of our birth, from the world to which we truly belong. They are the voice of the living spirit, unborn, undying, ancient, perpetual and constant. They are the voice of the inner God, speaking in the body of man.

T P O 441–442. Life teaches us in two ways, by tuition that the world gives us, and by intuition, the working of the inner self. As men develop, their intuition increases, and they do not depend so much as before on the instruction that the world gives. That is another way of saying that the man who uses his inner powers can learn much more from a little experience than other men can from a great deal. Because of the activity of his innate intelligence, the developed man is able to see the great significance of even small things ; but the undeveloped mind is full of curiosity. It is eager for novelty, because, not being good at thinking, it soon exhausts the obvious significance of commonplace things. This mind is the one that craves miracles in connection with its religious experience, as it is blind to the countless miracles that surround it all the time.

T P O 797. What we call the dictates of conscience come from above, and represent usually the knowledge of the ego on the subject. But here a word of caution is necessary. The ego himself is as yet but partially developed. His knowledge on any given subject may be quite small, or even inaccurate, and he can reason only from the information before him.

Because of this, a man's conscience often misleads him, for an ego who is young, and knows but little, may yet be able to impress his will upon the personality. But as a general rule the undeveloped ego is also undeveloped in his power of impressing himself upon his lower vehicles: and perhaps this is just as well.

Sometimes, however, as said, an ego, who lacks development in tolerance and wide knowledge, may yet have a will sufficiently strong to impress upon his physical brain orders which show that he is a very young ego, and does not understand.

Hence, when conscience seems to dictate something *T P O* 798.
which is clearly against the great laws of mercy and truth and justice (as, possibly, was the case with some of the inquisitors), the man should think carefully whether the universal rule is not a greater thing than the particular application which seems to conflict with it. The intellect should always be used in such a way that it will be an instrument of the ego, not an obstacle in the path of his development.

A curious example of the way in which an ego may *H S I* 347.
manifest himself to the personality is that described in *The Mental Body*, p. 280. A certain orator, whilst speaking one sentence of a lecture, habitually sees the next sentence actually materialise in the air before her, in three different forms, from which she consciously selects that one which she thinks the best. This is evidently the work of the ego, though it is a little difficult to see why he takes that method of communication, instead of himself selecting the form he thinks best, and impressing that form alone on the personal consciousness.

That which is known to mystics as the "Voice of the *I L I* 343-
Silence" differs for people at different stages. The 344. *T P O* 369-
voice of the silence for any one is that which comes 370.
from the part of him which is higher than his conscious- *M* 21.
ness can reach, and, naturally, that changes as his evolution progresses.

For those now working with the personality, the voice of the ego is the voice of the silence, but when one has dominated the personality entirely, and has made it one with the ego, so that the ego may work perfectly through it, it is the voice of the ātmā—the triple spirit on the nirvānic plane. When this is reached, there will still be a voice of the silence—that of the Monad. When the man identifies the ego and the Monad, and attains Adeptship, he will still find a voice of the silence coming down to him from above, but then it will be the voice, perhaps, of one of the Ministers of the Deity, one of the Planetary Logoi. Perhaps for Him in turn it will be the voice of the Solar Logos Himself. The "Voice of the Silence," therefore, from whatever level it may come, is always essentially divine.

T N P 40–42. The ego works in the physical body through the two great divisions of the nervous system—the sympathetic and the cerebro-spinal. The sympathetic system is connected mostly with the astral body, the cerebro-spinal system with the mental body, this system coming more and more under the influence of the ego as he advances in intellectual power.

As the cerebro-spinal system developed, the ego passed on to the sympathetic system more and more of the parts of his consciousness, definitely established, towards which he no longer needed to turn his attention, in order to keep them in working order. It is possible, by the methods of Hatha Yoga, for example, for the ego to re-establish direct control over portions of the sympathetic system: to do so, however, is obviously not a step forward, but a step backward, in evolution.

T N P 64. The student should recollect that the ego is always striving upwards, trying to get rid of the lower planes, endeavouring to throw off the burdens which prevent his climbing. He does not want to be troubled, for example, with looking after the vital functions of the body, and gives his attention to the machinery only when anything goes wrong. As previously said, all such workings are recoverable, but it is not worth while to do so. On the contrary, the more we can hand over to that automatism, the better; for the less we have to utilise the waking consciousness, for the things that are constantly recurring, the more shall we have to work for the things that really need attention, and that are probably vastly more important, at any rate from the point of view of the ego.

Occasionally a man may become dominated by a "fixed idea," this resulting, in some cases, in madness, in other cases, in the unshakable devotion or determination of the saint or the martyr. These two classes of cases have diverse psychological origins, which we may now study. *T N P* 42–46.

A fixed idea that is madness is an idea which the ego has handed over to the sympathetic system, so that it has become part of the "sub-conscious." It may be a past mood or notion, that the ego has outgrown; or a forgotten fact, suddenly reasserting itself, unaccompanied by its proper surroundings; or the connection of two incongruous ideas; and so on.

There are countless such ideas, with which the ego has had to do in the past, and which he has not entirely thrown out of the mechanism of consciousness: so that they have lingered there, though the ego himself has outgrown them. So long as any part of the mechanism of consciousness can respond to them, for so long those ideas may emerge above the horizon, or "threshold," of consciousness.

When such an idea comes up, as it does, without reason, without rationality, with the rush and surge and passionate strength of the past, it overbears the subtler mechanism that the ego has evolved for his higher purposes. For ideas, such as those we are considering, are stronger on the *physical* plane than those we call the ordinary mental ideas, because, their vibrations being slower and coarser, they produce more result in the denser matter. It is far easier to affect the physical body, for example, by the surge of a barbaric emotion, than by the subtle reasoning of a philosopher.

We may state, then, that the fixed idea of the madman is usually an idea which has left its trace on the sympathetic system, and which, during some disturbance or weakening of the cerebro-spinal system, is able to assert itself in consciousness. It arises from below.

The fixed idea of the saint or the martyr, on the other hand, is a very different thing. This comes down from the ego himself, who is striving to impress upon the physical brain his own loftier emotion, his own wider knowledge. The ego, who can see further on the higher planes than he can in the physical encasement, tries to impress upon that physical encasement his own will, his own desire for the higher and nobler. It comes with all-dominating power ; it cannot approve itself to the reason, for the brain is not yet ready to reason on those lines of higher knowledge and of deeper vision and intuition ; but it comes down, with the force of the ego, on a body prepared for it, and thus asserts itself as the dominant power, guiding the man to heroic action, to martyrdom, to saintship. Such fixed ideas come, not, as in the previous class, from below, but from *above ;* not from the sub-conscious, but from the super-conscious.

As was said in *The Mental Body*, p. 279, we need not shrink from the fact that there is frequently a psychological instability associated with genius, as expressed in the saying that genius is akin to madness, and in the statement of Lombroso and others that many of the saints were neuropaths. The more delicate the machinery, the more easily may it be over-strained, or thrown out of gear ; hence it is sometimes true that the very instability of the genius or the saint is the very condition of their inspiration, the normal brain being not yet sufficiently developed, nor delicate enough, to answer to those subtle waves coming from the higher consciousness.

T N P 69–71. Thus those impulses, which we call the promptings of genius, come down from the super-conscious, from the realm of the ego himself. Not only do these inspirations from the higher consciousness sometimes cause brain-instability, but, as is well known, they are frequently accompanied by great irregularity of moral conduct. The reason for this is interesting and important.

When any force comes down, from a higher to a

lower plane, it is subject to transmutation in the vehicle into which it comes. According to the nature of the vehicle will be the transmutation of the force, a portion of the force being changed by the vehicle, into which it plays, *into the form of energy to which that vehicle lends itself most readily*.

Hence, for example, if an organism have a tendency to sexual excitement, the downflow of the force of genius will immensely increase the force of sexuality, by that part of it which is transmuted into vitality. We may note here, as an example of the working of this principle, that in the Third Race, the downflow of the spiritual life, into the channels of the animal man, so enormously increased his animal powers, that it was necessary that the Sons of Mind should come to his assistance, or humanity would have plunged down into the vilest of animal excesses, the very force of the spiritual life increasing the depth of the plunge into degradation. The lesson to be learnt here is clearly that, before we invite the inflow of the higher forces, it is all-important first to purify the lower nature. As the Buddha taught, the first rule is: "Cease to do evil."

In the words of *The Voice of the Silence*: "Beware lest thou shouldst set a foot still soiled upon the ladder's lowest rung. Woe unto him who dares pollute one rung with miry feet. The foul and viscous mud will dry, become tenacious, then glue his feet unto the spot; and like a bird caught in the wily fowler's lime, he will be stayed from further progress. His vices will take shape and drag him down. His sins will raise their voices like as the jackal's laugh and sob after the sun goes down; his thoughts become an army, and bear him off a captive slave.

"Kill thy desires, Lanoo, make thy vices impotent, ere the first step is taken on the solemn journey.

"Strangle thy sins, and make them dumb for ever, before thou dost lift one foot to mount the ladder.

"Silence thy thoughts, and fix thy whole attention on thy Master, whom yet thou dost not see, but whom thou feelest."

The student will scarcely need to be told that *one* meaning of " thy Master " is his own ego.

T P O 659. A man on the Path must do his work thoroughly. On the threshold mistakes can easily be corrected. But unless the disciple gets rid entirely, for example, of the desire for power, in the early stages of his spiritual apprenticeship, it will become stronger and stronger. If he does not weed it out where it is based in the physical, astral and mental planes, but allows it to take root in the spiritual plane of the ego, he will find it very difficult to eradicate. Ambition thus established in the causal body is carried on from life to life. So the pupil should beware of permitting spiritual ambition to touch the causal body, and so build into it elements of separateness, which more and more encase the life.

T P O 358. A man who is a genius on some line may often find it easy to apply tremendous concentration to his particular line of work ; but, when he relaxes from that, his ordinary life may quite possibly be still full of whirlpools in his mental and astral bodies. Such whirlpools may and do constantly crystallise into permanent prejudices, and make actual congestions of matter closely resembling warts upon the mental body (*vide The Mental Body*, p. 31). This, of course, is not what is required : the student of occultism aims at nothing less than the complete destruction of the whirlpools, so as to comb out the lower mind and make it the calm and obedient servant of the higher self *at all times.*

I L I 487. During the sleep of the physical body, although the ego leaves the body, yet he always maintains a close connection with it, so that under ordinary circumstances he would be quickly recalled to it by any attempt that might be made upon it, *e.g.*, to obsess it.

I L I 492–494. Whilst there are several widely different causes of sleep-walking (*vide The Astral Body*, pp. 90–1), there are some instances in which it appears that the ego is able to act more directly upon his physical body during the absence of the intermediate mental and astral vehicles—instances in which the man is able, during his sleep, to write poetry, or to paint pictures, which would be far beyond his powers when awake.

The ego often impresses his ideas upon the person- *I L II* 159–
ality in dreams, using sets of symbols, of which each 160.
ego has his own system, though some forms seem *D* 48–49 : 54.
general in dreams. Thus it is said that to dream of water signifies trouble of some sort, although there does not seem any real connection between the two. But, even though there be no real connection, an ego—or for that matter some other entity who desires to communicate—may use the symbol, merely because it is understood by the personality, and, by means of it, warn the personality of some impending misfortune.

Prophetic dreams must be attributed exclusively to *D* 51–52.
the action of the ego, who either foresees for himself, or is told of some future event, for which he wishes to prepare his lower consciousness. This may be of any degree of clearness and accuracy, according to the power of the ego to assimilate it himself, and, having done so, to impress it upon his waking brain.

Sometimes the event is one of serious moment, such as death or disaster, so that the motive of the ego, in endeavouring to impress it, is obvious. On other occasions, however, the fact foretold is apparently unimportant, so that it is difficult to understand why the ego should take any trouble about it. But, in such cases, it must be borne in mind that the fact remembered may be merely a trifling detail of some far larger vision, the rest of which has not come through to the physical brain. Stories of such prophetic dreams are, of course, quite common. Several are to be found in *Dreams*, by Bishop C. W. Leadbeater, p. 52 *et seq.*

In order to bring through, into the physical brain, *I L II* 221.
impressions from the ego, it is obvious that the brain must be calm. Everything from the causal body *must* pass through the mental and astral bodies, and, if either of these is disturbed, it reflects imperfectly, just as the least rippling of the surface of a lake will break up and distort images reflected in it. It is necessary

also to eradicate absolutely all prejudices, otherwise they will produce the effect of stained glass, colouring everything which is seen through them, and so giving a false impression.

T P O 367. If a man is to hear the " still, small voice " with certainty and accuracy, he *must* be still : the outer man must be unshaken by all external things, by the clamour of the big breakers of life that dash against him, as well as by the delicate murmur of the softer ripples. He must learn to be very still, to have no desires and no aversions. Except on rare occasions, when it is unusually strong, it is only when personal desires and aversions have ceased to exist, when the voice of the outer world can no longer command him, that a man can hear the inner voice which should be his unfailing guide.

CHAPTER XXVIII

THE EGO AND THE PERSONALITY: SACRAMENTAL AIDS

THE sacraments of the Christian religion, and also the ceremonies of Freemasonry, have such an intimate bearing on the relationship between the ego and the personality, as to justify a separate chapter being devoted to considering this important aspect of our subject.

We will consider first the sacraments of Christianity, as they are performed in the Liberal Catholic Church.

The Christian Church sets out to meet the soul, or *S O S* 250.
ego, as soon as he comes into his new set of bodies, offering him welcome and assistance: this is achieved through the ceremony of baptism.

As it is not practicable to get at the ego himself, his *S O S* 251–
vehicles are dealt with on the physical plane. As we 252.
have seen, what the ego most needs is to get his new set of vehicles into order, so that he can work through them. Coming, as he does, laden with the results of his past lives, he has within him seeds of good qualities, and also seeds of evil qualities. Those seeds of evil have often been called "original sin," and quite wrongly connected with the fabled action of Adam and Eve.

It is obviously of great importance to the child that everything possible should be done to starve out the germs of evil, and to encourage those of good: it is to this end that the sacrament of baptism is especially designed. The water used is magnetised, with a special view to the effect of its vibrations upon the higher vehicles, so that all the germs of good qualities, in the unformed astral and mental bodies of the child, may thereby receive a strong stimulus, while at the same time the germs of evil may be isolated and deadened.

The ceremony has also another aspect, that of consecrating and setting apart the new vehicles to the true expression of the soul within, and, when it is properly and intelligently performed, there can be no doubt that its effect is a powerful one, which may affect the whole future life of the child.

S O S 253–254. The baptismal ceremony brings a new force into activity, on the side of the ego, in order to influence his vehicles in the right direction. Underlying the belief, that at baptism a guardian angel is given to the child, is the fact that a new thought-form, or artificial elemental, is built, which is filled by the divine force, and also ensouled by a higher kind of nature-spirit, known as a sylph. This remains with the child as a factor on the side of good, so that to all intents and purposes it is a guardian angel. Incidentally, through this work the sylph becomes individualised, and grows from a sylph into a seraph, through its association with a thought-form, permeated by the life and thought of the Head of the Church Himself.

The sacrament of baptism cannot alter the disposition of a man, but it can make his vehicles a little easier to manage. It does not suddenly make a devil into an angel, or a very evil man into a good one, but it certainly gives the man a better chance. This is what it is intended to do, and that is the limit of its power.

S O S 257. In addition, and more specifically, the baptismal ceremony is intended to open up the chakrams, or force-centres, and to set them moving much more rapidly. When this has been done (for details the student is referred to *The Science of the Sacraments*), and the "guardian-angel" thought-form has been
S O S 260. built, the pouring-in of the triple spiritual force takes place at the actual baptism itself, through the medium of the consecrated water.

S O S 262. As the names of the Trinity are invoked, the force unquestionably flows from the Three Persons of the Solar Deity Himself, though it reaches us through the intermediate stages of the Christ, Who is the Head of the Church, and the ordained priest. The thought which fills the guardian-angel thought-form is, in fact, really that of the Christ Himself.

Baptism is primarily intended for infants, and its omission in infancy cannot be fully supplied by baptism in later life. The adult has necessarily long ago verified the matter of his vehicles for himself, and his currents are flowing much in the same way as baptism would have caused them to flow ; but it will usually be found that the " corners " are not cleaned up, much of the aura seems unvivified, and there is a large amount of indeterminate matter, with which nothing is being done ; it has, therefore, a tendency to get out of the general circulation, to settle and form a deposit, and so gradually to clog the machinery and interfere with its efficient working. Baptism in infancy obviates much of this unpleasant result. *S O S* 270. *S O S* 271.

In the case of older people, quite a different type of sylph is given, a more worldly-wise entity, capable of development into a keener intelligence. About him there is something half-cynical: he has unwearying patience, but he does not seem to be expecting much, while the angel of the baby is optimistic—vaguer, it may be, than the other, but full of love and hope, and schemes for the future.

Still, a wholesome and beneficent influence is exercised by the baptism of adults ; the anointing with the the sacred chrism is not without its use, in cleansing the gateway through which the man passes in and out of his body in sleep, and even the making of the shield, before and behind, is good, especially for those who are young and unmarried.

In the sacrament of Confirmation, the bishop pronounces a preliminary blessing, which is intended to widen out the connection between the ego and his vehicles, in order to prepare the way for what is coming. We might say that the object is to stretch both soul and vehicles to their utmost capacity, that they may be able to receive more of the Divine outpouring. *S O S* 275–279.

As he makes the sign of the cross, at the appropriate places, the bishop pours into the candidate power, which is definitely that of the Third Person of the Trinity. This comes in three waves, and acts at the three levels, upon the principles of the candidate.

The divine power rushes through the ego of the bishop, into the higher mind of the candidate: then it pushes upwards into buddhi, and finally presses upwards into the ātmā. In each case, it is through the Third-Person aspect of each of these principles that the work is done.

Some candidates are, of course, far more susceptible to the process of opening-up than others. Upon some the effect produced is enormous and lasting; in the case of others, it is often but slight, because as yet that which has to be awakened is so little developed as to be barely capable of any response.

When the awakening, so far as it may be, has been achieved, there comes what may be called the filling and sealing of ātmā, buddhi and manas. The effect on ātmā is reflected into the etheric double, so far as the development allows, that on buddhi is reproduced in the astral body, and that on higher manas is mirrored in the mental body.

The intention of Confirmation is thus to tighten the links all the way up, to bring about a closer connection between the ego and the personality, and also between the ego and the monad. The result is not merely temporary; the opening-up of the connections makes a wider channel, through which a constant flow can be kept going. Confirmation arms and equips a boy or girl for life, and makes it easier for the ego to act on and through his vehicles.

S O S 290-299. Passing to the Minor Orders, we find that the Cleric is intended to aim at the control of his physical body: the Doorkeeper to purify and control his astral body: the Reader has to learn to wield the forces of his mind: the ordination of the Exorcist is aimed at the causal body, and is intended to develop the will, and to give the ego fuller control of the lower vehicles. The degree of Acolyte is intended to help the man to quicken his intuition, the buddhic faculty

In this series of diagrams, the following symbols are employed :— *S O S* 317. *I L I* 344.

Dormant or latent principle.

Slightly awakened.

Partly awakened and glowing.

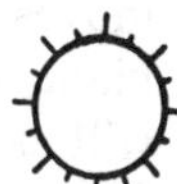

Awakened and glowing.

First degree of connection with the Christ.

Second and stronger connection.

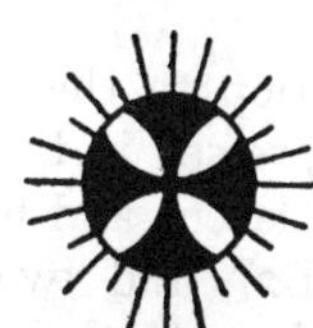

Fullest connection with the Christ.

Connection with the Logos.

DIAGRAM XXX.—Symbols used in Diagrams XXXI–XXXV.

In Diagram XXXI we have illustrated the condition of an intelligent and cultured layman. The true man, the Monad, is shown on his own plane, that of Anupādaka. He expresses, or manifests himself in his three aspects on the plane of ātmā: these we will term Ātmā (1), Ātmā (2) and Ātmā (3), and have marked on the diagrams as A1, A2 and A3 respectively.

Of these three aspects, the first (A1), remains on the plane of ātmā: the second descends, or moves outwards, to the plane of buddhi, where we will call it Buddhi (1), marking it B1. The third descends or moves out through two planes, and shows itself in the higher mental world as Manas, or M: this aspect, also, as it descends or moves through the plane of Buddhi, we will call Buddhi (2) or B2.

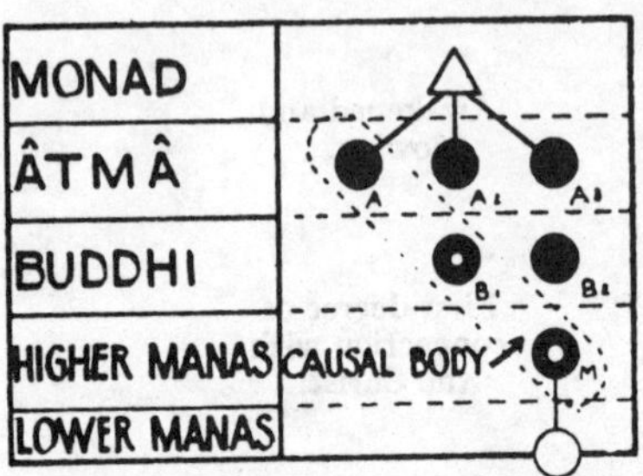

DIAGRAM XXXI.—The Principles of an "Intelligent and Cultured Layman."

These three outer or lower manifestations, A1, B1 and M, taken together, constitute, as we know, the soul, or ego, in his causal body, as indicated in the diagram by the dotted line which encloses them.

Thus we see that, in addition to the principles of ātmā, buddhi and manas, expressed in the ego as A1, B1 and M, there is also, still latent and undeveloped, another aspect of Buddhi (B2), and two aspects of ātmā (A1 and A2), making three further aspects still to be brought out of latency, and developed into activity.

Now in the Christ Himself, the Perfect Man, these principles also exist, in exactly the same order: but in His case, they are, of course, fully developed, and, moreover, mystically one with the second Person of the Trinity. One of the gifts conferred by ordination is the linking of certain of these principles, in the ordinand, with the corresponding principles of the Christ, so that a definite channel is made, down which spiritual strength and wisdom will flow, up to the fullest limit of the ordinand's receptivity.

The Ordination to the degree of Sub-Deacon confers *S O S* 325–328. no powers, but assists in preparing the way for Ordination to the degree of Deacon, the lowest of the three Major Orders. The bishop therefore attempts gently to widen the connection (the antahkarana, see p. 190) between the ego and the lower vehicles of the Sub-Deacon (see Diagram XXXIIA).

At the Ordination of a deacon, the link between the *S O S* 318–319 : 331–332. ego and his vehicles is widened to become a channel, and also the higher manas (M) is linked with the corresponding principle of the Christ. In some cases, buddhi (B1) may also be awakened, and made to glow slightly, thereby establishing a slight line of connection between it and the higher manas. These effects are indicated in Diagram XXXIIB.

MONAD
ÂTMÂ
BUDDHI
HIGHER MANAS
LOWER MANAS
A B

DIAGRAM XXXII.—The Principles of a Sub-Deacon and Deacon.

This opening of the channel is so great a departure from ordinary life that it can be done only by stages, and the first step towards it, in the Ordination of a deacon, may be regarded as practically a psychic surgical operation.

The threefold influence, of which a bishop is so *S O S* 333–334. especially the custodian (as we shall see presently), is called strongly into manifestation, and poured forth, so that, by playing upon the corresponding principles in the ordinand, it stirs them into sympathetic vibration ; they therefore become, at any rate for the time, enormously more active and receptive than ever before.

At the conclusion of the ceremony of ordination, the bishop makes a final cross, of which the express purpose is to thicken the walls of the much-expanded link between the ego and the personality, to harden them, and hold them more firmly in their new form. It is as though a sort of framework were erected within, a lining to prevent the widened channel from contracting.

S O S 321. The establishment of the link between the deacon and the Christ enables the higher manas of the Christ to influence that of the deacon, and to stir it into beneficent activity. Needless to say, it does not at all follow that it *will* so affect it; that depends on the deacon. At least the way is laid open, the communication is established, and it is for him to make of it what he can.

S O S 319–323 : 338–340. In the case of the priest, the connection is carried a stage further, and several important developments take place.

At the first imposition of hands, ātmā and buddhi in the priest (A1 B1 and M) are made to glow with indescribable fervour, by sympathetic vibration, in harmony with the blinding light of the corresponding principles in the Christ. The glow is usually slight in ātmā, but more marked in buddhi. The influx rushes into the ordinand's ātmā, buddhi and manas, through the corresponding principles of the bishop himself.

Further, a line between ātmā and buddhi is established, while that already existing between buddhi and higher manas is intensified. The channel between higher manas and the lower vehicles is also widened (see Diagram XXXIIIc).

At the second imposition of hands, the hitherto latent principle of buddhi (B2) is called into activity, and linked with that of the Christ, while the link between it and higher manas is strengthened.

The link between the priest's own ātmā, buddhi and manas (A1, B1 and M) is opened still more, to permit the flow of more force (see Diagram XXXIIID).

Thus the priest becomes, in a very real sense, an outpost of the consciousness of the Christ, so that he becomes "His man"—the "parson," in fact, that word meaning the same as the *person* (see p. 213), who represents the Christ in a certain parish.

S O S 309. At the ordination of the priest, his ego is more

definitely awakened, so that he can act directly upon other egos at the level of the causal body. It is, in fact, this relation which gives him that power to straighten out the distortion, caused by deviation from the path of right, which, in ecclesiastical terminology, is known as the power to "remit sin."

The anointing of the hands of the priest, with oil of catechumens, which is constructive in its effects, is a setting of them apart for the purpose of his office, and a moulding of them for the transmission of the power of the Christ. The hand of the priest is thus a specialised instrument that can transmit blessing. The anointing brings the opening forces to bear upon the hands, and endues them with power, whereby, along the lines that are made in the anointing, the influence can pour out. *S O S* 344–345.

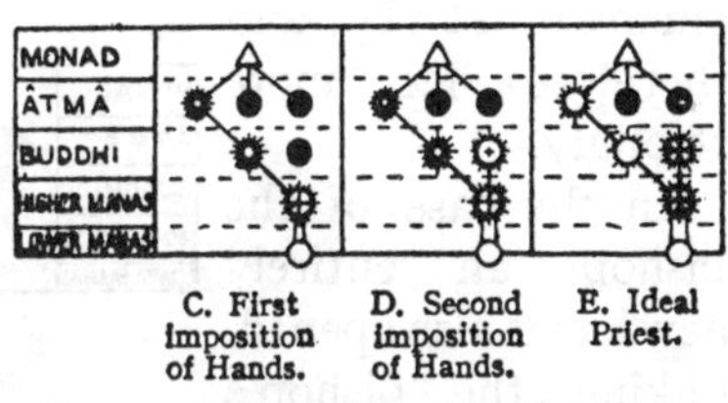

DIAGRAM XXXIII.—The Principles of a Priest.

The process is something like the magnetisation of steel: the anointing operates so that forces can pass through the hands, and at the same time tempers the hands, so that they can bear those forces, and transmit the power safely.

The bishop makes one cross, which is intended to arrange for the distribution of the force which rushes down the diagonal line between Ātmā (1), Buddhi (1) and Manas, and a second cross which arranges for the dispensing of the force which flows from Buddhi (2).

The development of an ideal priest is possible to a man of great determination, who for years works at strengthening the connections between his own principles and those of the Christ. He can intensify the link made with Buddhi (2) and Manas, and can arouse to vigorous action Ātmā (1) and Buddhi (1), thereby making himself a channel of extraordinary power (*vide* Diagram XXXIIIE).

At the consecration of a bishop, when the actual *S O S* 356–357 : 319.

words of consecration are said, a connection is made between Buddhi (2) and Ātmā (3), and the channels between Buddhi (2) and Manas, and the corresponding principles of the Christ, are enormously widened (*vide* Diagram XXXIVF).

Thus, through Ātmā (3), Buddhi is linked directly with the Triple Spirit of the Christ, so that blessing from that level flows through him, for those Three Aspects are, of course, truly one: hence the rationale of the bishop signing the people with a triple cross, instead of with one, as the priest does.

The priest draws his blessing down through his own principles, Ātmā (1), Buddhi (1) and Manas, and emits through his causal body. The bishop, being more fully developed, is able to let the power shine through more immediately, and therefore far more strongly.

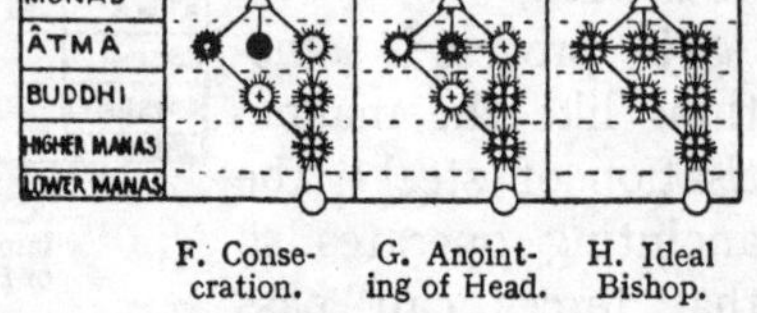

F. Consecration. G. Anointing of Head. H. Ideal Bishop.

DIAGRAM XXXIV.—The Principles of a Bishop.

In the case of the bishop, an entirely new line is also opened, linking the bishop's Buddhi (1) directly with that of the Christ, and thus giving it the potentiality of a development far beyond our imagination. It is this wonderful Christ-force which enables him to hand on his power to others.

S O S 358. Next, the way is opened for the influence of the amazing development of Buddhi, which has just been made possible, to pour down into the mental and astral vehicles.

S O S 360: 319. At the anointing of the head of the bishop with chrism, the power of reflection of the triple spirit in the lower vehicles is intensified, the triple spirit Ātmā (1), Ātmā (2) and Ātmā (3), glowing, and the way being cleared, down into the physical brain, for the flow of the new forces (see Diagram XXXIVG).

The three lines connecting Ātmā (3), Buddhi (2) and Manas (see Diagram XXXIV), indicate that a bishop can draw into the causal body, and thus ray forth in blessing, the threefold power of the Triple Spirit.

The action of the chrism tends in the direction of making the force-centre at the top of the head—the brahmarandra chakram—which in most men is a saucer-like depression—into a rapidly rotating cone, projecting upwards from the head. *S O S* 361.

The anointing of the hands of the bishop with chrism arranges the mechanism of the distribution of the three kinds of force, from the Three Aspects of the Trinity. *S O S* 362.

The direct line of communication between buddhi and the astral body is opened fully, so that, if and when that buddhi, or intuition, is developed, it may flow through at once, into what is intended to be its expression in physical life. *S O S* 363.

The development of an ideal bishop is possible to one who takes advantage of every opportunity. All of his principles become responsive channels to the power of the Christ, and he becomes a veritable sun of spiritual energy and blessing. This stage is indicated in Diagram XXXIVh). *S O S* 319.

The Perfect Man is not only linked with the Christ, and with his own Highest Self, the Monad, but becomes ever more and more an epiphany of the Logos, or Deity, who brought forth the solar system. He becomes the Master, for Whom incarnation is no longer necessary. Diagram XXXV indicates this stage.

Another provision in the Christian religion is the power of Absolution, vested in the priests. As this affects the relations between the various bodies of man, we may usefully consider it briefly here. *S O S* 82–86.

The bodies of man are not, of course, separate in space, but interpenetrating. Looked at from below, however, they give the impression of being joined by innumerable fine wires or lines of fire. Every action which works against evolution puts an unequal strain upon these—twists and entangles them. When a man goes badly wrong, the confusion becomes such that communication between the higher and lower bodies is seriously impeded; he is no longer his real self, and only the lower side of his character is able to manifest itself fully.

Whilst natural forces will straighten out the distortion in due time, yet the Church provides for the work being done more speedily, for the power of straightening out this tangle in higher matter is one of those powers specifically conferred upon a priest at ordination. The co-operation of the man himself is, of course, also needed: for, "if we confess our sins, He is faithful and just to forgive us our sins, and to cleanse us from all unrighteousness."

The effect of "absolution" is strictly limited to the correction of the distortion above described. It re-opens certain channels, which have been to a large extent closed by evil thought or action; but it in no way counteracts the physical consequences of that action, nor does it obviate the necessity of restitution, where wrong has been done.

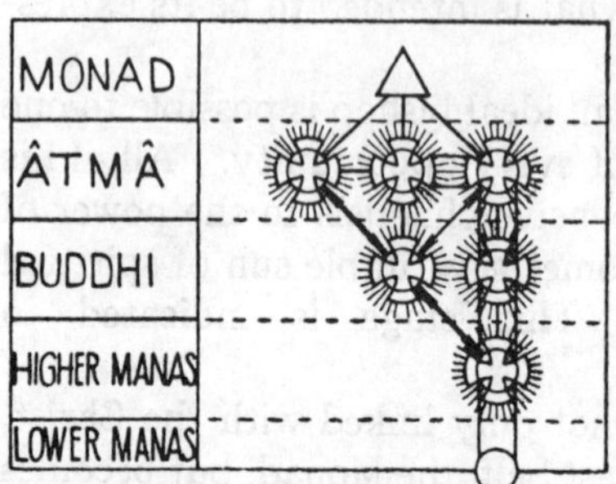

Diagram XXXV.—The Perfect Man.

The priest's action straightens out the etheric, astral and mental entanglement, produced by the wrong action, or rather by the mental attitude which made that action possible; but it does not in any way relieve the man from the karmic penalty of his action. "Be not deceived; God is not mocked: for whatsoever a man soweth, that shall he also reap."

S O S 176. One other item of information, regarding the work of the priest in the Holy Eucharist, may be mentioned. In making the three crosses, at "bless, approve and ratify," over the offerings, the priest pushes his "tube" through the etheric, astral and the lower mental matter respectively, and the two crosses, made separately over the wafer and the chalice, carry the same tube, now in two branches, on through the higher mental into the plane above. In doing this, he should use the forces of his own causal body, pressing his thought upward to the highest possible level.

H L F 162–163.

Turning now to Freemasonry, we find that the three Principal Officers represent Ātmā, Buddhi and Manas in man, and that the three Assistant Officers represent the lower mind, the emotional nature or astral body, and the etheric double: the O.G. or Tyler represents the physical body. As we are in this book concerned principally with the causal body, we may note especially that the higher mind is represented by the J.W.

H L F 169–171.

In the devas, nature-spirits and elementals associated with the J.W., a golden hue predominates.

H L F 220.

When the R.W.M. creates, receives and constitutes the candidate as an E.A.F., the three touches of the f . . . s . . . convey different aspects of power, corresponding to the three Aspects of the Trinity, the first conveying strength to the brain, the second love to the heart, and the third executive ability to the right arm.

The general effect of this downpouring of force is to widen somewhat the channel of communication between the ego and the personality of the candidate.

The degree of E.A.F. corresponds to the sub-deacon in the Christian system.

H L F 257–258.

At a similar point in the Second Degree ceremony, there is a more decided widening of the link between the ego and the personality, so that it is opened up as a definite channel for the downpouring of force. This channel the candidate can utilise with marked effect, if he sets himself to work upon it and through it.

In this Degree, there is a certain parallel between the Passing of a F.C. and the ecclesiastical ordination to the diaconate. At the same time, a link is made between the candidate and the H.O.A.T.F., in those Lodges where He is acknowledged.

As in the case of the widening of the consciousness, the link that is made is for the candidate to utilise as he pleases. It may be of the greatest benefit to him; it may change the whole of his life, and enable him to make rapid progress along the path that leads to Initiation. Or, on the other hand, if he entirely neglects it, it may make but very little difference to him.

H L F 262–263. The proving of a M.M. by the square and compasses indicates that a M.M. may be tested and known by the fact that both the higher self and the lower self are in working order, are functioning together and in harmony.

The M.M. is symbolical of the Initiate of the fourth degree, the Arhat. At that stage of attainment, on the occult path, the battle against the lower quaternary is practically over, and the latter has become an obedient instrument in the hands of the higher triad, which is awake and active in all its three parts.

H L F 264. The M.M. has to find the g . . . s . . . on the c . . . : in other words, it is by finding in himself that deeper Self, which is the Monad, beyond even the higher triad, that the M.M. will at last discover the supreme secret of life, and will then find in very truth, by his own living experience, that he is, and always has been, one with God.

H L F 265. In earlier Degrees, the consciousness of the candidate had to be raised from the s . . . to the c . . . , that is, from the quadrilateral to the triangle, from the lower to the higher self. But now, as a M.M., it has to be raised from the triangle to the point—as is clearly indicated by the W.T.—from the higher self to the Monad.

The Monad is now beginning to work his will in the higher self, as before the higher self worked his will in the lower. The s . . . t represents the action of that Monad, as it turns upon a centre pin, and sends out a line from its own body as it spins the web of life, just as a spider spins its web from its own body.

The p . . . marks that chosen path, or ray of the Monad, the line of life and work which the Arhat must discover, and on which he must specialise, in order to make rapid progress. And the c . . . once more represent the triangle, the powers of the triple spirit, which he must use in his work.

H L F 274–276. The currents of etheric force, which flow through and around the spine of every human being, are stimulated into activity, in Freemasonry, in order that the evolution of the candidate may be quickened. This stimulation is applied at the moment when the R.W.M. creates, receives and constitutes. In the First Degree, it affects Īda, the feminine aspect of the force, thus making it easier for the candidate to control passion and emotion. In the Second Degree, it is the Pingalā, or masculine aspect, which is strengthened, in order to facilitate the control of mind. In the Third Degree, the central energy itself, the Sushumnā, is aroused, thereby opening the way for the pure spirit from on high.

It is by passing up this channel of the sushumnā that a *yogi* leaves his physical body at will, in such a manner that he can retain full consciousness on higher planes, and bring back into his physical brain a clear memory of his experiences.

Īda is crimson in colour, pingalā is yellow, and sushumnā is deep blue.

The stimulation of these nerves, and the forces which flow through them, is only a small part of the benefit conferred by the R.W.M., when he wields the sword at the moment of admission. The widening of the connection between the individuality and the personality has already been mentioned, also the formation of a link between certain principles of the candidate and the corresponding vehicles of the H.O.A.T.F. The changes induced are somewhat of the same nature as those described on p. 233 *et seq.*, but of a less pronounced character.

Whilst these effects are real, unmistakable and universal, yet their result in the spiritual life of the candidate depends, of course, upon himself.

The E.A. should, as a personality, be employed on organising his physical life for higher use ; but at the same time, as an ego, he should be developing active intelligence in his causal body, exactly as does the pupil of a Master, who is preparing himself for Initiation. H L F 285.

In the same way, the F.C. is organising his emotional

life, while he unfolds intuitional love in his buddhic body.

The M.M., while arranging his mental life down here, should, as an ego, be strengthening his spiritual will, or ātmā.

CHAPTER XXIX

MEMORY OF PAST LIVES

A GLANCE at Diagram XXV on p. 147 should be sufficient to indicate the mechanical reason why the physical brain of a man cannot normally remember his past lives. For it is obvious that the physical body can have neither a memory, nor a record, of a past incarnation in which it did not participate. Precisely the same consideration applies to his astral and mental bodies, since all these vehicles are new for each incarnation.

I L II 218.
T B 44.
M 51.
S P 36–37.
R 18.
T 61.
C 123.

We thus see that, as the causal body is the only one that persists from one incarnation to another, the lowest level, at which we can hope to get really reliable information about past lives, is that of the causal body, for nothing below that can give us first-hand evidence.

In these past lives, the ego in his causal body was present—or rather a certain small part of him was present—and so he is an actual witness. All the lower vehicles, *not* being witnesses, can report only what they may receive from the ego. Consequently, when we bear in mind how imperfect is the communication between the ego and the personality in the ordinary man, we shall see at once how entirely unreliable such second, third, or fourth-hand testimony is likely to be.

I L II 219.
T B 44.
S C 288.

Although one may sometimes obtain from the astral and mental bodies isolated pictures of events in a man's past life, we cannot get a sequential and coherent account of it; and even those pictures are but reflections from the causal body, and probably very dim and blurred reflections, which occasionally find their way through to the lower consciousness.

It is thus abundantly clear that, in order to read accurately past lives, it is necessary first of all to

I L II 220 develop the faculties of the causal body. The thing, however, could be done at lower levels, by psychometrisation of the permanent atoms, but, as this would be a much more difficult feat than the unfolding of the senses of the causal body, it is not at all likely to be attempted successfully.

Including the method just mentioned, there are four methods of reading past lives :—

(1) Psychometrisation of the permanent atoms.

(2) To take the ego's own memory of what happened.

(3) To psychometrise the ego, or rather his causal body, and see for ourselves the experiences through which he has passed. This method is safer than (2), because even an ego, having seen these things through a past personality, may have imperfect or prejudiced impressions of them.

(4) To use the buddhic faculties, becoming completely one with the ego under investigation, and to read his experiences as though they were our own, *i.e.*, from within, instead of from without. This method obviously demands much higher development.

Methods (3) and (4) have been employed by those who prepared the series of incarnations, which have been published during the past few years in *The Theosophist*, some of them having also been produced in book form. The investigators had also the advantage of the intelligent co-operation of the ego, whose incarnations were described.

I L II 221. The physical presence of the subject, whose lives are being read, is an advantage, but not a necessity. He is useful, provided he can keep his vehicles perfectly calm, but, if he becomes excited, he spoils everything.

The surroundings are not specially important, but quiet is essential, because, if impressions are to be brought through clearly, the physical brain must be calm.

It is necessary also to eradicate absolutely all prejudices, otherwise they will produce the effect of stained glass, colouring everything which is seen through them, and so giving a false impression.

We may say that there are two sources of error possible: (1) personal bias; (2) limited views. *I L II* 229.

In view of the fact that there are fundamental differences of temperament, these cannot but colour the views taken of other planes. Every one below the level of an Adept is sure to be influenced in this manner to some extent. The man of the world magnifies unimportant details, and omits the important things, being in the habit of doing this in daily life. On the other hand, a man starting on the Path may, in his enthusiasm, lose for a time his touch with the ordinary human life, from which he has emerged. But even so, he has the advantage, for those who see the inside of things are nearer to the truth than those who see only the outside.

In order to minimise this source of error, it is usual for people, of radically different types, to work together at these investigations. *I L II* 230-231.

The second danger we have mentioned is that of a limited view, of taking a part for the whole. Thus, one may take a view of a small portion of a given community, and apply it to the whole community, *i.e.*, one may fall into the common error of generalising on an insufficient basis of observation.

There is, however, a general aura of a time or a country, which usually prevents any great mistakes of this sort. A psychic, who has not been trained to sense this general aura, is often unconscious of it, and may thus fall into many errors. Long-continued observation shows that all untrained psychics are sometimes reliable, and sometimes unreliable, and those who consult them therefore run a risk of being misled.

In looking at past lives, it is safer to retain full physical consciousness, so as to be able to make a note of everything, while it is being observed, than to leave the physical body during the observations, and trust to memory for their reproduction. This latter plan, however, has to be adopted when the student, though able to use the causal body, can do so only while the physical body is asleep. *I L II* 221-222.

The identification of egos is sometimes difficult, because egos naturally change considerably in the course of some thousands of years. Some investigators feel an intuition as to the identity of a particular ego, and, although such an intuition may often be right, it may certainly also sometimes be wrong. The safer, but more laborious, method of identification, is to pass the records rapidly in review, and trace the ego concerned through them, until he is found at the present day.

I L II 223. In some cases, the egos of ordinary people are instantly recognisable, even after thousands of years: that does not speak particularly well of the people concerned, because it means that they have made but little progress. To try to recognise, twenty thousand years ago, one whom one knows at the present day, is somewhat like meeting as an adult some one whom one knew long ago as a child. Sometimes recognition is possible, sometimes the change has been too great.

Those who have since become Masters of the Wisdom are often instantly recognisable, even thousands of years ago, but that is for a different reason. For, when the lower vehicles are already fully in harmony with the ego, they form themselves in the likeness of the Augoeides, and so change little from life to life. Similarly, when the ego himself is becoming a perfect reflection of the Monad, he also changes but little, though he gradually grows: hence he is readily recognisable.

The nature of the Ākāshic Records having been already described in *The Mental Body*, a few of the more immediately relevant points only will be mentioned here.

In examining a past life, the easiest way is to let the record drift past at its natural rate: but, as this *I L II* 224. would mean a day's work to look up the events of each day, it is clearly impracticable, except for short periods. It is, however, possible to accelerate or retard the passage of events to any degree required, so that a period of thousands of years may be run through rapidly, or any particular picture may be held as long as desired.

What is described as the unrolling of the record is, in reality, not a movement of the record, but of the consciousness of the seer. But the impression which it gives is exactly as though the record itself were unrolled. The records may be said to lie upon one another in layers, the more recent on the top and the older ones behind. Yet even this simile is misleading, because it suggests the idea of thickness, whereas the records occupy no more space than does the reflection on the surface of a mirror. The consciousness does not *I L II* 225–228.
really move in space at all, but rather puts on itself, as a kind of cloak, one or other of the layers of the record, and, in doing so, it finds itself in the midst of the action of the story.

The method of arriving at dates has been described in *The Mental Body*, page 242.

It is, on the whole, somewhat easier to read lives forwards than backwards, because in that case we are working with the natural flow of time, instead of against it.

The languages employed are almost always unintelligible to the investigator, but, as the thoughts behind the words lie open before him, that matters little. On several occasions, investigators have copied down public inscriptions, which they could not understand, and have afterwards had them translated on the physical plane, by some one to whom the ancient language was familiar.

The records must not be thought of as originally *I L II* 231–232.
inhering in matter of any kind, though they are reflected in it. In order to read them, it is not necessary to come into direct contact with any particular grouping of matter, since they can be read from any distance, when a connection has once been made.

Nevertheless, it is true that each atom contains the record, or perhaps possesses the power to put a clairvoyant *en rapport* with the record, of all that has ever happened within sight of it. It is, in fact, on account of this phenomenon that psychometry is possible.

But there is attached to it a very curious limitation, in that the normal psychometer sees, by means of it, only what he would have seen if he had been standing at the spot from which the object psychometrised has been taken.

For example, if a man psychometrises a pebble, which has been lying for ages in a valley, he will see only what has passed during those ages in that valley. His view will be limited by the surrounding hills, just as if he had stood for all those ages where the stone lay, and had witnessed all those things.

There is, however, an extension of the psychometric power, by which a man may see the thoughts and feelings of the actors in his drama, as well as their physical bodies. There is also another extension by which, having first established himself in that valley, he may make it the basis of further operations, and so pass over the surrounding hills and see what lies beyond them, and also what has happened there since the stone was removed, and even what occurred before it in some manner arrived there.

But the man who can do all this will soon be able to dispense with the stone altogether.

When using the senses of the causal body, it is seen that every object is throwing off pictures of the past.

I L II 233. We have already seen that, as the inner faculties are developed, life becomes continuous. Not only can the consciousness of the ego be reached, but it is possible to travel back, even as far as the animal group-soul, and look through animal eyes at the world which then existed. The difference of outlook is said to be so different as to make description impossible.

Short of such continuous consciousness, there is no detailed memory of the past, not even of the most important facts. There is, however, this fact, that whatever we have known in the past we are almost sure to recognise and instantly accept, as soon as it is again presented to us in the present.

Hence, though one may appreciate intellectually *I L II* 234–
the truth of reincarnation, actual proof can be obtained 235.
only in the causal body, where the ego is cognisant of his past.

When a man, using the consciousness of his causal *I L I* 377.
body, has always with him the memory of all his past lives, he is, of course, capable of consciously directing the various lower manifestations of himself at all points of his progress.

During the stages in which the man is not yet fully *I L I* 91.
capable of this, the ego can nevertheless impress his purpose upon his permanent atoms, so that that purpose will be carried over from life to life. Knowledge of this will not be born inherent in the man, as part of his stock-in-trade, so to speak, but the moment it comes before him, in any form, in his next incarnation, he will immediately recognise its truth, seize upon it, and act accordingly.

In the case of a very quick re-birth, the possibility *T C* 123.
of recovering the memory of the past incarnation is considerably increased. Diagram XXV, page 147, should make the mechanism of this possibility easy to understand. There have been a large number of atoms and molecules, in the old mental and astral bodies, which have preserved a certain affinity with the mental unit and astral permanent atom, and consequently a good deal of the old material may be used in building the new mental and astral bodies. With their assistance, it is clear that memory of the last incarnation should be more easily attained than in cases where there has been a long interval between lives, and the old materials have all been dissipated and spread through the various planes.

We do not yet understand the laws which govern *I L II* 455–
the power to impress the detailed knowledge of one 456.
life upon the physical brain of the next. Such evidence as is at present available seems to show that details are usually forgotten, but that broad principles appear to the new mind as self-evident.

It is a common experience, on hearing of a truth for

the first time, to feel that one has known it before, though one has never been able to formulate it in words. In other cases, there is scarcely even that degree of memory: yet, when the new truth is presented, it is instantly recognised as true.

Assuming the truth of tradition, even the Buddha Himself, who incarnated with the definite intention of helping the world, knew nothing clearly of His mission after He had entered His new body, but regained full knowledge only after years of searching for it. Undoubtedly He could have known from the first, had He so chosen, but He did not so chose, submitting Himself rather to what seems to be the common lot.

I L II 457–485. On the other hand, it may be that the Buddha did not take the body of Prince Siddartha from birth, but only when it fainted, after the long austerities of the six years searching for truth. If this be so, there would be no memory, because the entity in the body was not the Buddha, but some one else.

In any case, however, we may be sure that the ego, who is the true man, always knows what he has once learned: but he is not always able to impress it upon his new brain without the help of a suggestion from without.

It seems to be an invariable rule that one who has accepted occult truth in one life always comes into contact with it in the next, and so revives his dormant memory. We may say, perhaps, that the opportunity of thus recovering the truth is the direct karma of having accepted it, and of having earnestly tried to live according to it in the previous incarnation.

CHAPTER XXX

THE EGO ON HIS OWN PLANE

We come now to consider the ego as a conscious entity on his own plane, *i.e.*, in the higher mental or causal world, quite apart from the partial expressions of himself on the lower planes.

From the moment that the ego breaks off from his group-soul, and commences his separate existence as a human being, he is a conscious entity: but the consciousness is of an exceedingly vague nature. The forces of the higher mental world pass through him practically without affecting him, because he cannot as yet respond to more than a very few of such extremely fine vibrations. The only physical sensation, to which this condition is at all comparable, is that which occasionally comes to some persons, at the moment of awakening in the morning. There is a state, intermediate between sleeping and waking, in which a man is blissfully conscious that he exists, and yet is not conscious of any surrounding objects, nor capable of any movement. Indeed, he sometimes knows that any movement would break the spell of happiness, and bring him down into the ordinary waking world, and so he endeavours to remain still as long as possible. *I L I* 373-375. *T B* 44.

This condition, which is a consciousness of existence, and of intense bliss, closely resembles that of the ego of the average man upon the higher mental plane. As we have seen previously, he is wholly centred there, only for the short time intervening between the end of one life in devachan and the commencement of his next descent into incarnation. During that short period, he obtains a fleeting glimpse of his past and his future, a flash of retrospect and prospect, and for many ages these glimpses are his only moments of full

awakening : and, after this momentary awakening, he
I L I 375 : 387. falls asleep again. As we have seen, it is his desire for a more perfect manifestation, his desire to feel himself more thoroughly alive, that drives him into the effort of incarnation.

D 18. A stanza in the *Book of Dzyan* states that " Those who received but a spark remained destitute of knowledge : the spark burned low " ; H. P. Blavatsky then explains that " those who received but a spark constitute the average humanity which have to acquire their intellectuality during the present manvantaric evolution." (*Secret Doctrine*, II, 177.) In the case of most men the spark is still smouldering, and it will be many an age before its slow increase brings it to the stage of steady and brilliant flame.

I L I 34. The causal body of the average man has thus as yet almost no consciousness of anything, external to itself,
D P 81. on its own plane. The immense majority of egos are but dreamily semi-conscious, though few are now in the condition of mere colourless films. The majority are not yet sufficiently definite, even in such consciousness as they possess, to understand the purpose or the laws of the evolution in which they are engaged.

I L I 387. Although the ordinary ego is still in a sleepy condition, he is yet, during physical life, capable to some extent of brooding watchfully over the personality, and of a little effort.

I L I 35. *D P* 31–32. The average ego in his causal body may be compared to the chicken within the egg, the chicken being entirely unconscious of the source of the heat, which nevertheless stimulates its growth.

When an ego reaches the stage where he breaks through his shell, and becomes capable of some sort of response, the whole process takes on a different form, and is enormously quickened.

The awakening process is greatly helped by the Masters of the Wisdom, who pour out their spiritual force like sunlight, flooding the entire plane, and affecting to some extent everything within its radius. As mentioned in Chapter XII, even the group-souls of animals on the lower mental plane are greatly affected and assisted by this influence.

It is on the mental plane that much of the most important work of the Masters is done: this is more especially the case upon the causal plane, where the individuality, or ego, can be acted upon directly. It is from this plane that They shower the grandest spiritual influences upon the world of thought: from it They impel great and beneficent movements of all kinds. Here, again, much of the spiritual force poured out by the glorious self-sacrifice of the Nirmānakayas is distributed. Here also direct teaching is given to those pupils who are sufficiently advanced to receive it in this way, since it can be imparted far more readily and completely here than on the lower planes.

With a developed man, the ego is fully awake. In *I L I* 387.
course of time the ego discovers that there are a good many things which he can do, and, when this happens, he may rise into a condition in which he has a definite life on his own plane, though in many cases it is even then but dreamy.

The ego of the ordinary person, as we have seen, has *I L I* 388.
rather a vegetable consciousness or life, and seems to be *M P* 181. *I L II* 68.
only just aware of other egos. But, as the ego becomes *T P O* 9:2.
sufficiently developed, he can not only help other egos, but lives a life of his own among his peers, among the great Arūpadevas, among all kinds of splendid Angels or Devas. The young ego is probably but little awake, as yet, to all that glorious life, just as a baby in arms knows little of the interests of the world surrounding him; but, as his consciousness gradually unfolds, he awakens to all this magnificence, and becomes fascinated by its vividness and beauty.

Such a developed ego enjoys the companionship of all the brightest intellects that the world has ever produced, including, as said, the deva or angel kingdom as well as the human. The life of the ego on his own plane is glorious beyond any conception possible to the personality. If one could imagine an existence in the company of the great men of the world—artists, poets, scientists, and even the Masters Themselves—and add to all that an understanding unattainable down here—then only would one begin to have some idea of the life of the ego.

The personality would not, of course, know what the ego does, unless the personality and ego have been unified. Thus, the ego may know the Master, while
I L I 378. the personality does not. The ego must have been fully conscious and active on his own plane for a long time before any knowledge of that existence can come through into his physical life.

I L II 68–69. This ego-consciousness must not be confused with the consciousness which comes from the *unification* of the higher and lower selves, mentioned in Chapter XXVI. When unification has been achieved, the man's consciousness resides in the ego all the time, and from the ego it plays through whatever vehicle he may happen to be using. But, in the case of a man who has not yet achieved that union, the consciousness of the ego on his own plane comes into activity only when he is no longer hampered by any lower vehicles, and exists only until he puts himself down into incarnation; for, as soon as he takes up a lower body, his consciousness can manifest for the time only through that body.

D P 17 : 20 : 77 : 35. The causal plane is the true and relatively permanent home of the ego, for here he is free of the limitations of the personality, and is simply himself, the reincarnating entity. Although his consciousness may be dim, dreamily unobservant and scarcely awake, yet his vision is true, however limited it may be. Not only is he free from the illusions of the personality, and the refracting medium of the lower self, but thought itself no longer assumes the same limited forms which it takes upon itself, at levels below the causal.

D 18–19. *S P* 53. In some of the older literature, there are statements which seem to imply that the higher ego needs no evolution, being already perfect and godlike on his own plane. Wherever such expressions are used, whatever may be the terminology employed, they must be taken to apply only to the ātmā, the true "god" within man, which is certainly far beyond the necessity of any kind of evolution of which we can know anything.

Again, H. P. Blavatsky states that Manas, or the higher Ego, as " part of the Universal Mind, is unconditionally omniscient on its own plane " : the meaning, of course, is that this is so only when it has fully developed self-consciousness by its evolutionary experiences, and " is the vehicle of all knowledge of the past and present, and the future."

The reincarnating ego most undoubtedly does evolve, as is perfectly evident to those who possess causal sight. At first, he has very little active power on any plane, and it is his purpose to become fully active on all planes, even the physical. *I L I* 388.

An ego who is awakened, and is truly alive upon his own plane, is a glorious object, giving us for the first time some idea of what man is intended to be. Such developed egos are still separate, yet intellectually they fully realise their inner unity, for they see one another as they are, and can no longer blunder, or fail to comprehend. *M* 52. *M P* 181.

It is not easy to explain, in physical words, the differences which exist between egos, since all of them are in many ways much greater than anything to which we are accustomed down here. Some faint reflection of the impression, produced by intercourse with them, may be conveyed by saying that an advanced ego reminds one of a dignified, stately and most courteous ambassador, full of wisdom and kindliness, while the less developed man has more of the type of the bluff, hearty, country squire. An ego who is already on the Path, and is nearing Adeptship, has much in common with the great Angels, and radiates spiritual influences of prodigious power. *M P* 182–183.

It is, therefore, not to be wondered at that the ego throws himself energetically into the whirl of intense activity of his own plane, and that it seems to him immensely more important and interesting than the faint, far-distant struggles of a cramped and half-formed personality, veiled in the dense obscurity of the lower world.

G E 76–77. One ego has been described, by a person who saw him, as a radiant youth, like a Greek Apollo carved out of glistening marble, and yet immaterial, with inspiration as his keynote. Another ego appeared somewhat like the sculpture of Demeter in the British Museum, a dignified, serene and peaceful figure, brooding as it were over the world which he helped to foster and protect. Thus every ego has his own radiantly beautiful appearance, expressing his particular mission or genius.

Among such beings, thoughts no longer take form and float about as they do at lower levels, but pass like lightning-flashes from one to another. Here we are face to face with the enduring body of the ego, a body older than the hills, an actual expression of the Divine Glory which ever rests behind it, and shines through it more and more in the gradual unfolding of its powers. Here we deal no longer with outer forms, but we see the things in themselves, the reality which lies behind the imperfect expression. Here cause and effect are one, clearly visible in their unity, like two sides of the same coin. Here we have left the concrete for the abstract ; we no longer have the multiplicity of forms, but the idea which lies behind all those forms.

D 41. The ego, on his own plane, is able to perceive with
M 118. absolute instantaneity, without, of course, the use of
nerves : hence arises a certain class of dream, where a
man is awakened from sleep by a physical sound or
touch. In the minute space of time, between the
impact and the awakening of the man, the ego will often
compose a kind of drama, or series of scenes, leading up
to and culminating in the event which awakens the
physical body. This habit, however, seems to be
peculiar to the ego which, as far as spirituality is con-
D 42. cerned, is still comparatively undeveloped. As the ego
develops, and comes to understand his position and his
responsibilities, he rises beyond these graceful sports
of his childhood.

It seems that, just as primitive man casts every natural phenomenon into the form of a myth, so the primitive ego dramatises every event that comes under his notice. But the man who has attained full consciousness finds himself so fully occupied in the work of the higher planes that he devotes no energy to such matters, and therefore dreams no more in this fashion.

D 48–49. *T P O* 859.

The use of symbols seems to be a characteristic of the ego, when out of the body during sleep: that is to say, that what in the physical world would be an idea, requiring many words to express, is perfectly conveyed to the ego by a single symbolical image. When such a thought is remembered in the physical brain, unless its key is also recollected, there is likely to be confusion. The activities of the ego on his own plane thus sometimes give rise to another class of dream; but there are, of course, many other causes of dreams (*vide The Astral Body*, page 93).

M 50–51: 118. *M P* 181–182.

The ego on his own plane uses abstractions just as we on the physical plane deal with concrete facts. On his plane, the essence of everything is available; he is no longer concerned with details: he need no longer talk round a subject or endeavour to explain it. He takes up the essence or the idea of a subject and moves it as a whole, as one moves a piece when playing chess. His world is a world of realities, where not only is deception impossible, but also unthinkable. He no longer deals with emotions, ideas, or conceptions, but with the thing in itself.

It is impossible to express in words the ordinary traffic between men in fully developed causal bodies. What down here would be a system of philosophy, needing many volumes to explain it, is there a single definite object—a thought which can be thrown down as one throws a card upon a table.

An opera or an oratorio, which here would occupy a full orchestra for many hours in the rendering, is there a single mighty chord. The methods of a whole school of painting are condensed into one magnificent idea. And ideas such as these are the intellectual counters, which are used by egos in their converse one with another.

M 51. *D P* 14.

On this plane, as we have said previously, the ego

has fully unrolled before him all the lives he has lived on this globe, the actual living records of the past. He sees his lives as one vast whole, of which his descents into incarnation have been but the passing days. He sees the karmic causes which have made him what he is: he sees what karma still lies in front of him, to be worked out before "the long sad count is closed," and thus he realises, with unerring certainty, his exact place in evolution. Here he perceives the great scheme of evolution, and what is the Divine will for him.

M 118–119. When dealing with matters on his own plane, and those below him, all the ideas of the ego are complete ideas, properly rounded off and perfect.

Furthermore, anything incomplete would be to him unsatisfactory, would, in fact, hardly be counted as an idea at all. For him a cause includes its effect, and therefore, in the longer view which he is able to take, poetic justice is always done, and no story can ever end badly.

These characteristics of his reflect themselves to a certain extent in his lower vehicles, and we find them appearing in ourselves in various ways. Thus, children always demand that fairy tales shall end well, that virtue shall be rewarded, and that vice shall be vanquished; and all unsophisticated and healthy-minded people feel a similar desire. Those who clamour for an evil realism are precisely those whose views of life have become unhealthy and unnatural, because, in their short-sighted philosophy, they can never see the whole of any incident, but only the fragment of it which shows in one incarnation, and usually only the merest outside husk even of that.

In the Fourth Root-Race, which is concerned chiefly with the development of the astral body and its emotions, this characteristic of rounding off stories, and exaggeration, is often very marked: this is clearly
M 120–122. seen, for example, in old Keltic stories. The desire for scientific accuracy and truth is comparatively a recent development, and belongs more specifically to the Fifth Root-Race, which is concerned principally

with the development of mind and the mental body. Fifth Race people thus demand first that a thing shall be true, otherwise it is of little interest to them: the old races, on the other hand, demand first of all that it shall be pleasing, and decline to be limited in their appreciation, by any such consideration as whether the thing had ever materialised, or could ever materialise, on the physical plane.

The desire for accuracy is thus the coming through of another quality of the ego, of his power to see truly, to see a thing as it is, as a whole and not only in part. Understanding this, we should clearly encourage and insist on the quality of accuracy, and keep our record of facts distinct from our thoughts and desires with regard to those facts.

Yet, in cultivating truthfulness, there is no need to extinguish romance. It is necessary to be accurate: it is not necessary to be a Gradgrind. We need not lose sight of the beauty and romance which lie behind things, merely because we have acquired a scientific knowledge of details, many of which may be arid and superficial. Thus sugar does not cease to be sweet and pleasant to the taste because we have learned that its chemical formula is $C_{12}H_{22}O_{11}$.

The ego's measure of time and space is so entirely different from that which we use in waking life, that from our view it seems as though neither time nor space existed for him. *D* 35.

Events which, on the physical plane, take place in succession, appear on the mental plane to be occurring simultaneously, and at the same point. That, at least, is the effect on the consciousness of the ego, though it appears probable that absolute simultaneity is the attribute of a still higher plane, and that the sensation of it on the mental plane is simply the result of a succession so rapid that the infinitesimally minute spaces of time are indistinguishable, just as the eye receives the impression of a continuous ring of fire, if a stick, with one end burning, is whirled round rapidly. The reason for this, of course, is that the *D P* 6.

human eye is not able to distinguish, as separate, similar impressions which follow one another at intervals of less than about the tenth part of a second.

Particular examples of what we may call the immense speed, at which the consciousness of the ego operates on its own plane, may be found in *Dreams* by Bishop Leadbeater, pages 36–40, where a number of dreams, dependent on this phenomenon, are recounted and explained.

D 42 : 51. A result, which follows from the ego's supernormal
C 131–132. method of time-measurement, is that in some degree prevision is possible to him. If he knows how to read them, the present, the past, and to a certain extent the future, lie open before him. He undoubtedly thus foresees, occasionally, events that will be of interest or importance to the lower personality, and makes more or less successful endeavours to impress them upon it.

D 43–44. Man undoubtedly possesses freewill: hence pre-
C 134–135. vision is possible only to a certain extent. In the case of an ordinary man, it is probably possible to a very large extent, since the man has developed no will of his own worth speaking of, and is consequently very largely the creature of circumstances. His karma places him amid certain surroundings, and their action upon him is so much the most important factor in his history, that his future course may be foreseen with almost mathematical certainty.

When we consider the vast number of events which can be but little affected by human action, and also the complex and wide-spreading relation of causes to their effects, it should not seem wonderful to us that, on the plane where the result of all causes at present in action is visible, a very large portion of the future may be foretold with considerable accuracy, even as to detail. That this can be done, has been proved again and again, not only by prophetic dreams, but by the second-sight of the Highlanders, and the predictions of clairvoyants; and it is on the forecasting of effects, from the causes already in existence, that the scheme of astrology is largely based.

When, however, we come to deal with a developed man, then prophecy fails us, for he is no longer the creature of circumstances, but to a great extent their master. The main events of his life may certainly be arranged beforehand, by his past karma ; but the way in which he will allow them to affect him, the method by which he will deal with them, and perhaps triumph over them—these are his own, and they cannot be foreseen, except as probabilities. Such actions of his, in their turn, become causes, and thus there are produced in his life chains of effect which were not provided for by the original arrangement, and, therefore, could not have been foretold with any exactitude.

We may say, therefore, that the course of the ordi- *D P* 14.
nary undeveloped man, who has practically no will of his own worth speaking of, may often be foreseen clearly enough, but, when the ego boldly takes his future into his own hands, exact prevision becomes impossible.

An ego, who is at all developed, will meditate upon *I L I* 331.
his own level, such meditation not necessarily synchronising with any meditation that the personality may be performing. The yoga of a fairly well-developed ego is to try to raise his consciousness, first into the buddhic plane, and then through its various stages. This he does, without reference to what the personality may be doing at the time. Such an ego would probably also send down a little of himself at the personal meditation, though his own meditations are very different.

It should ever be remembered that the ego is not *I L I* 346.
manas or mind only, but the spiritual triad of Ātmā-Buddhi-Manas. At our present stage of consciousness, the ego rests in the causal body on the higher mental plane, but, as he develops, his consciousness will be centred on the buddhic plane : later still, when he attains Adeptship, it will be centred on the plane of ātmā.

But it must not be supposed, that when this further development takes place, the manas is in any way lost.

For, when the ego draws himself up into the buddhic plane, he draws up manas with him, into that expression of manas which has all the time existed on the buddhic plane, but has not been fully vivified until now.

Similarly, when he draws himself up into the plane of ātmā, manas and buddhi exist within him, just as fully as ever, so that now the triple spirit is in full manifestation, on its own plane, in all its three aspects.

The spirit is, therefore, truly sevenfold, for he is triple on his own plane, that of ātmā, dual on the buddhic, and single on the mental, the unity which is his synthesis making seven. Thus, though he draws himself into the higher, he retains the definiteness of the lower.

S P 59. What has been stated to be the clearest and best description of the human trinity, Ātmā-Buddhi-Manas, is to be found in *The Key to Theosophy* by H. P. Blavatsky :—

THE HIGHER SELF is Ātmā, the inseparable ray of the Universal and ONE SELF. It is the God *above*, more than within us. Happy the man who succeeds in saturating his *inner Ego* with it.

THE SPIRITUAL *divine* EGO is the spiritual soul, or *Buddhi*, in close union with *Manas*, the mind-principle, without which it is no Ego at all, but only the Ātmic vehicle.

THE INNER OR HIGHER EGO is *Manas*, the fifth principle, so called, independently of Buddhi. The mind-principle is the Spiritual Ego only when merged into one with Buddhi. . . . It is the permanent individuality, or the reincarnating Ego (*The Key to Theosophy*, pages 175–176).

I L I 378–380. As soon as an ego becomes at least partially conscious of his surroundings, and of other egos, he leads a life, and has interests and activities, on his own plane. But even then we must remember, as we have seen in earlier chapters, that he puts down into the personality only a very small part of himself, and that that part constantly becomes entangled in interests which, because they are so partial, are often along lines different from the general activities of the ego himself, who consequently does not pay any particular attention to the lower life of the personality, unless something rather unusual happens to it.

When this stage is reached, the ego usually comes under the influence of a Master. In fact often his first clear consciousness, of anything outside himself, is his touch with that Master. The tremendous power of the Master's influence magnetises him, draws his vibrations into harmony with its own, and multiplies many-fold the rate of his development. It rays upon him like sunshine upon a flower, and he evolves rapidly under its influence. This is why, while the earlier stages of progress are so slow as to be almost imperceptible, when the Master turns His attention upon the man, develops him, and arouses his own will to take part in the work, the speed of his advancement increases in geometrical progression.

In the chapters on devachan, we saw that an ego, who is much loved by many people, may have part in many heavens simultaneously, ensouling the thought-images which his friends make of him. These images are, of course, of great evolutionary benefit to the ego concerned, affording him additional opportunities of developing qualities, such, for example, as affection. This is clearly the direct result and reward of those lovable qualities, which draw towards the man the affectionate regard of so many of his fellow-men.

D P 47. *L A D* 34. *O S D* 432. *I L II* 74. *S O S* 173–174.

Occasionally the action of such a force, upon the ego of a surviving friend, may manifest even in the personality of that friend upon the physical plane. For, while the action is upon the ego, through the special thought-image, yet the personality of the surviving friend is a manifestation of that same ego, and, if the ego be considerably modified, it is at least possible that that modification may show itself in the physical manifestation on this lower plane.

I L II 74.

It is obvious, however, that there are two possible limitations to the perfection of the intercourse between the ego concerned, and those who make images of

O S D 432–433.

him. First, the image may be partial and imperfect, so that many of the higher qualities of the ego may not be represented, and may therefore be unable to show themselves through it.

Secondly, it is just possible that the ego is not in reality, so to speak, as good as the image which has been made of him, so that he is unable to fill it completely. This, however, is unlikely to occur, and could take place only when a quite unworthy object had been unwisely idolised. These aspects of the matter have, however, been fully dealt with in *The Mental Body*, pages 197–198.

D P 49. *I L II* 59. The more highly the ego is developed, the more fully is he able to express himself through the thought-images, these becoming steadily fuller expressions of himself. When he gains the level of a Master, he consciously employs them as a means of helping and instructing his pupils.

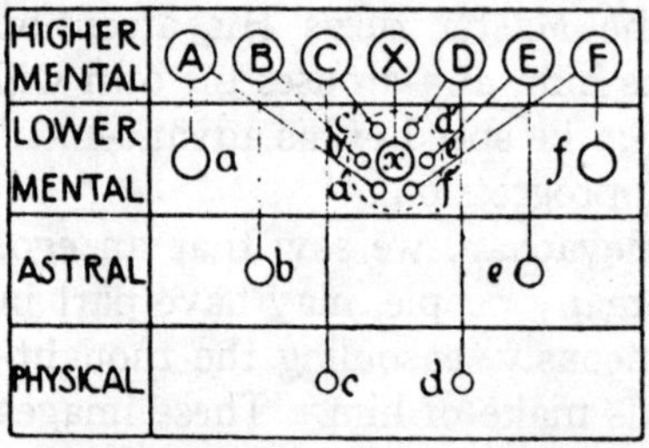

Diagram XXXVI.—An Ego and his Thought-Images in Devachan.

To assist the student in obtaining a thoroughly clear grasp of the mechanism and results of thought-images in devachan, Diagrams XXXVI and XXXVII are appended.

Diagram XXXVI illustrates an ego X, in his mental body x, in devachan, surrounded by thought-images a′, b′, c′, d′, e′ and f′ of his six friends A, B, C, D, E, and F, respectively.

Of these A and F are also in devachan, in their respective mental bodies a and f : B and E are on the astral plane, in their respective astral bodies b and e ; C and D are still "alive" in the physical world in their physical bodies c and d.

The diagram shows that the thought-images, made by X, of his six friends, are ensouled by, and therefore directly connected with, the *egos* A, B, C, D, E, and F, *not* with the personal expressions of those egos, whether those personal expressions be on the physical, astral or mental planes.

It is also clear from the diagram that the personalities a, b, c, etc., can know nothing of what is happening through the thought-images a′, b′, c′, etc., except through their own egos A, B, C, etc.

Diagram XXXVII illustrates four egos A, B, C and D, all mutual friends, A, B and C being in devachan, whilst D is still in his physical body.

Each of A, B and C makes a thought-image of each of his three friends, these images being ensouled by the respective egos.

A, B and C each possess three expressions of themselves: one through their own mental bodies, and two through the thought-images in the devachans of the others.

D, on the other hand, possesses four expressions of himself: one through his own physical personality, and three more through the thought-images which his three friends have made of him.

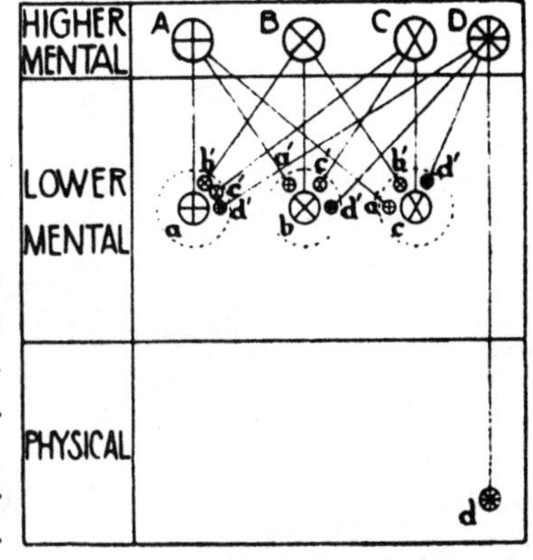

DIAGRAM XXXVII.—Egos in Devachan.

An understanding of the way in which an ego can appear simultaneously in the devachanic images of a number of people (as well, of course, as other phenomena of the ego world) shows that, in order to go from one place to another, travelling is not necessary for the ego. *T P O* 423.

In *The Mental Body* (page 236) we described the chord of a man, and explained how this chord is used to find a man, wherever in the three worlds he may be. That chord consists of his own note, and those of the *I L II* 209.

I L II 206–208 : 210. three lower vehicles—mental, astral and physical. If the man has none of these lower vehicles at the time, the same mechanism holds good, for the causal body has always attached to it the mental unit, and the astral and physical permanent atoms, these being quite sufficient to give out the distinctive sound.

The combination of sounds, which produce a man's chord, is his true occult name. This must not be confused with the hidden name of the Augoeides, which is the chord of the three principles of the ego, produced by the vibrations of the atoms of ātmā, buddhi and manas, and the Monad behind them.

CHAPTER XXXI

INITIATION

In *The Astral Body* and *The Mental Body* the subject of Discipleship was dealt with, so far as it concerns the astral and mental bodies of the disciple, or pupil, of a Master. It will now be desirable briefly to recapitulate the leading facts concerning the stages of Probation, Acceptance, and Sonship, because in each of these the causal body is also in some degree affected: then we shall proceed to describe, so far as the ego in his causal body is concerned, the great step of Initiation, which is the culmination of Discipleship.

In the stage of *Probation*, the Master makes a living *M P* 79–80.
image of the pupil, moulding out of mental, astral and *I L I* 43–44.
etheric matter an exact counterpart of the causal, mental, astral and etheric bodies of the neophyte, and keeps this image at hand, so that He may look at it periodically. This image is placed in magnetic *rapport* with the man himself, so that every modification of thought or or feeling, in the man's own vehicles, is faithfully reproduced in the image. The Master is thus able to follow the progress of the pupil, and estimate when he will be ready to take the next step.

When the pupil is *Accepted*, the Master dissolves the *M P* 113–114.
"living images," because they are no longer necessary. *I L I* 44–45.
The consciousness of the pupil is then united with that of his Master, in such a way that whatever the pupil feels or thinks is within the astral and mental bodies of his Master. If and when necessary, the Master can erect a barrier, and so for the time shut off the consciousness of the pupil from His own consciousness.

At the stage of *Sonship*, the link with the Master is *M P* 163.
such that not only the lower mind, but also the ego in *I L I* 52–53.
the causal body of the pupil, is enfolded within that of

the Master, and the Master can no longer draw a veil to shut off the pupil.

Whilst these stages naturally help very greatly, in preparing a man to take the first great Initiation, yet, technically speaking, they have nothing to do with Initiation, or steps on the Path, which belong to an entirely different category. Probation, Acceptance and Sonship represent the relationship of the pupil to his own Master: Initiations, on the other hand, are tokens of the man's relation to the Great White Brotherhood, and to its august Head.

I L I 54–55. Strictly speaking, therefore, the Great White Brotherhood has nothing to do with the relations between the Master and His pupil; that is a matter solely for the private consideration of the Master Himself. Whenever the Master considers that the pupil is fit for the first Initiation, He gives notice of that fact, and presents him for it, and the Brotherhood asks only whether he is ready for the Initiation, and not what is the relationship between him and any Master.

At the same time, it is true that a candidate for Initiation must be proposed and seconded by two of the higher members of the Brotherhood, and it is certain that the Master would not propose a man for the tests of Initiation unless He had, with regard to him, the certainty of his fitness, which could come only from such close identification with his consciousness as that of which we have spoken.

T P O 17: 15. It has already been mentioned (see Chapter XIII, page 80) that, in a man's existence, there are three great stages which outweigh in importance all others: they are:—

I. Individualisation: When the man begins his career as a human ego.

II. The First Initiation: When the man becomes a member of the Great White Brotherhood.

III. The Fifth Initiation: When he leaves the human kingdom, and enters the superhuman stage; this is the goal which is set before all humanity.

A man who has taken the First Initiation is said to

" enter the stream." The words used in admitting the candidate to the Brotherhood include this statement : " You are now safe for ever ; you have entered upon the stream ; may you soon reach the further shore." The Christian calls him the man who is " saved " or " safe." The meaning is, that he is quite sure to go on, in this present stream of evolution, that he is certain not to drop out at the " day of judgment," or the " great separation " in the next (fifth) Round, like a child in school who is too backward to go on with the rest of his class.

The importance of Initiation does *not* lie in the exaltation of the individual, but in the fact that he has now become definitely one with a great Order, the " Communion of Saints," as it is called in the Christian terminology. *M P* 139–140.

The candidate has now become more than an individual man, because he is a unit in a tremendous force. The Brotherhood is not only a body of men, each of whom has his own duties to perform ; it is also a stupendous unity—a flexible instrument in the hand of the Lord of the World, a mighty weapon that He can wield. No unit in the whole scheme loses the least fraction of his individuality, but he has added to it something a thousand times greater.

When an ego is Initiated—the student will notice that it is the *ego* who is Initiated, not the personality—he becomes part of the closest organisation in the world, one with the great sea of consciousness of the Great White Brotherhood. For a long time the new Initiate will not be able to understand all that this union implies, and he must penetrate far into the sanctuaries before he can realise how close is the link, and how great is the consciousness of the King Himself, the Lord of the World, which all Brothers to a certain extent share with Him. It is incomprehensible and inexpressible down here ; metaphysical and subtle it is beyond words, but, nevertheless, a glorious reality, real to such an extent that, when we begin to grasp it, everything else seems unreal. *M P* 84 : 141–142.

We saw previously (*vide The Mental Body*, page 302) that the Accepted pupil may lay his thought beside that of his Master; so now the Initiate may place his thought beside that of the Brotherhood, and draw into himself just as much of that tremendous consciousness as he, at his level, is able to respond to.

M P 157–159. At the point in the great ceremony when the Star of Initiation appears, a line of dazzling light extends from the Star to the heart of the Initiator, and from Him to the heart of the candidate. Under the influence of that tremendous magnetism, the tiny Silver Star of Consciousness, which represents the Monad in the candidate, swells out in glowing brilliancy, until it fills his causal body, and for a wonderful moment the Monad and the ego are one, even as they will be permanently one when Adeptship is attained.

On this occasion, the Monad identifies himself for the time with the fraction of himself that is the ego, and it is he, the Monad, who takes the vows.

The effect of Initiation on the astral body has already been described in *The Astral Body*, page 254.

M P 143–144. So wonderful is the expansion of the consciousness of the Initiate, that it is most apt to speak of the change as a new birth. He begins to lead a new life "as a little child," the life of the Christ; the Christ, the buddhic or intuitional consciousness, is born within his heart.

He has now also the power to give the blessing of the Brotherhood, a tremendous and overwhelming force, which he is able to give or send to any one, as he judges to be most appropriate and useful. The power of the Brotherhood will flow through him just as much as he will let it flow. It is for him to use the power, and to remember that he has the entire responsibility of directing it, for whatever purpose he may choose. The blessing given by the Officiant at Initiation means: "I bless you; I pour my force and blessing into you; see that you in your turn constantly pour out this blessing to others."

If the Initiate possesses the qualification of Shraddhā

—perfect trust in his Master and in the Brotherhood, and the utter certainty that, because he is one with Them, all things are possible to him—he may go through the world as a veritable Angel of light, shedding joy and benediction around his path.

Before Initiation, the pupil has probably already *M P* 162.
practised himself in the development of the buddhic *T P O* 828–
consciousness, so that he has usually had experience 829.
at that level. But if he has not, then at Initiation his first experience takes place.

Nevertheless, at Initiation the man does not attain the full buddhic consciousness, nor does he in any way develop a buddhic vehicle at that time. But, in view of the fact that some of the teachings which must be given at the buddhic level could not otherwise be understood, a certain amount of development of the buddhic vehicles seems to be required.

When the consciousness is raised to the buddhic *I L I* 93-94.
vehicle, a very remarkable thing happens to the causal *I L II* 519.
body: *it vanishes,* and the Initiate is under no compulsion ever again to take it up; but, naturally, this cannot be done until all the karma of the lower planes is exhausted.

For a man is not free from binding results, on lower planes, until he is perfectly selfless on those planes. If a man, when helping another, feels perfectly the unity with him, then he obtains the result of his action on the buddhic plane only, and not on any of the lower planes.

Another interesting factor to bear in mind is that *I L II* 520.
there is always a general karma, belonging to an order or a nation, and that each individual is, to a certain extent, responsible for the action of the whole. Thus, for example, a priest has a certain responsibility for all that the collective priesthood does, even though he may not personally approve of it.

It is the mere act of focussing oneself in the buddhic *T P O* 605.
vehicle that causes the causal body to vanish. As soon, however, as the consciousness is brought down again on to the higher mental plane, the causal body

reappears. It is not the same as it was before, because the particles have been dissipated, but it seems in every way exactly the same body.

T P O 697. On the buddhic plane, the finest thread which we can conceive represents the ordinary man. As soon as he regularly thinks of higher matters, and turns his attention to them, the thread begins to thicken. It becomes more and more like a cable, and later on it appears as a funnel, because, as it seems to clairvoyant vision, it widens out above, and comes down into the causal body. Later on, the causal body is enlarged by the inrushing of forces, and the funnel becomes very much larger, widening out at the bottom as well as the top. At the First Initiation (for many, however, this experience comes before that), the man, as we have seen, abandons the causal body, and plunges into the buddhic plane. When that occurs, the funnel shapes itself into a sphere. At that level there are, of course, more dimensions, so that the phenomenon cannot be fully described, but this is how it appears to one who is able to see it.

I L I 94. In view of what was said above, *i.e.*, that there is no compulsion to re-form the causal body, it follows that the time which remains to the Initiate, before he reaches the level of Adeptship, need not involve a descent to the physical plane at all, and therefore he may not take what we ordinarily mean by incarnations.

Nevertheless, in the great majority of cases, incarnations upon the physical plane are taken, because the man has work to do, upon that plane, for the Great Brotherhood.

T P O 60–61. The buddhic consciousness gives one a realisation of the One Consciousness, penetrating all—the One Consciousness of God, in fact. Such realisation gives a sense of the utmost safety and confidence, the most tremendous impulse and stimulus imaginable. Yet at first it might be alarming, because a man might feel that he was losing himself. This is, of course, not the case. The Christ said: "He that loseth his life for My sake shall find it." Christ represents the buddhic principle, and is saying: " He who, for My sake—*i.e.* for the development of the Christ within him—will put aside the causal vehicle, in which he has been living for so long, will find himself, will find the far grander and higher life." To do this needs some courage, and it is a startling experience the first time that one is wholly in the buddhic vehicle, and finds that the causal body, upon which one has been depending for thousands of years, has vanished. But, when the experience does come, the man will know with absolute certainty that the Self is one. The idea cannot be conveyed, but it will be known when experienced, and nothing will ever again shake that certainty.

When the buddhic consciousness fully impresses the physical brain, it gives such a new value to the factors of life that a man no longer *looks upon* a person or object, but *is* that person or object. He is able to recognise the motives of others as his own motives, even though he perfectly understands that another part of himself, possessing more knowledge, or a different viewpoint, may act quite differently. *M* 53-56. *M P* 191. *T P O* 700.

It must not, however, be supposed that when a man enters upon the lowest sub-division of the buddhic plane he is at once *fully* conscious of his unity with all that lives. That perfection of sense comes only as the result of much toil and trouble, when he has reached the highest sub-division of the buddhic plane. Step by step, sub-plane by sub-plane, the aspirant must win his way for himself, for, even at that level, exertion and effort are still necessary, if progress is to be made.

This work of developing himself on sub-plane after sub-plane now lies before the candidate. He is now definitely upon the Path of Holiness, and is described in the Buddhist system as the Sotāpatti or Sohan, " he who has entered the stream " ; among the Hindus he is called the Parivrājaka, which means the " wanderer," *M P* 192.
one who no longer feels that any place in the three lower worlds is his abiding-place or refuge.

The subject of buddhic consciousness will be considered rather more fully in the next chapter.

M P 165–167. Three factors, all interdependent, are involved in a man's fitness for the first Initiation. *First :* he must be in possession of a sufficient amount of the well-known "Qualifications" (*vide The Mental Body*, page 294). *Second :* the ego must have so trained his lower vehicles that he can function perfectly through them, when he wishes to do so : expressed in another way, he must have effected what is called the junction of the lower and higher selves. *Third :* he must be strong enough to stand the great strain involved, which extends even to the physical body.

All Initiates, however, are by no means equal in development, any more than all men who take the degree of Master of Arts are equal in knowledge. Whilst there is a certain attainment required for Initiation, some may have achieved far more than the minimum demanded in some directions.

Hence, for similar reasons, there may be considerable variation in the interval between Initiations. A man who has just taken the First Initiation may, nevertheless, possess a considerable share of the qualifications for the Second ; therefore for him the interval between the two may be unusually short. On the other hand, a candidate who had only just sufficient strength in all directions to enable him to pass through the First, would have slowly to develop within himself all the additional faculties and knowledge necessary for the Second, so his interval would probably be long.

T P O 581. Initiation has the effect of altering the "polarity" of the man's mental and causal vehicles, so that he can be used as others cannot, however highly they may be developed along other lines.

T P O 37–38. *M P* 188. Comparing the First with the Fifth Initiation, we have seen that for the First, the higher and lower self must be unified, so that there shall be nothing but the ego working in the personality: for the Fifth, there shall be nothing in the ego that is not approved or inspired by the Monad.

Whenever the Monad touches our lives down here, he comes as a god from above. In all cases of Initiation he flashes down, and for a moment becomes one with the ego, just as the Monad and ego will be permanently one when Adeptship is attained. At certain other important and critical times the Monad flashes down, as in the case mentioned in *The Lives of Alcyone*, when Alcyone took a pledge to the Lord Buddha.

Thus, at the First Initiation, the personality ceases to have a will of its own—except when it forgets—and lives only to serve the higher. The ego is now active through the personality in the lower planes, and is beginning to realise the existence of the Monad, and to live according to its will. The Monad himself has determined the path for the ego's evolution ; and he can choose no other, because he is becoming himself, gaining release from the bondage even of the higher planes. *T P O* 239.

Another way of expressing this truth is to say that, just as the man on the Probationary Path has to learn to get rid of all that we speak of as the personality, so the Initiate must get rid of his individuality, of the reincarnating ego, so that at the end of the Path his life will be entirely under the direction of the Monad. *T P O* 627.

The individuality, or ego, is a very wonderful thing—complex, exceedingly beautiful and marvellously adapted to its surroundings, a glorious being indeed. The idea of the separated self is ingrained in us, and is part of the very ego which is the one permanent thing about us, so far as we know. In the earlier stages this idea of the separated self had to be developed and strengthened, it being, in fact, the source of our strength in the past. But, nevertheless, this "giant weed" has to be killed out at one time or another. The strong can tear it out from themselves at the beginning of their development. The weak must wait and let it go on growing while they are developing sufficient strength to kill it out. For them that is unfortunate, because the longer it is allowed to persist the more closely it becomes intertwined with the nature of the man. *T P O* 688–689.

Hence, all systems of occult teaching agree in advising students to try from the very beginning to get rid of the illusion of separateness. The man has to learn that behind the individuality itself there is the Monad; that will seem the true Self, when he has laid aside the individuality. Beyond even that he will in due time learn and realise for himself that even the Monad is but a spark in the Eternal Flame.

S P 56–57. Only as the lower self or personality becomes pure from all breath of passion, as the lower manas frees itself from kāma, can the "shining one" impress it. H. P. Blavatsky writes: "It is when this trinity—Ātmā-Buddhi-Manas—in anticipation of the final triumphant reunion beyond the gates of corporeal death, became for a few seconds a unity, that the candidate is allowed, at the moment of initiation, to behold his future self. Thus we read in the Persian *Desatir* of the 'resplendent one'; in the Greek philosopher–initiates of the Augoeides—the self-shining 'blessed vision resident in the pure light'; in Porphyry, that Plotinus was united to his 'god' six times during his life-time, and so on." (*Isis Unveiled*, II., pages 114–115.)

This "trinity" made into unity is the "Christ" of all mystics. When, in the final Initiation, the candidate has been outstretched on the floor, or altar stone, and has thus typified the crucifixion of the flesh, or lower nature, and when from this "death" he has "risen again" as the triumphant conqueror over sin and death, he then, in the supreme moment, sees before him the glorious presence, and becomes "one with Christ," is himself the Christ. Thenceforth he may live in the body, but it has become his obedient instrument; he is united with his true Self, Manas made one with Ātmā-Buddhi, and, through the personality which he inhabits, he wields his full powers, as an immortal spiritual intelligence.

While he was still struggling in the toils of the lower nature, Christ, the spiritual ego, was daily crucified in him; but, in the full Adept, the Christ has risen triumphant, lord of himself and of nature. The long pilgrimage of manas is over, the cycle of necessity is trodden, the wheel of re-birth ceases to turn, the Son of Man has been made perfect by suffering.

Until this point is reached, " the Christ " is the object of aspiration. The " ray " is ever struggling to return to its source, the lower manas ever aspiring to re-become one with the higher. It is this continual yearning towards reunion which clothes itself as prayer, as inspiration, as " seeking after God." " My soul is athirst for God, for the living God," cries the eager Christian. This cry is the inextinguishable impulse upwards of the lower self to the higher. Whether the person pray to the Buddha, to Vishnu, to Christ, to the Virgin, to the Father, is, of course, merely a question of dialect, not of essential fact. *S P* 57–58.

In all, the Manas united to Ātmā-Buddhi is the real object, variously called the ideal man, the personal God, the God-Man, God-Incarnate, the Word made flesh, the Christ who must be " born in " each, with Whom the believer must be made one.

When once a man enters upon the Path, and converges all his energies upon it, his rate of progress is enormously accelerated. His progress will not be by arithmetical progression, *i.e.*, in the ratio 2, 4, 6, 8, etc., nor by geometrical progression, *i.e.*, in the ratio 2, 4, 8, 16, etc., but by powers, in the ratio 2, 4, 16, 256, etc. This fact should afford great encouragement to the serious student. *T P O* 770.

CHAPTER XXXII

BUDDHIC CONSCIOUSNESS

In view of the fact that the First Initiation involves experiencing the buddhic consciousness, it is desirable to amplify what was said in the preceding chapter regarding the nature of consciousness on the buddhic plane.

T B 26–27. The student will scarcely need to be told that all description of buddhic consciousness is necessarily and essentially defective. It is impossible in physical words to give more than the merest hint of what the higher consciousness is, for the physical brain is incapable of grasping the reality.

It is difficult enough to form a conception even of astral plane phenomena, there being four dimensions in the astral world. In the buddhic world there are no less than six dimensions, so that the difficulties are evidently enormously enhanced.

A E P There is an ingenious diagram (for which the present writer is indebted to the unknown designer), reproduced as Diagram XXXVIII, on p. 279, which illustrates graphically the fundamental difference between the buddhic plane and all the planes below it.

The diagram is seen to consist of a number of spikes or spokes which *overlap at a certain point.* That point of overlap is the beginning of the buddhic plane.

The tips of the spokes represent the physical consciousness of men: they are separate and distinct from one another. Passing up the spokes towards the centre, we see that the astral consciousness is a little wider, so that the consciousnesses of separate men approach a little nearer to one another. The lower mental consciousnesses approach still more nearly to one another, whilst the higher mental consciousnesses, at their very highest level, meet at the point where the buddhic consciousness commences.

It will now be seen that the buddhic consciousness, of each individual and separate " man," overlaps that of the other separate consciousnesses on either side of him. This is a graphic illustration of the " overlapping " aspect of buddhic consciousness, where a sense of union with others is experienced.

As the consciousness rises still further up into the higher planes, it will be seen that it overlaps those on

Diagram XXXVIII.—**Unity in Diversity.**

either side of it more and more, until eventually, when the " centre " is reached, there is practically a complete merging of consciousness. Nevertheless, each separate spoke still exists, and has its own individual direction and outlook. Looking *out* towards the lower worlds, each consciousness looks in a different direction: it is an aspect of the one central consciousness. Looking inwards, on the other hand, these diverging directions all meet together, and become one with one another.

The sense of union is characteristic of the buddhic plane. On this plane, all limitations begin to fall *D P* 101–102.

away, and the consciousness of man expands until he realises, no longer in theory only, that the consciousness of his fellows is included within his own, and he feels and knows and experiences, with an absolute perfection of sympathy, all that is in them, because it is in reality a part of himself.

S G O 348–349. On this plane a man knows, not by mere intellectual appreciation, but by definite experience, the fact that humanity is a brotherhood, because of the spiritual unity which underlies it all. Though he is still himself, and his consciousness is his own, yet it has widened out into such perfect sympathy with the consciousness of others that he realises he is truly only part of a mighty whole.

A W 224–225. As a being, standing in the sun, suffused with its light, and pouring it forth, would feel no difference between ray and ray, but would pour forth along one as readily and easily as along another, so does a man on the buddhic plane *feel* brotherhood, and pours himself into any one who needs his help. He sees all beings as himself, and feels that all he has is theirs as much as his: in many cases, more theirs than his, because their need is greater, their strength being less.

A W 297. *I L II* 116. As the predominant element in the causal body is knowledge, and ultimately wisdom, so the predominant element of consciousness in the buddhic body is bliss and love. The serenity of wisdom marks the one, whilst tenderest compassion streams forth inexhaustibly from the other.

A W 218–219. *M B* 82. *S S* 102. Hence the buddhic body is called by the Vedāntins the Ānandamayakosha, or bliss-sheath. This is the "house not made with hands, eternal in the heavens," of which St. Paul, the Christian Initiate, spoke. He raised charity, pure love, above all other virtues, because by that alone can man on earth contribute to that glorious dwelling. For a similar reason is separateness called the "great heresy" by the Buddhists, and "union" or yoga is the goal of the Hindu.

I L I 348–349. A selfish man could not function on the buddhic plane, for the very essence of that plane is sympathy and perfect comprehension, which excludes selfishness.

There is a close connection between the astral and the buddhic bodies, the astral being in some ways a reflection of the buddhic. But it must not therefore be supposed that a man can leap from the astral consciousness to the buddhic, without developing the intervening vehicles.

Although, on the highest levels of the buddhic plane, a man becomes one with all others, we must not therefore assume that he feels alike to all. There is, in fact, no reason to suppose that we shall ever feel absolutely alike towards everybody. For even the Lord Buddha had His favourite disciple Ānanda, and the Christ regarded St. John the Beloved in a different way from the rest. What is true is that presently men will love every one as much as they now love their nearest and dearest, but by that time they will have developed, for those nearest and dearest, a type of love of which they have no conception now.

There is no separation on the buddhic plane. On *T P O* 696. that plane, as said, consciousnesses do not necessarily merge instantly at the lowest level, but they gradually grow wider and wider until, when the highest level is reached, a man finds himself consciously one with humanity. That is the lowest level at which the separateness is absolutely non-existent ; in its fullness the conscious *unity* with all belongs to the ātmic or nirvānic plane.

To each ego, who can reach this state of conscious- *M P* 190. ness, it would seem that he had absorbed or included all others ; he perceives that all are facets of a greater Consciousness ; he has, in fact, arrived at the realisation of the ancient formula : " Thou art That."

It must be recollected that, whilst the buddhic *T P O* 710. consciousness brings a man into union with all that is glorious and wonderful in others, into union, in fact, with the Masters Themselves, yet it also, and necessarily, brings him into harmony with the vicious and the criminal. Their feelings must be experienced, as well as the glory and the splendour of the higher life. When separateness is abandoned, and unity is realised, a man finds that he is merged in the Divine Life, and that the attitude of love is the only one which he can adopt, towards any of his fellow-men, whether they be high or low.

M P 189. *N* 186. *M* 52 : 54. An ego, whilst living in the causal body, already recognises the Divine Consciousness in all; when he looks upon another ego, his consciousness leaps up, as it were, to recognise the Divine in him.

But, on the buddhic plane, it no longer leaps to greet him from *without*, for it is already enshrined in his heart. He *is* that consciousness, and it is *his*. There is no longer the "you" and the "I," for both are one—facets of something which transcends, and yet includes them both.

M 53. It is not only that we understand another man, but that we feel ourselves to be acting through him, and we appreciate his motives as our own motives, even though, as said in the preceding chapter, we may perfectly understand that another part of ourselves, possessing more knowledge, or a different view-point, might act quite differently.

The sense of personal property in qualities and in ideas is entirely lost, because we see that these things are truly common to all, because they are part of the great reality which lies equally behind all.

Hence personal pride in individual development becomes an utter impossibility, for we see now that personal development is but as the growth of one leaf, among the thousands of leaves on one tree, and that the important fact is not the size or shape of that particular leaf, but its relation to the tree as a whole; for it is only of the tree as a whole that we can really predicate permanent growth.

M 54. *I L I* 349. We have ceased altogether to blame others for their differences from ourselves: instead, we simply note them as other manifestations of our own activity, for now we see reasons which before were hidden from us. Even the evil man is seen to be part of ourselves—a weak part ; so our desire is not to blame him, but to help him by pouring strength into that weak part of ourselves, so that the whole body of humanity may be vigorous and healthy.

Thus, when a man rises to the buddhic plane, he can gain the experience of others ; hence it is not necessary for every ego to go through every experience, as a separate individual. If he did not want to feel the suffering of another, he could withdraw : but he would choose to feel it, because he wants to help. He enfolds in his own consciousness one who is suffering, and although the sufferer would know nothing of such enfoldment, yet it will, to a certain extent, lessen his sufferings. *I L I* 350.

On the buddhic plane there is a quite new faculty, having nothing in common with faculties on the lower planes. For a man recognises objects by an entirely different method, in which external vibrations play no part. The object becomes part of himself, and he studies it from the inside instead of from the outside. *C* 18–19.

With such a method of apprehension, it is clear that many familiar objects become entirely unrecognisable. Even astral sight enables one to see objects from all sides at once, as well as from above and below : adding to that the further complication that the whole inside of the body is laid out before us, as though every particle were separately placed upon a table : adding to that again the fact that, while we look at these particles, we are yet at the same time within each particle, and are looking through it, it is apparent that it becomes impossible to trace any resemblance to the object which we knew in the physical world. *M* 56–57.

Whilst the intuition of the causal body recognises the *outer*, the intuition of buddhi recognises the *inner*. Intellectual intuition enables one to realise a thing *outside* oneself : with buddhic intuition, one sees a thing from *inside*. *T C* 148–149.

Thus if, when working in the causal body, we want to understand another person, in order to help him, we turn our consciousness upon his causal body, and *T P O* 799. *M* 70.

study its peculiarities ; they are quite well marked, and plainly to be seen, but they are always seen from without. If, wanting the same knowledge, we raise our consciousness to the buddhic level, we find the consciousness of the other man as part of ourselves. We find a point of consciousness which represents him—we might call it a hole rather than a point. We can pour ourselves down that hole, and enter into his consciousness, at any lower level that we wish, and therefore can see everything precisely as he sees it—from inside him, instead of from outside. It will easily be understood how much that lends itself to perfect understanding and sympathy.

M 54–55. Yet, as has been said, in all this strange advance, there is no sense of loss of individuality, even though there is an utter loss of sense of separateness. Whilst that may seem a paradox, yet it is true. The man remembers all that lies behind him. He is himself the same man who did this action, or that, in the far-off past. He is in no way changed, except that now he is much more than he was then, and feels that he *includes* within himself many other manifestations as well.

If, here and now, a hundred of us could simultaneously raise our consciousness into the buddhic world, we should all be one consciousness, but to each man that consciousness would seem to be his own, absolutely unchanged, except that now it included all the others as well.

N 187. Buddhic vision reveals a person, not as an enclosure, but as a Star radiating out in all directions : the rays of that star pierce the consciousness of the observer, so that it is felt to be a part of himself, and yet not perfectly so. All observers agree that it is impossible, except by a series of contradictions, to describe the buddhic state of consciousness.

T P O 701–702. The power of identification is gained, not only with regard to the consciousness of people, but with regard to everything else, on the buddhic plane. Everything is learnt, as said, from the inside, instead of from the outside. That which we are examining has become a part of ourselves ; we examine it as a kind of symptom in ourselves. This characteristic obviously constitutes a fundamental difference. Before it can be attained, utter selflessness must be acquired, because so long as there is anything personal in the disciple's point of view, he cannot make any progress with the buddhic consciousness, which depends on the suppression of the personality.

H. P. Blavatsky states that: " Buddhi is the faculty of cognising, the channel through which divine knowledge reaches the Ego, the discernment of good and evil, also divine conscience, and the spiritual Soul, which is the vehicle of Ātmā." (*The Secret Doctrine,* I., page 2.) It is often spoken of as the principle of spiritual discernment. *S P* 60.

In the Yoga system, turīya, a lofty state of trance, is related to the buddhic consciousness, just as sushupti is related to the mental consciousness, svapna to the astral, and jāgrat to the physical. These terms, however, are used also with other significances, being relative rather than absolute, *vide The Mental Body,* page 146. *I Y* 16.

In the Six Stages of Mind, given in *The Mental Body,* page 146, that of niruddha, or Self-controlled, corresponds to activity on the buddhic plane. *I Y* 35.

In the physical body, the yellow prāna which enters the heart chakram or force-centre represents the principle of buddhi. *Ch.* 34.

Although, at the buddhic level, a man still has a definite body, yet his consciousness seems equally present in vast numbers of other bodies. The web of life, which is constructed of buddhic matter, is extended so that it includes these other people, so that, instead of many small separate webs, there is one vast web, which enfolds them all in one common life. *M* 57-58.

Many of these others may, of course, be entirely unconscious of this change, and to them their own private little part of the web will still seem as much separated as ever—or would do so if they knew anything at all about the web of life. So, from this standpoint, and at this level, it seems that all mankind are bound together by golden threads, and make one complex unit, no longer *a* man, but *man* in the abstract.

C 136–137: 109. On the buddhic plane, in some manner which is naturally quite incomprehensible to the physical brain, past, present and future all exist simultaneously. Neither is a man, on this plane, any longer subject to limitations of space such as we know on the physical plane. Hence, in reading the Ākāshic Records (*vide The Mental Body*, page 238) he no longer needs, as on the mental plane, to pass a series of events in review because, as said, past, present and future are simultaneously present to him.

C 139. With consciousness fully developed on the buddhic plane, therefore, perfect prevision is possible, though, of course, the man may not—in fact, will not—be able to bring the whole result fully through into his lower consciousness. Nevertheless, a great deal of clear foresight is obviously within his power, whenever he chooses to exercise it; and even when he is not exercising it, frequent flashes of foreknowledge come through into his ordinary life, so that he often has an instantaneous intuition as to how things will turn out, even before their inception.

I L I 354. *C* 81–82. *S G O* 148. *T P O* 505. The extension of the buddhic plane is so great, that what may be called the buddhic bodies of the different planets of our chain meet one another, so that there is but one buddhic body for the whole chain. Hence it is possible for a man, in his buddhic body, to pass from one of these planets to another.

T B 21. We may note here that an atom of buddhic matter contains 49^3 or 117,649 "bubbles in koilon."

I L II 214. A man who can raise his consciousness to the atomic level of the buddhic plane finds himself so absolutely in union with all other men that, if he wishes to find another man, he has only to put himself out along the line of that other person in order to find him.

M 73. The following may be taken as an example of the working of buddhic consciousness. All beauty, whether it be of form or of colour, whether it be in nature or in the human frame, in high achievements of art or in the humblest household utensil, is but an expression of the One Beauty ; and therefore, in the lowliest thing that is beautiful, all beauty is implicitly contained, and so, through it, all beauty may be realised, and He, Who Himself is Beauty, may be reached. To understand this fully needs the buddhic consciousness, but even at much lower levels the idea may be useful and fruitful.

As a Master has expressed it : " Do you not see that as there is but One Love, so there is but One Beauty ? Whatever is beautiful, on any plane, is so because it is part of that Beauty, and, if it is pushed back far enough, its connection will become manifest. All Beauty is of God, as all Love is of God ; and through these His Qualities the pure in heart may always reach Him."

The full development of the buddhic vehicle, how- *M* 63.
ever, belongs to the stage of the Arhat, though those who are as yet far from that level can gain in various ways touches of the buddhic consciousness.

Buddhi in the human spirit is the pure and com- *C W* 160.
passionate Reason, which is the Wisdom Aspect, the Christ in man.

In the normal course of evolution, the buddhic *C W* 240–
consciousness will be gradually unfolded in the sixth 242.
sub-race of the Fifth Root Race, and still more so in the Sixth Root Race itself.

One may trace the coming of the sixth sub-race in *C W* 216–
the scattered people found in the fifth sub-race, in whom 220.
tenderness is the mark of power. It is a synthesising spirit which characterises the sixth sub-race ; its members are able to unite diversity of opinion and of character, to gather round them the most unlike elements, and blend them into a common whole, having the capacity to take into themselves diversities, and send them out again as unities, utilising the most different capacities, finding each its place, and welding all together into a strong whole.

Compassion is strongly marked ; it is that quality which is at once affected by the presence of weakness, answering to it with patience, with tenderness, and with protection. The sense of unity and compassion will be a strength and a power which will be used for service, the measure of strength being the measure of responsibility and of duty.

CHAPTER XXXIII

THE EGO AND THE MONAD

In Chapter III we studied the Coming Forth of the Monads, and considered briefly the general nature of the Monads. In the chapter on Initiation, we dealt with the effects which Initiation produces on the relation between the Monad and the ego. It will now be fitting to consider such further information as is available regarding the relation between the ego and the Monad, and also to deal a little more fully with the nature of the Monad himself, and his attitude towards his manifestations in the lower worlds.

Turning first to the nature of the Monad himself, we are confronted with the difficulty that no direct observation of the Monad, on his own plane, is at present possible to our investigators. The plane on which the Monad resides—the Anupādaka plane—is at present beyond the reach of our clairvoyant investigators, the highest which those investigators can actually know of man, from direct observation, being the manifestation of the Monad as the Triple Spirit on the plane of Ātmā. Even at that stage he is incomprehensible: for his three aspects are quite distinct and apparently separate, and yet are all fundamentally one and the same. *S O S* 317. *M* 6 : 20. *T* 23.

Whilst no one below the rank of the Adept can see the Monad, yet the Arhat can know of its existence. For, on the plane of ātmā, the triple manifestation can be perceived, and the rays which make that triple manifestation are obviously converging as they rise to the highest point. It can therefore be seen that they must become one, though the actual unity is out of the sight. *T P O* 824.

We have already referred (*vide* page 124) to the *T P O* 689.

possibility of focussing the consciousness in the highest level of the causal body, looking up the line that joins the ego and the Monad, and, through that vision, realising the identity with the Deity.

M P 176. Perhaps the least misleading manner, in which we can image the true nature of the Monad to ourselves, is to think of him as a part of God—a part, however, of That which cannot be divided. Although, unfortunately, this is a paradox to the finite intellect, yet it enshrines an eternal truth which is far beyond our comprehension.

M 17–18. For each Monad is literally a part of God, apparently temporarily separated from Him, while he is enclosed in the veils of matter, though in truth never for one moment really separated. He can never be apart from God, for the very matter in which he veils himself is also a manifestation of the Divine. Although matter seems to us evil, because it weighs us down, clogs our faculties, and holds us back upon the road, yet this is only because as yet we have not learned to control it, because we have not realised that it also is divine in its essence, because there is nothing but God.

S C 55. It is a mistake to think of the Monad as something very far away. For the Monad is very near to us, is our SELF, the very root of our being, the one and only reality. Hidden, unmanifest, wrapt in silence and darkness though he be, yet our consciousness is the limited manifestation of that SELF, the manifested God in our bodies, which are his garments.

T 23.
M 20.
T P O 239.
I L I 343.
R 14.

The Monad has been variously described as the Eternal Man: a fragment of the Life of God: a Son of God, made in His image: a spark *in* the Divine Fire: the "hidden God," as he was known to the Egyptians: he is the God within us, our personal God: our true Self: a fragment of the Eternal: the real, and *only* permanent "I" in man. The Monads have been described also as centres of force in the Logos.

S P 67–68. Instead of speaking of human Monads, it might perhaps be more accurate to speak of "the Monad manifesting in the human kingdom," though such pedantic accuracy might be still more puzzling. H. P. Blavatsky wrote : " The Spiritual Monad is one, universal, boundless, and impartite, whose rays, nevertheless, form what we, in our ignorance, call the ' individual Monads ' of men." (*The Secret Doctrine*, I, 200.)

As the Occult Catechism expresses it :—

" I sense one Flame, O Gurudeva ; I see countless undetached sparks burning in it.

" Thou sayest well. And now look around and into thyself. That light which burns inside thee, dost thou feel it different in any wise from the light that shines in thy brother-men ?

" It is in no way different, though the prisoner is held in bondage by Karma, and though its garments delude the ignorant into saying, ' thy soul ' and ' my soul.' " (*The Secret Doctrine*, I, 145.)

To take a physical plane analogy, we recognise that electricity is *one* all the world over ; and, though it may be active in this machine or in that, the owner of no machine can claim it as distinctively *his* electricity. So also is the Monad *one* everywhere, though manifesting in different directions, through apparently separate and different human beings.

But, in spite of having the same source, and the *I L I* 343.
same fundamental nature, yet each Monad possesses *M* 20.
a very distinct individuality of his own : in his manifestation on the plane of Ātmā, as a triple light of blinding glory, even at that stage, each Monad possesses certain qualities which make him distinct from every other Monad.

The consciousness of the Monad on his own plane is *T C* 46.
complete : he shares the divine knowledge in his own world. But, in the lower world, he is to all intents and purposes unconscious : he cannot in any way touch the lower planes of life, the matter there being of a character which is not amenable to his influences. He, who has been in union with all around him, would, if plunged into denser matter, find himself in uttermost isolation, as in empty space, unconscious of all impacts and contacts of matter.

T C 48. Nevertheless, everything is in him, by virtue of the One Life that he shares : but it has to be brought out : hence we speak of awakening the latent consciousness into life. Literally everything is in the Monad, all divine knowledge ; but, to bring that out, so that on any plane of matter he may *know*, is the whole work of evolution.

T C 46. Hence the rationale of his evolutionary journey, down and again upwards, is for the purpose of acquiring that consciousness, of subjugating matter completely as a vehicle, until on each plane he answers to the vibrations of similar matter outside, and is able to bring out *moods* of consciousness, which answer to those outside impressions, and thereby make it possible for him to be conscious of them.

N 8–9. Bishop Arundale gives an interesting account of the appearance and evolution of the Monads. Looking upon the world, he writes, he sees our Lord the Sun expressed in myriad suns. Each Monad is a sun in miniature, the Sun Divine throwing off sparking suns, charged with all His attributes. The process of evolution begins, and these sparks burst into colour ; rainbows with sun-hearts, or centres. Every atom of light is an atom of unconscious Divinity, slowly but surely fulfilling the will of the Sun that it shall become unfolded into self-conscious Divinity. Every atom is a Sun unconscious, and shall become a Sun self-conscious.

S P 63. When manifestation begins, the Monad is " thrown downwards into matter," to propel forwards and force evolution (*vide The Secret Doctrine*, II, 115) : it is the mainspring of all evolution, the impelling force at the root of all things.

T C 48. This accounts for that mysterious pressure, which so much puzzles orthodox science, as to why things move onwards : as to what is the force which makes evolution : as to what gives rise to all the variety we find in the world, and the ever-present " tendency to variation."

L I 343 The Monad knows from the first what is his object

in evolution, and he grasps the general trend of it. But, until that portion of him, which expresses itself in the ego, has reached a fairly high stage, he is scarcely conscious of the details down here, or at any rate he takes little interest in them. He seems at that stage not to know other Monads, but rests in indescribable bliss, without any active consciousness of his surroundings.

The purpose, then, of the descent of the Monad into *M P* 15.
matter, is that through his descent he may obtain definiteness and accuracy in material detail. To this end, as we have seen in the earlier chapters of this book, an atom of each of the planes of Ātmā, Buddhi and Manas is attached to the Monad : the distinction of *T C* 18.
these atoms gives a precision that did not exist in the consciousness of the Monad on his own plane.

But, it may be asked, if the Monad is of the essence *M V*
of divinity in the beginning, and returns to divinity at 63.
the end of his long pilgrimage, if the Monad is all-wise and all-good, when he starts on his journey through matter, why is it necessary for him to go through all this evolution, including, as it does, much sorrow and suffering, simply to return to his source in the end ?

The question is based on a misconception of the facts. When that which we call the human Monad came forth from the Divine, it was not, in reality, a human Monad, still less an all-wise and all-good Monad : it returns, eventually, in the form of thousands of millions of mighty Adepts, each capable of himself developing into a Logos.

As a man who cannot swim, flung into deep water, at *T* 24–25.
first is helpless, yet eventually learns to swim and move freely in the water, so with the Monad. At the end of his pilgrimage of immersion in matter, he will be free of the Solar System, able to function in any part of it, to create at will, to move at pleasure. Every power that he unfolds through denser matter, he retains for ever under all conditions : the implicit has become explicit, the potential the actual. It is his own Will to

live in all spheres, and not in one only, that draws him into manifestation.

For there was no developed individualisation in the Monad at first: it was simply a mass of monadic essence. The difference between its condition when issuing forth, and when returning, is exactly like that between a great mass of shining nebulous matter, and the solar system which is eventually formed out of it. The nebula is beautiful, undoubtedly, but vague and, in a certain sense, useless. The sun formed from it by slow evolution pours forth life, heat and light upon many worlds and their inhabitants.

Or we may take another analogy. The human body is composed of countless millions of tiny particles, and some of them are constantly being thrown off from it. Suppose that it were possible for each of these particles to go through some kind of evolution, by means of which it would in time become a human being, we should not say that, because it had been, in a certain sense, human at the beginning of that evolution, it had therefore not gained anything when it reached the end.

So, the monadic essence comes forth as a mere outpouring of force, even though it be Divine force.

T C 18–19. The appearance and evolutionary course of the Monad may be compared with the appearance of the long day of Brahmā, of the Saguna-Brahman, Sachchidānanda, the Divine Triplicity. That coming forth into cosmic manifestation we have reproduced, in our solar system, by the Solar Logos, and again by the Monad, who is a fragment of the Logos. When the human evolution is over, he gathers himself up again, and the superhuman evolution begins. Thus we have the long swing of the opening life, from the nirvānic, back to the nirvānic, the whole of human evolution lying between these two. It is completed with the Initiation of the Jīvanmukta, the Master, where superhuman evolution begins.

M 27–28: 2–3. Whilst the Monad in his own world is practically without limitations, at least so far as our solar system is concerned, yet at every stage of his descent into matter he not only veils himself more and more deeply in illusion, but he actually loses his powers.

If, in the beginning of his evolution, we may suppose the Monad able to move and to see, in an infinite number of those directions in space which we call dimensions, then at each downward step he cuts off one of these, until, for the consciousness of the physical brain, only three of them are left. Thus, by involution into matter, the Monad is cut off from the knowledge of all but a minute part of the worlds which surround him. Furthermore, even what is left to him is but imperfectly seen. For those who can train themselves to appreciate more than three dimensions, there is available an excellent method of arriving at some sort of comprehension of what consciousness on planes higher than the physical is like, and what it involves: though at the same time such a method of approach brings home the hopelessness of expecting fully to understand the Monad, who is raised by many planes and dimensions above the point from which we are attempting to regard him.

All the sacrifices and limitations, caused by descent *M P* 343. into matter, may rightly be described as necessitating suffering. But, as soon as the *ego* fully understands the situation, they are undertaken gladly: the ego has not the perfection of the Monad, and so he does not fully understand at first: he has to learn. Thus the quite tremendous limitation at each further descent into matter is an unavoidable fact, so that there is that much of suffering inseparable from manifestation. We have to accept that limitation as a means to an end, as part of the Divine Scheme.

There are two senses in which all manifested life is *M P* 341–342. sorrowful, unless man knows how to live it. One of these is to a certain extent inevitable, but the other is an entire mistake, and is easily to be avoided. As we have seen, to the Monad, who is the true Spirit of man, all manifested life is a sorrow, just because it *is* a limitation: a limitation which we in our physical brain cannot in the least conceive, because we have no idea of the glorious freedom of the higher life.

It is in this sense that it has always been said that the Christ—the Second Person of the Trinity—offers Himself as a Sacrifice, when He descends into matter. Undoubtedly it is a sacrifice, because it is an inexpressibly great limitation, for it shuts off from Him all the glorious powers which are His, on His own level.

The same is true of the Monad of man ; undoubtedly he makes a great sacrifice, when he brings himself into connection with lower matter, when he hovers over it through the long ages of its development up to the human level, when he puts down a tiny fragment of himself, a finger-tip as it were, and thereby makes an ego, or individual soul.

M P 343–345. The second kind of sorrow, which it is possible entirely to avoid, is due to " desire," using that word in the wide sense to include all desires for lower things, such as craving for power, money, position, and so forth. All such desires necessarily cause disturbance and suffering : hence, from this point of view, what is most needed for progress is serenity.

Hence we have the two first of the Four Noble Truths which the Lord Buddha taught : the Existence of Sorrow, and the Cause of Sorrow.

S P 67. *R* 14. Passing now to consider, more specifically, the ego in his relation to the Monad, we should realise that the individualising process, by means of which the ego comes into being, *does not take place on the spiritual plane,* but that Ātmā-Buddhi, as seen through Manas, *appears* to share in the individuality of Manas.

M 17. Even the ego is not the true, eternal man : for the ego had a beginning—he came into existence at the moment of individualisation : and whatever has a beginning must also have an end. Therefore even the ego, which has lasted since emergence from the animal kingdom, is also impermanent. The Monad, and the Monad alone, is the only real, permanent man.

M 7. We may look upon the ego as a manifestation of the Monad on the higher mental plane : but we must understand that he is infinitely far from being a perfect manifestation. Each descent from plane to plane means much more than a mere veiling of the Spirit: it means also an actual diminution in the *amount* of Spirit expressed.

Although to speak of Spirit in terms of quantity is inaccurate and misleading, yet, if an attempt is to be made to express these higher matters in human words at all, such incongruities cannot be wholly avoided. The nearest that we can come, in the physical brain, to a conception of what happens to the Monad, when he involves himself in matter, is to say that only part of him can be shown, and even that part must be shown in three separate aspects, instead of in the glorious totality which he really *is* in his own world.

So, when the second aspect of the triple spirit comes *M* 7–8.
down a stage, and manifests as buddhi or intuition, it *T B* 61. *T P O* 258.
is not the whole of that aspect which so manifests, but *M P* 16:
only a fraction of it. So again when the third aspect 177.
descends two planes, and manifests as intellect, it is only a fraction of a fraction of what the intellect-aspect of the Monad really is. Therefore the ego is not a veiled manifestation of the Monad, but a veiled representation of a minute fraction of the Monad.

Following the ancient maxim, " as above, so below," as the ego is to the Monad, so is the personality to the ego. By the time we have reached the personality, the fractionisation has been carried so far that the part we are able to see bears no appreciable proportion to the reality of which, nevertheless, it is the only possible representation to us. Yet with and from this hopelessly inadequate fragment, we strive to comprehend the whole. Our difficulty in trying to understand the Monad is the same in kind, but much greater in degree, as that which we found when we tried really to grasp the idea of the ego.

Diagram XXXIX is an attempt, however inadequate, to represent graphically the relationship between the Monad, the ego and the personality.

The Monad has been compared with the flame: the *T P O* 443.

ego or triple spirit with the fire: and the personality with the fuel.

I L II 209. I L I 344–345. T P O 761: 764. The correspondence between the Monad in its relation to the ego, and the ego in its relation to the personality, will bear a little further amplification. As the ego is triple, so is the Monad: the three constituents of the Monad exist on the first three planes of our System, viz., the Ādī, the Anupādaka and the Ātmā planes. On the ātmic plane the Monad takes to itself a manifestation, which we call the Monad in its ātmic vesture, or sometimes the triple ātmā, or triple spirit. *This is for the Monad what the causal body is for the ego.*

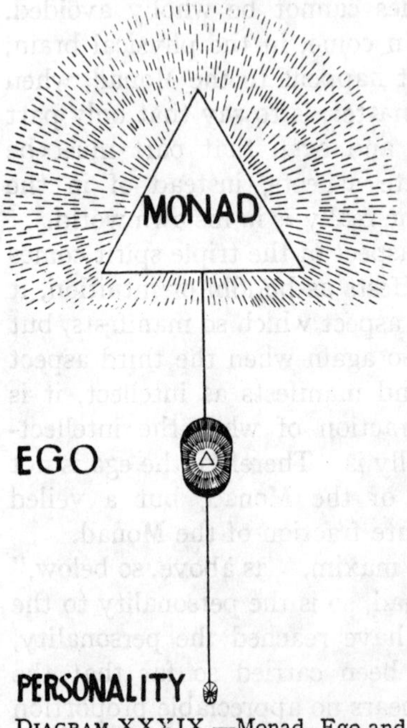

Diagram XXXIX.—Monad, Ego and Personality (I).

Just as the ego takes on three lower bodies (mental, astral and physical), the first of which (the mental) is on the lower part of his own plane, and the lowest (the physical) two planes below, so the Monad—regarding him now as the triple ātmā or spirit—takes on three lower manifestations (ātmā, buddhi, manas), the first of which is on the lower part of his own plane, and the lowest two planes below that.

It will thus be seen that the causal body is to the Monad what the physical body is to the ego. If we think of the ego as the soul of the physical body, we may consider the Monad as the soul of the ego in turn.

For, just as the causal body takes, from the personality, whatever is of a nature to help its growth, so the causal body, through its inner or upper side, passes on, into the third aspect of ātmā, the essence of all experiences which may have entered into it. What is thus poured into the manasic aspect of ātmā renders it capable of acting without the causal body, that is, without a permanent vehicle which limits it. This throws light on the phenomenon of the perishing of the causal body, or the individuality, with which we have already dealt in Chapter XXXI.

Diagram XL is an attempt to illustrate these somewhat complex correspondences and relationships.

The entire higher triad, ātmā-buddhi-manas, may *T P O* 409.
also be regarded as the buddhi of the still more inclusive triad of Monad, Ego and Personality. That larger buddhi is triple—will, wisdom and activity—and its third aspect, kriyāshakti, in due course comes into operation in the body, to awaken its organs and liberate its latent powers.

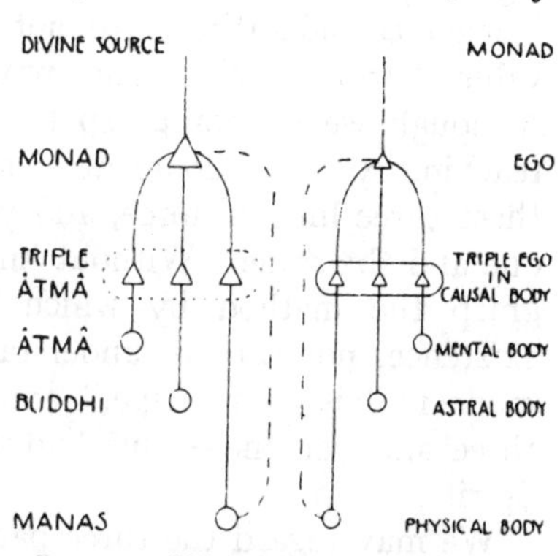

DIAGRAM XL.—Monadic and Egoic Relationships.

The statement, in *Light on the Path*, that the "war- *T P O* 841–
rior" in man is "eternal and sure," may be taken as 842.
relatively true of the ego in relation to the lower self, and *absolutely* true with regard to the Monad in relation to the ego. The ego, as we have seen, may make mistakes at an earlier stage, but is far less likely to do so than is the personality. The Monad, on the other hand, makes no mistakes, although his knowledge of conditions down here may be somewhat vague. But his instinct must be on the side of right, for he is divine. Neither the ego nor the Monad have as yet accurate knowledge, because their evolution is not complete. They are for us as guides, and one cannot

do other than follow them. But even as guides they are themselves unfolding.

I L I 344–345. *T P O* 829. We may note here that the triple manifestation of the Monad is that which Christianity speaks of as the "three persons in one God," teaching, in the Athanasian creed, that men should worship "One God in Trinity and Trinity in Unity, neither confounding the persons nor dividing the substance"—that is to say, never confusing the work and function of the three separate manifestations, each on its own plane, yet never for a moment forgetting the eternal unity of the "substance," that which lives behind all alike, on the highest plane, where these three are one.

Such considerations are not merely of theoretical value, but have also some practical bearing on life. Although we cannot grasp the full meaning of such teaching, yet we should at least know that there are these three lines of force, and yet that all the force is one and the same. Without knowing that, we cannot grasp the method by which our world came into existence, nor can we understand man, whom "God made in His own image," and who therefore is also three and yet one—ātmā-buddhi-manas, and yet one Spirit.

T P O 356–357. We may regard the three parts of the higher self as three aspects of a great consciousness or mind. They are all three modes of cognition. Ātmā is not the Self, but is this consciousness knowing the *Self*. Buddhi is this consciousness knowing the *life in the forms*, by its own direct perception. Manas is the same consciousness looking out upon the world of *objects*. Kāma-Manas is a portion of the last, immersed in that world, and affected by it. The true self is the Monad, whose life is something greater than consciousness, which is the life of this complete mind, the Higher self.

T P O 375. The same truth may be expressed in a slightly different form—indeed in many forms. Ātmā, Buddhi and Manas in man reflect in their smaller spheres the characteristics of the great Trinity. Ātmā is the consciousness of *self*, and also the *will*, which gives self-direction. Manas, at the other pole, is consciousness of the *world*, and its *thought-power* does all our work, even that which is effected through the hands. But buddhi, between the two, is the very *essence* of consciousness, of *subjectivity*.

Beyond this middle member, triple in character, is *T P O* 376.
the Monad in man, representative in him of Parabrahman, the state of his true and absolute nirvāna, beyond consciousness. The ātmā is the state of his false and relative nirvāna, of the nirvānic or ātmic plane, his last illusion, that persists between the Fourth (Arhat) and Fifth (Adept) Initiations.

As the Monad lies *above* the trinity of consciousness, so the personal bodies lie outside or *beneath* it—they are known only in reflection in manas.

We may perhaps presume—though here we are *M* 19–20.
going far beyond actual knowledge—that when we *M P* 177.
have finally and fully realised that the Monad is the true man, we shall find, beyond that again, a yet further and more glorious extension. We shall find that the Spark has never been separated from the Fire, but that, as the ego stands behind the personality, as the Monad stands behind the ego, so a Planetary Angel stands behind the Monad, and the Solar Deity Himself stands behind the Planetary Angel. Perhaps, even further still, it may be that, in some way infinitely higher, and so at present utterly incomprehensible, a greater Deity stands behind the Solar Deity, and behind even that, through many stages, there must rest the Supreme over all. But here even thought fails us, and silence is the only true reverence.

In the average man the Monad is, of course, but *I L I* 343.
little in touch with the ego and the lower personality, although both of these are yet somehow expressions of him. Just as it is evolution for the personality to *M P* 179.
learn to express the ego more fully, so it is evolution for the ego to learn to express the Monad more fully. And just as the ego in time learns to control and dominate *M P* 20.
the personality, so the Monad, in his turn, learns to dominate the ego.

Diagram XLI is a rough illustration of the relation between Monad, Ego and Personality, and the stages by which these three gradually come more and more into touch with one another.

At the left-hand side of the diagram, we see the ego represented as very small: he is just a baby ego: complete, but small and undeveloped: the personality is also slender, indicating its primitive condition. As evolution proceeds, the personality gradually widens out, until eventually it becomes equilateral, indicating that it is well developed, all-round, symmetrical. Also, it will be observed, the link between the personality and the ego, at first very narrow, has widened out,

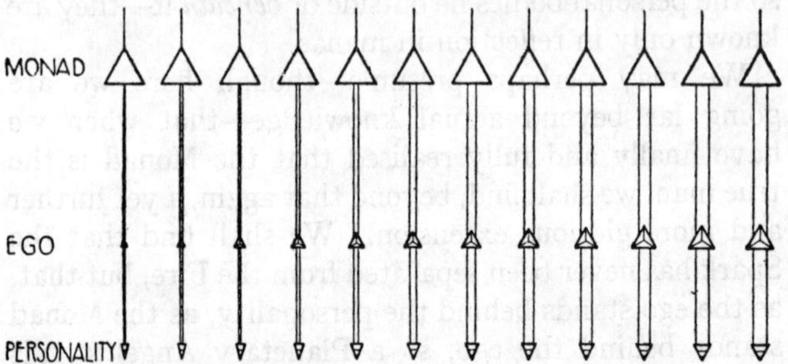

DIAGRAM XLI.—Monad, Ego and Personality (II).

until it becomes almost as wide as the full width of the personality.

Whilst this has been going on, at the same time, the ego has been steadily growing in size, and the channel between him and the Monad has also been steadily increasing in width.

Thus, at the right-hand side of the diagram, we have a strong and wide channel between Monad and Ego, the Ego himself being fully developed, exercising, through a wide and well-developed link, full control over a symmetrically developed personality.

Finally, the time will come when, just as the personality and ego have become one, the Monad and ego also become one. This is the unification of the ego with the Monad, and when that is achieved the man has attained the object of his descent into matter, he has become the Superman, the Adept.

Diagram XLII illustrates this consummation. Here we see the Monad, Ego and Personality in perfect alignment, veritably an " at-one-ment." The same life permeates all three of its manifestations, but the per-

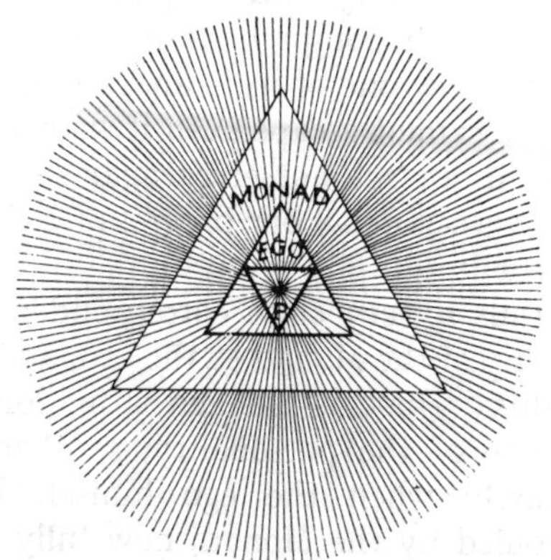

DIAGRAM XLII.—Monad, Ego and Personality : " At-one-ment."
This diagram is an attempt to indicate :—

I. The complete alignment, or unification of Monad, Ego and Personality.
II. The consequent *one* centre of consciousness.
III. The *one* life flowing through all three.
IV. The limitations imposed upon the manifestations of the one life by the outline-barriers of Personality, Ego and Monad.
V. The fact that Personality, Ego and even Monad are but māyāvic or illusory veils imposed upon the Divine Life.
VI. The fact that the One Life itself is unlimited and universal, as indicated by the circularity of the aura of radiation, thus transcending its expressions through Monad, Ego and Personality. " With one portion of Myself I manifest, but I remain."

sonality, owing to its size and its constitution, is able to express less of the one life than the ego is able to do, and the ego, in his turn, for similar reasons, is able to express less than can the Monad.

Even the Monad cannot confine, contain, or express the whole of the divine life which radiates out from and beyond that veil, however thin, of separative matter—which makes him a distinct being.

When this consummation is reached, then only, for the first time, does the entity enter upon his real life, for the whole of this stupendous process of evolution is but a preparation for that true life of the spirit, which begins only when man becomes more than man. Humanity is the final class of the world-school, and, when a man passes out of this, he enters the life of the glorified Spirit, the life of the Christ.

That life has a glory and a splendour beyond all comparison and all comprehension : but the attainment of it by every one of us is an absolute certainty, from which we cannot escape even if we would. If we act selfishly, if we set ourselves against the current of evolution, we can delay our progress : but we cannot finally prevent it.

M 5. There is thus a very close correspondence between the relationship of the Monad to the ego, and the ego to the personality. Just as the ego is for long ages the ensouling force of the personality, so there comes a time eventually when the ego himself becomes a vehicle, ensouled by the Monad, now fully active and awakened. All the manifold experiences of the ego, all the splendid qualities developed in him, all these pass into the Monad himself, and find there a vastly fuller realisation than even the ego could have given them.

M 22. The question arises, does the Monad, in the case of the ordinary man, ever do anything which affects, or can affect, his personality down here? Such interference appears to be most unusual. The ego is trying, on behalf of the Monad, to obtain perfect control of the personality, and to use it as an instrument : but, because that object is not yet fully achieved, the Monad may well feel that the time has not yet come for him to intervene from his own level, and to bring the whole of his force to bear, when that which is already in action is more than strong enough for the required purpose. But, when the ego is already beginning to succeed, in his effort to manage his lower vehicles, then the Monad does sometimes intervene.

In the course of investigating some thousands of human beings, traces of such intervention were found in only a few. The most prominent instance is that given in the twenty-ninth life of Alcyone, when he pledged himself to the Lord Buddha to devote himself in future lives to the attainment of the Buddhahood, in order to help humanity.

This being a promise for the far-distant future, it was obvious that the personality, through which it was given, could by no means keep it. Investigation revealed that even the ego, though full of enthusiasm at the idea, was being impelled by a mightier force from within, which he could not have resisted, even had he wished to do so. Following the clue still further, it was found that the impelling force came forth unmistakably from the Monad. He had decided, and he registered his decision. His will, working through the ego, will clearly have no difficulty in bringing all future personalities into harmony with his great intention. *M* 23.

Other examples of the same phenomenon were found. Certain Monads had already responded to the call of the higher Authorities, and had decided that their representative personalities should assist in the work of the Sixth Root Race in California, some hundreds of years hence. Because of that decision, nothing that these personalities might do during the intervening time could possibly interfere with the carrying out of that decision.

The compelling force is thus not from without, but from within, from the real man himself. When the Monad has decided, the thing will be done, and it is well for the personality to yield gracefully and readily, recognising the voice from above, and co-operating gladly. If he does not do this, then he will lay up for himself much useless suffering. It is always the man himself who is doing this thing; and he, in the personality, has to realise that the ego *is* himself, and he has for the moment to take it for granted that the Monad is still more himself—the final and greatest expression of him.

What is known as the great Company of Servers affords another instance; the Servers are a type apart, to which Monads seem to be attached *ab initio*, how- *N* 75–76.

ever long it may take for the type to be expressed in the outer consciousness. In a certain sense, it is a kind of predestination, the Monad having taken the resolve. (For a fuller account of the Servers, *vide* article, entitled *The Servers*, by C. W. Leadbeater, in *The Theosophist*, September, 1913.)

I L II 389–390. In view of the general consideration that in a perfectly ordered universe there is no room for chance, it seems probable that the very mode of individualisation from the animal kingdom was somehow predetermined, either for or by the Monad himself, with a view to preparation for whatever portion of the great work he is to undertake in the future.

For there will come a time when we shall all be part of the great Heavenly Man : not in the least as a myth or a poetic symbol, but as a vivid and actual fact, which certain investigators have themselves seen. That celestial body has many members ; each of these members has its own function to fulfil, and the living cells which are to form part of them need widely different experiences to prepare them. It may well be that, from the dawn of evolution, the parts have been chosen, that each Monad has his destined line of evolution, and his freedom of action is concerned chiefly with the *rate* at which he shall move along that line.

S O S 196–198. In the Celebration of the Holy Eucharist, there is a good deal of symbolism concerned with the Monad, the Ego and the Personality. Briefly, speaking first of the Three Persons of the Trinity, the Host typifies God the Father, and also stands for the Deity, whole and indivisible ; the Wine stands for God the Son, Whose life is poured down into the chalice of material form ; the Water represents God the Holy Ghost, the Spirit Who brooded over the face of the waters, and yet at the same time is Himself symbolised by water.

Speaking next of the Deity in man, the Host signifies the Monad, the totality, the unseen cause of all : the paten means the Triple Ātmā or Spirit through which the Monad acts on matter : the Wine indicates the individuality, poured into the chalice of the causal body : the Water represents the personality which is so intimately mixed with it.

Passing to the effect of Communion upon the communicant, the force of the Host is essentially Monadic, and acts most powerfully upon whatever within the man represents the direct action of the Monad : the force of the Chalice is more that of the ego : the Wine has a very powerful force upon the higher astral levels, and the Water sends out even etheric vibrations.

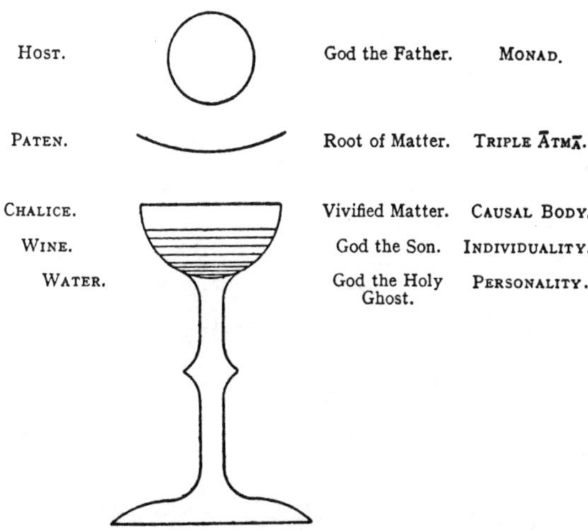

DIAGRAM XLIII.—The Symbolism of the Holy Eucharist.

When the priest makes the three crosses with the Host over the Chalice, he wills strongly that the influence from the Monadic level should descend into the ego in its threefold manifestation of Ātmā, Buddhi and Manas : and then, as he makes the two crosses between the Chalice and his own breast, he draws that influence into his own mental and astral bodies, that through him it may radiate fully upon his people. *S O S* 214–215.

This symbolises the earlier stages of evolution, when the Monad hovers over his lower manifestations, brooding over them, acting upon them, but never touching them. So the priest holds the Host above the Chalice, yet never touches the one with the other until the appointed time has come.

S O S 228. When the priest drops the fragment of the Host into the Chalice, he thereby signifies the descent of a ray of the Monad into the ego.

To facilitate memorisation of this system of symbols, Diagram XLIII is appended.

CHAPTER XXXIV

THE SECOND AND HIGHER INITIATIONS

EACH stage of the Path proper is divided into four steps :— *M P* 196–197.

The First is its *Maggo*, or way, during which the student is striving to cast off the fetters.

The Second is its *Phala*, literally fruit or result, when the man finds the result of his efforts showing themselves more and more.

The Third is its *Bhavagga*, or consummation, the period when, the result having culminated, he is able to fulfil satisfactorily the work belonging to the step on which he now firmly stands.

The Fourth is its *Gotrabhu*, which means the time when he has arrived at a fit state to receive the next Initiation. This means complete and entire freedom from the fetters of his stage on the Path.

The first of the three fetters, or Samyojana, which have to be cast off, before the candidate can take the Second Initiation, is *Sakkāyadiṭṭhi*, the delusion of self. This is the " I-am-I " consciousness which, as connected with the personality, is nothing but an illusion, and must be got rid of at the very first step of the real upward Path. But to cast off the fetter completely means even more than this, for it involves the realisation of the fact that the individuality also is, in very truth, one with the All, that it can therefore never have any interests opposed to those of its brethren, and that it is most truly progressing when it most assists the progress of others. *M P* 192–193.

The second fetter is *Vichikichcha*, doubt or uncertainty. The candidate must arrive at the certainty of conviction, founded on individual experiment, or mathematical reasoning. He believes, not because he *M* 195.

has been told, but because the facts are now self-evident. This is the only method of resolving doubt known to occultism.

M P 195–96. The third fetter is *Silabbataparamasa*, or superstition. This includes all kinds of unreasoning and mistaken belief, and all dependence upon outward rites and ceremonies to purify the heart. The man must realise that within himself deliverance must be sought, and that, however valuable aids such as ceremonies, etc., may be in developing will, wisdom and love, yet they can never take the place of that personal effort by which alone he can achieve. The knowledge of the spiritual permanence of the true ego brings reliance on one's own spiritual strength, and so dispels superstition.

P O 829. The buddhic consciousness is directly related to these three fetters, for they are all dispelled by that consciousness. Recognising the unity, the man can have no delusion of separateness. Seeing for himself the great laws of life in operation, he can no longer doubt. He sees all the roads that lead to the one Bliss, and that all roads are good, so that he can no longer hold to the superstition that any one form of belief is necessary, to one who has attained that level.

M P 197. The Second Initiation takes place in the lower mental world, so that the candidate must have developed the power to function freely in his mental body.

M P 209. This Initiation rapidly continues the development of the mental body, and at or near this point the pupil learns to use the māyāvirūpa (*vide The Mental Body*, page 169).

M P 208. At the Second Initiation, the Key of Knowledge is given, the Initiator pouring out, from His own mental and causal bodies, rays of power which, falling on the mental and causal bodies of the Initiate, stimulate into sudden and splendid growth the germs of similar powers therein existing. As though a bud, stimulated by the sun-rays, should suddenly burst into all the glory of the opened flower, so do the mental and causal bodies suddenly unfold the powers latent within them, expanding into radiant beauty. Through them, now expanded, buddhi or intuition can play freely, the great new power being thus set free to work.

The period after the Second Initiation is in many *M P* 211–
ways the most dangerous anywhere on the Path: it is 214.
at this stage that, if there is any weakness in a candidate's character, it will find him out. In nearly all cases, the danger comes through pride. It is indicated in the Gospel story by the temptation in the wilderness.

As the First Initiation corresponds to a new birth, so may the Second Initiation be compared to the baptism of the Holy Ghost and Fire, for it is the power of the Third Person of the Trinity that is outpoured at that moment, in what may but inadequately be described as a flood of fire.

The man at this stage is known to the Buddhists as a Sakadāgāmin, the man who returns but once, the meaning being that he should need but one more incarnation before attaining Arhatship, the Fourth Initiation.

The Hindu name for this step is the Kitichaka, the man who builds a hut, he who has reached a place of peace.

At this stage no additional fetters are cast off, but it is usually a period of considerable psychic and intellectual advancement. The man must have the astral consciousness at his command during physical waking life, and, during sleep, the heaven-world will be open before him.

When the Third Initiation is passed, the man becomes *M P* 214–
the Anāgāmin, which means literally "he who does 215.
not return," for it is expected of him that he will attain the next Initiation in the same incarnation. The Hindu name for this stage is the Hamsa, which means a swan, but the word is also considered to be a form of the sentence So-ham, "That am I." There is a tradition, too, that the swan is able to separate milk from water, and the Sage is similarly able to realise the true value, for living beings, of the phenomena of life.

This Initiation is typified, in the Christian symbolism,

by the Transfiguration of the Christ. He went up into a high mountain apart, and was transfigured before His disciples: "his face did shine as the sun, and his raiment was white as the light," "exceeding white as snow, so as no fuller on earth can white them." This description suggests the Augoeides, the glorified man, and it is an accurate picture of what happens at this Initiation, for, just as the Second Initiation is principally concerned with the quickening of the lower mental body, so at this stage the causal body is especially developed. The ego is brought more closely into touch with the Monad, and is thus transfigured in very truth.

Even the personality is affected by that wondrous outpouring. The higher and the lower self became one at the First Initiation, and that unity is never lost, but the development of the higher self, that now takes place, can never be measured in the lower worlds of form, although the two are one to the greatest possible extent.

At this stage, the man is brought before the Spiritual King of the World, the Head of the Occult Hierarchy, Who, at this step, either confers the Initiation Himself, or deputes one of His Pupils, the three Lords of the Flame, to do so. In the latter event, the man is presented to the King soon after the Initiation has taken place. Thus the "Christ" is brought into the presence of His "Father"; the buddhi in the Initiate is raised, until it becomes one with its origin on the nirvānic plane, and a very wonderful union between the first and second principles in man is thus effected.

M P 216. The Anāgāmin enjoys, while moving through the round of his daily work, all the splendid possibilities given by full possession of the faculties of the higher mental plane, and during the sleep of the body he enters the buddhic plane.

In this stage, he has to throw off any lingering remains of the fourth and fifth fetters—attachment to the enjoyment of sensation, typified by earthly love,
M P 217. and all possibility of anger or hatred. He must become free from the possibility of being enslaved in

any way by external things. He must rise above all considerations connected with the mere personality of those around him, recognising that the affection which flourishes upon the Path is an affection between egos. Therefore it is strong and permanent, without fear of diminution or fluctuation, for it is that " perfect love which casteth out fear."

The Fourth Initiation is known as that of the Arhat, *M P* 219.
which means the worthy, the capable, the venerable or perfect. The Hindus call the Arhat the Paramahamsa, the one above or beyond the Hamsa. In the Christian system the Fourth Initiation is indicated by the suffering in the Garden of Gethsemane, the Crucifixion, and the Resurrection of the Christ.

This Initiation differs from the others in that it has *M P* 222–
the double aspect of suffering and victory, hence a 223.
series of events has been employed to represent it. The type of suffering, which accompanies the Initiation, clears off any arrears of karma which may still stand in the Initiate's way. The patience and joyousness, with which he endures them, have great value in the strengthening of his character, and help to determine the extent of his usefulness in the work which lies before him.

The Initiate has to experience for a moment the *M P* 221–
condition called *Avīchi*, which means the " waveless," 222. *T P O* 704.
that which is without vibration. The man stands absolutely alone in space, and feels cut off from all life, even from that of the Logos ; it is without doubt the most ghastly experience that it is possible for any human being to have. It seems to have two results : (1) that the candidate may be able to sympathise with those to whom *Avīchi* comes as a result of their actions : and (2) that he may learn to stand cut off from everything external, and test and realise his own utter certainty that he is one with the Logos, and that any such feeling of loneliness must be but an illusion.

Avīchi for the black magician corresponds to nirvāna *I Y* 83.
for the White Adept. Both of these types of men, antitheses of each other, are *yogis*, and each gets the

result of the law he has followed. One attains the *kaivalyam*—realisation of oneness, complete isolation—of Avīchi, the other the kaivalyam of Nirvāna.

M P 225. For the Arhat, while still in the physical body, the
T P O 592. consciousness of the buddhic plane is his, this being its normal home.

I L I 93. In fact, to stand at the level of the Arhat involves the power fully to use the buddhic vehicle.

T P O 769. When the Arhat draws himself up into the buddhic
I L I 346. plane, it must not be supposed that manas is in any way lost. For he draws up manas with him into that expression of manas which has all the time existed on the buddhic plane, but has not been fully vivified until now. He still remains triple, but instead of being on the three planes, he is now on two, with ātmā developed on its own plane, buddhi on its own plane, and manas level with buddhi, drawn up into the intuition. Then he discards the causal body, because he has no further need of it. When he wishes to come down again, and manifest on the mental plane, he has to make a new causal body, but otherwise he does not need one.

Much in the same way, at a later stage, the buddhi and the glorified intellect will be drawn up into the ātmic plane, and the triple spirit will be fully vivified. Then the three manifestations will converge into one. That is a power within the reach of the Adept, because, as we shall see in due course, He unifies the Monad and the ego, just as the disciple is trying to unite the ego with the personality.

This drawing up of the higher manas from the causal body, so that it is on the buddhic plane side by side with the buddhi, is the aspect or condition of the ego which H. P. Blavatsky called the spiritual ego, which
T P O 771. is buddhi plus the mānasic aspect of the One, which was drawn up into buddhi when the causal vehicle was cast aside. That state—that of the Arhat—is called by Christian mystics that of spiritual illumination, of the Christ in man.

T P O 357. H. P. Blavatsky has also a classification in which she speaks of four divisions of the mind :—

(1) Manas-taijasi, the resplendent or illuminated manas, which is really buddhi, or at least that state of man when his manas has become merged in buddhi, having no separate will of its own.

(2) Manas proper, the higher manas, the abstract thinking mind.

(3) Antahkarana, the link or channel or bridge between the higher manas and kāma-manas during incarnation.

(4) Kāma-manas which, on this theory, is the personality.

M P 225: 218. *T P O* 592: 505.

When the Arhat leaves the physical body in sleep or trance, he passes at once into the unutterable glory of the nirvānic plane. His daily effort is now to reach further and further up into the nirvānic plane, up the five lower sub-planes on which the human ego has being. He has a number of planes open to him, and can focus his consciousness at any particular level he chooses, although there will always be a background of the buddhic and nirvānic consciousness.

M P 228.

Even at the ātmic level, there is a sheath of some sort for the Spirit, for in one sense it seems as though it were an atom, and yet in another it seems to be the whole plane. The man feels as if he were everywhere, but could focus anywhere within himself, and wherever for a moment the outpouring of force diminishes, that is for him a body.

M P 230.

The Arhat has to work at the casting off of the remaining five of the ten great fetters, which are :—

(6) Rūparāga—desire for beauty of form, or for physical existence in a form, even including that in the heaven-world.

(7) Arūparāga—desire for formless life.

(8) Mano—pride.

(9) Uddhachcha—agitation or irritability, the possibility of being disturbed by anything.

(10) Avijjā—ignorance.

M P 218–219. *I L I* 93: *T P O* 376.

The Arhat Initiation may be thought of as half-way between the First and the Fifth Initiations.

On the first half of the Path—from the First to the

Fourth Initiation—the man is busy shaking himself free from those personal limitations, from the illusion of "it." On the second half, he is engaged in releasing himself from the illusion of "you." It is usually said that seven lives are occupied, in the average case, at normal times, between the First and Fourth Initiations, and seven lives also between the Fourth and Fifth. But these figures are capable of very great reduction or increase. In most cases the actual period is not very great, since usually the lives are taken in immediate succession, without interludes in the heaven-world.

T P O 261 : 591–592. *M P* 213. The Arhat, whose ego is working perfectly in the causal body, need not incarnate again in a physical body, and go through the wearisome round of birth and death, which is so unpleasant—at any rate, from the point of view of the ego himself. He must, however, descend as far as the astral plane. While in the astral body, he may at any moment that he chooses enjoy the nirvānic consciousness. If he is in the physical body, he can reach that nirvānic consciousness only when he leaves the body in sleep or trance, as already explained above.

T P O 505. Nirvānic consciousness means consciousness anywhere in the solar system.

M P 231–232. *T P O* 750 : 831. The Fifth Initiation makes a man a Master, an Adept, a Superman. The Buddhists call Him the Asekha—literally, the not-disciple—because He has no more to learn, and has exhausted the possibilities of the human kingdoms of nature. The Hindus speak of Him as the Jīvanmukhta, a liberated life, a free being, because His will is one with the Universal Will, that of the One without a second. He stands ever in the light of Nirvāna, even in His waking consciousness, should He choose to remain on earth in a physical body. When out of that, He rises still higher into the Monadic plane, beyond not merely our words but our thought.

I Y 20–21. As *The Secret Doctrine* expresses it : the Adept "begins his Samādhi on the Ātmic plane," all planes below the ātmic being one to Him.

A man attains Adeptship when he raises His ordinary consciousness to the nirvānic level: the fact that differentiates Him, and makes Him an Adept, is that He has unified the Monad with the ego. And, since He has become one with the Monad, He has already reached the level of the third or lowest manifestation of the Deity or Logos.

In Christian symbolism, the Ascension and the Descent of the Holy Spirit stand for the attainment of Adeptship, for the Adept does ascend above humanity, beyond this earth, although, if He chooses, as did the Christ, He may return to teach and help. As He ascends, he becomes one with the Holy Spirit, and invariably the first thing He does, with His new power, is to pour it down upon His disciples, even as the Christ poured down tongues of fire upon the heads of His followers at the Feast of Pentecost.

At the Asekha Initiation, the ātmā is seen as a clear light, a star, and, when it spreads out, at the last breaking down of the wall, it becomes the infinite light. *T P O* 784.

Before that, the Arhat can feel the underlying peace of ātmā when in meditative mood, but constantly he returns to the sorrow. But when a man rises to the ātmic plane in full consciousness, and the buddhic consciousness merges into that, there is but one light seen. This is expressed in *The Voice of the Silence:* "The Three that dwell in glory and in bliss ineffable, now in the world of Māyā have lost their names. They have become one star, the fire that burns but scorches not, that fire which is the Upādhi of the flame."

While the man was in the causal body, he saw the Sacred Three as separate, but now he sees them as the three aspects of the triple ātmā. Buddhi and manas, which were "twins upon a line" in the buddhic consciousness of the previous stage, are now one with ātmā, the fire which is the vehicle of the monadic flame.

Then says the Teacher: "Where is thy individuality, Lanoo, where the Lanoo himself? It is the spark lost in the fire, the drop within the ocean, the ever present ray become the All and the eternal

Radiance." He who was a disciple is now a Master. He stands in the centre, and the triple ātmā radiates from Him.

T P O 591. The Adept has the power to get at any knowledge that He wants, almost in a moment. He can make Himself one with it, and get at the core of it instantly, and then observe the surrounding details as He may require them. Somewhere on the buddhic or nirvānic plane, He would grasp the idea that lies at the back, for example, of any particular science or department of knowledge, and make Himself one with that. Then, from that point of view, He would reach down into any details He might require.

T P O 903–904. A Master does not appear to need all the knowledge stored within His brain as we do, but is able to turn a certain faculty on to anything that is wanted, and, by the use of that faculty, then and there, to know all about it. He would not need to read up a subject, but He would turn His all-seeing eye on the subject, and thereby somehow absorb the knowledge.

This may be the explanation of getting rid of avidyā—ignorance. With the buddhic faculty, as we have seen, it is no longer necessary to collect facts from outside, but one plunges into the consciousness of anything, whether it be mineral or plant or deva, etc., and understands it from inside.

T P O 764. H. P. Blavatsky has pointed out that a Master's physical body is a mere vehicle. It hands nothing on, but is simply a point of contact with the physical plane, a body kept as an instrument, needed for the work He does, and dropped when done with. The same consideration applies to the astral and mental bodies.

M P 241–242. The Masters aid, in countless ways, the progress of humanity. From the highest sphere, They shed down on all the world light and life, that may be taken up and assimilated, as freely as the sunshine, by all who are receptive enough to take it in. As the physical world lives by the Life of God, focussed by the sun, so does the spiritual world live by that same Life, focussed by the Occult Hierarchy.

Certain Masters are specially connected with religions, and use these religions as reservoirs, into which They pour spiritual energy, to be distributed to the faithful in each religion through the duly appointed " means of grace."

Then there is the great intellectual work, wherein the Masters send out thoughts of high intellectual power, to be caught up by men of genius, assimilated by them and given out to the world. On this level also, They send out Their wishes to Their disciples, notifying them of the tasks to which they should set their hands.

In the lower mental world, the Masters generate the thought-forms which influence the concrete mind, and guide it along useful lines of activity in this world, and teach those who are living in the heavenly world.

In the intermediate world, They undertake the work of the helping of the so-called dead, generally direct and supervise the teaching of the younger pupils, and send out aid in numberless cases of need.

In the physical world, They watch the tendencies of events, correct and neutralise, so far as law permits, evil currents, constantly balance the forces that work for and against evolution, strengthening the good and weakening the evil. They work also in conjunction with the Angels or Devas of the Nations, guiding the spiritual forces as the others guide the material.

The whole earth is divided into special areas, each in *M P* 243. the charge of a Master. These areas, consisting of huge countries or even continents, correspond somewhat to " parishes " in the Church organisation. Thus one Adept may be said to be in charge of Europe : another looks after India : and so on.

The Adept has all the different grades and forms of evolution to regard—not only humanity, but also the great kingdom of the Angels or Devas, the various classes of nature-spirits, the animals, vegetables and minerals, the elemental kingdoms, and many others of which so far nothing has been heard by mankind.

A large part of the work of the Adepts lies at levels *M P* 245. far beyond the physical, as They are engaged in pouring out Their own power, and also the force from the great store filled by the Nirmānakāyas. It is the karma of the world that it shall have a certain amount of this uplifting force at its service; on account of this, humanity is evolving as a unit, the fact of brotherhood enabling every one to make much more progress than would be even remotely possible were he standing entirely by himself.

M P 246. The Great White Brotherhood rays out the supply of force from the great reservoir upon all egos, without exception, on the higher mental plane, thus giving the greatest possible assistance to the unfolding of the indwelling life.

M P 246–247. Whilst an Adept may ray out His force upon enormous numbers of people, running often into many millions simultaneously, yet such is the wonderful quality of this power, which He pours forth, that it adapts itself to each one of these millions, as though he were the only object of its influence, and it appears as though what, for us, would be full attention, were being given to that one.

This arises from the fact that the Master's nirvānic or ātmic consciousness is a kind of point, which yet includes the entire plane. He can bring that point down through several planes, and spread it out like a kind of bubble. On the outside of that huge sphere are all the causal bodies, which He is trying to affect, and He, filling the sphere, appears all in all to each individual.

In this way He fills with His Life the ideals of millions of people, and is for them respectively the ideal Christ, the ideal Rāma, the ideal Krishna, an Angel, or perhaps a spirit guide.

M P 248–249. *I L I* 35–36. In this department of Their work, the Masters frequently take advantage of special occasions, and of places where there is some strong magnetic centre. Where some holy man has lived and died, or where some relic of such a person creates a suitable atmosphere, They take advantage of such conditions, and cause Their own force to radiate along the channels already prepared. When some vast assemblage of pilgrims comes together in a receptive attitude, again They take advantage of the occasion, by pouring Their forces out upon the people, through the channels by means of which they have been taught to expect help and blessing.

Another example of the methods of work of the *H S II* 216–
Masters at the causal level is afforded in the case of 217.
talismans, which a Master may link with His own causal body, so that its influence will last through the ages. This was done with certain physical objects, buried at various points of future importance, by Apollonius of Tyana.

The Adept having become one with the Third Aspect of the Logos, manifesting on the plane of ātmā, His next step is to become one with that Aspect which is represented by the Christ in the bosom of the Father. Later on, it may be presumed that He will draw ever nearer and nearer to the Deity of the Solar system.

When human life is completed, the Perfected Man *M P* 21.
usually drops his various material bodies, but He retains the power to take up any of them, if ever He should need them in the course of His work. In the majority of cases, one who gains that level no longer needs a physical body. He no longer retains an astral, a mental, or even a causal body, but lives permanently at His highest level.

Of those who attain Adeptship, comparatively few *M P* 238.
remain on our earth as members of the Occult Hierarchy, as will be explained more fully presently.

Beyond the Fifth or Asekha Initiation, the higher *M P* 235–
Path opens up in seven great ways, among which the 237. *T P O* 605:
Adept must take His choice. These seven are as 598.
follows :—

I. He may enter into the blissful omniscience and omnipotence of Nirvāna, with activities far beyond our knowing, to become, perhaps, in some future world, an Avatāra, or Divine Incarnation. This is sometimes called "taking the Dharmakāya vesture." The Dharmakāya keeps nothing below the Monad, though what the vesture of the Monad may be on its own plane we do not know.

II. He may enter on "the Spiritual Period"—a phrase covering unknown meanings, among them probably that of "taking the Sambhogakāya vesture." He retains His manifestation as a triple spirit, and, probably, can reach down and show Himself in a temporary Augoeides.

III. He may become part of that treasure-house of spiritual forces, on which the Agents of the Logos draw for Their work, "taking the Nirmānakāya vesture." The Nirmānakāya appears to preserve His Augoeides, that is, His causal body, and keeps all His permanent atoms, and therefore has the power to show Himself at whichever level He chooses. The Nirmānakāyas are spoken of in *The Voice of the Silence* as forming a Guardian Wall, which preserves the world from further and far greater misery and sorrow.

IV. He may remain a member of the Occult Hierarchy, which rules and guards the world in which He has reached perfection.

V. He may pass on to the next Chain, to aid in building up its forms.

VI. He may enter the splendid Angel or Deva Evolution.

VII. He may give himself to the immediate service of the Logos, to be used by Him in any part of the Solar System: His Servant and Messenger, who lives but to carry out His will, and do His work over the whole of the System which He rules. This is called joining the "Staff." It seems to be considered a very hard path, perhaps the greatest sacrifice open to the Adept, and is therefore regarded as carrying with it great distinction.

A member of the General Staff has no physical body, but makes one for Himself by Kriyāshakti—the "power to make"—of the matter of the globe to which He is sent. The Staff contains Beings at very different levels, from that of Arhatship upwards.

M P 232: 267. Above the Initiation of the Adept lies the Sixth Initiation, that of the Chohan, a word which means

"Lord." The same word is used also for the Heads of Rays Three to Seven.

The Ray to which an Adept belongs affects not only His appearance, but also that work that He has to do. The following table sets out briefly certain facts regarding the Rays :— *M P* 280–288.

Ray.	Head of Ray.	Characteristics of Ray.	Remarks
I.	Chohan Morya.	Strength.	The Master Jupiter is also on this Ray, and is the Guardian of India. He is a great student of the abstruser sciences, of which chemistry and astronomy are the outer shells.
II.	Chohan Kuthumi : formerly He was Pythagoras (6th century, B.C.).	Wisdom.	This Ray gives great Teachers to the world.
III.	The Venetian Chohan.	Adaptability : Tact.	Astrology is concerned with this Ray.
IV.	Chohan Serapis.	Beauty and Harmony.	Many artists are on this Ray.
V.	Chohan Hilarion : formerly Iamblichus (4th century).	Science : detailed knowledge.	
VI.	Chohan Jesus : formerly Apollonius of Tyana (1st century), and also Rāmanūjachārya (11th century).	Bhakti or Devotion.	The Ray of mystics.
VII.	Chohan Rakoczi : formerly the Comte de St. Germain (18th century) ; Francis Bacon (17th century) ; Robertus the monk (16th century) ; Hunyadi Janos (15th century) ; Christian Rosencreuz (14th century) ; Roger Bacon (13th century) ; Proclus the Neo-platonist (5th century) ; St. Alban (3rd century).	Ordered Service : Ceremonial.	Works through ceremonial magic, and employs the services of great Angels.

M P 279. The following are examples of the methods likely to be employed by representatives of the different rays :—

The First Ray man would attain his object by sheer force of resistless will, without condescending to employ anything in the nature of means at all.

The Second Ray man would also work by force of will, but with the full comprehension of the various possible methods, and the conscious direction of his will into the channel of the most suitable one.

The Third Ray man would use the forces of the mental plane, noticing very carefully the exact time when the influences were most favourable to success.

The Fourth Ray man would employ the finer physical forces of the ether.

The Fifth Ray man would set in motion the currents of what used to be called the astral light.

The Sixth Ray man would achieve his result by the strength of his earnest faith in his particular Deity, and in the efficacy of prayer to Him.

The Seventh Ray man would use elaborate ceremonial magic, and probably invoke the aid of non-human spirits, if possible.

M P 280. In attempting the cure of disease :—

The First Ray man would simply draw health and strength from the great fountain of Universal Life.

The Second Ray man would thoroughly comprehend the nature of the malady, and know precisely how to exercise his will-power upon it to the best advantage.

The Third Ray man would invoke the Great Planetary Spirits, and choose a moment when astrological influences were beneficent for the application of his remedies.

The Fourth Ray man would trust chiefly to physical means, such as massage.

The Fifth Ray man would employ drugs.

The Sixth Ray man would employ faith-healing.

The Seventh Ray man would use mantras, or magical invocations.

Beyond the Chohan Initiation, on Rays Three to Seven, the highest Initiation that can be taken on our globe is that of the Mahāchohan : it is possible, however, to go further on the First and Second Rays, as is indicated in the following table of Initiations, in which it will be seen that the Buddha Initiation is possible on the Second and First Rays, and that the Adept may go still further on the First. *M P* 307. *T P O* 598.

INITIATIONS								
		Silent Watcher.						
	9	Lord of the World.						
	8	Pratyeka Buddha	Buddha					
	7	Manu	Bodhisattva	Mahāchohan				
	6	Chohan	Chohan	Chohan	Chohan	Chohan	Chohan	Chohan
	5	Asekha	Asekha	Asekha	Asekha	Asekha	Asekha	Asekha
	4	First Ray	Second Ray	Third Ray	Fourth Ray	Fifth Ray	Sixth Ray	Seventh Ray
	3							
	2							
	1							

TABLE OF INITIATIONS

The Occult Government is in three departments, ruled by three officials, who are not merely reflections of the Three Aspects of the Logos, but are in a very real way actual manifestations of Them. These three are (1) the Lord of the World, who is one with the First Aspect, on the Ādi plane, and wields the divine Will on earth ; (2) the Lord Buddha, who is one with the Second Aspect, which dwells on the Anupādaka plane, and sends the divine Wisdom down to mankind ; and (3) the Mahāchohan, who is one with the Third Aspect, which resides on the nirvānic or ātmic plane, and *M P* 303-304.

exercises the divine Activity—representing the Holy Ghost. The following table sets out these facts :—

Logos.	Divine Powers.	Planes of Nature.	Triangles of Agents.	Ray.
First Aspect.	Will.	Ādi or Originating.	The Lord of the World.	1
Second Aspect.	Wisdom.	Anupādaka or Monadic.	The Lord Buddha.	2
Third Aspect.	Activity.	Ātmic or Spiritual.	The Mahā-chohan.	3–7

In this great Triangle, the Lord of the World and the Lord Buddha are different from the Mahāchohan, being

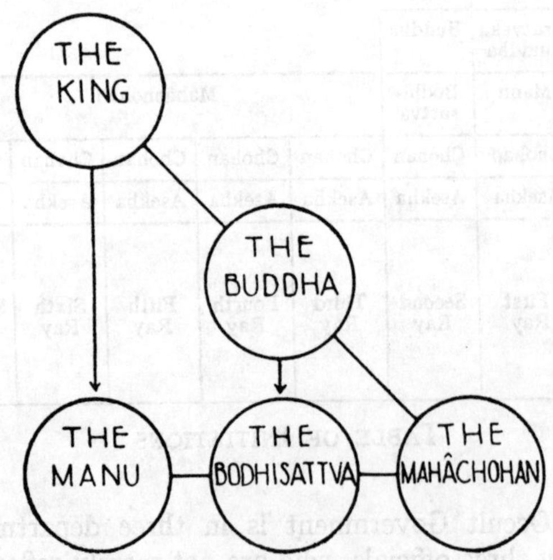

DIAGRAM XLIV.—The Great Triangles of the Hierarchy.

engaged in work which does not descend to the physical plane, but only to the level of the buddhic body, in the case of the Lord Buddha, and the ātmic plane, in that of the Lord of the World. Yet, without Their work, none of that at lower levels would be possible, so They provide for the transmission of Their influence, even to the lowest plane, through Their representatives, the Manu and the Bodhisattva, respectively.

The Manu and the Bodhisattva stand parallel with the Mahāchohan, thus forming another Triangle, to administer the powers of the Logos down to the

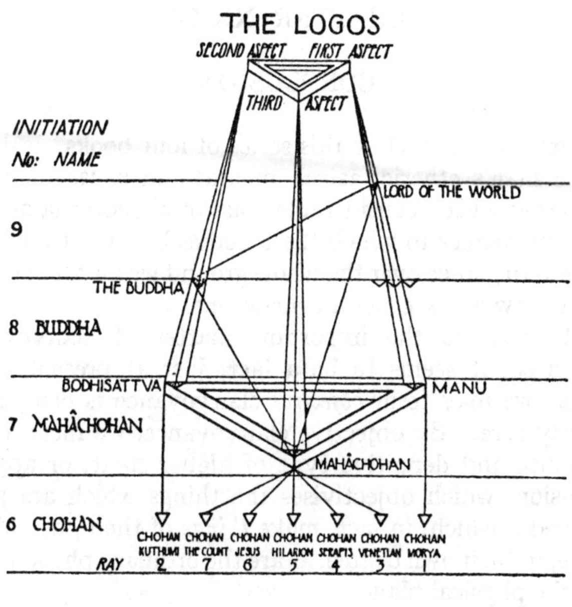

Diagram XLV.—The Occult Hierarchy.

physical plane. These two triangles are expressed in Diagram XLIV.

The various relationships described above are summarised in Diagram XLV, which is reproduced, with very slight modifications, from *The Masters and the Path.*

CHAPTER XXXV

CONCLUSION

In bringing to a close this series of four books, dealing with man's etheric, astral, mental and causal bodies, together with a considerable mass of phenomena of the various planes to which these bodies belong, it may be useful to glance over the whole ground we have covered, and draw a few general conclusions.

Turning to the important matter of clairvoyant research, it seems to be a fact, just at present, that what we may term *objective* clairvoyance is comparatively rare. By objective clairvoyance, we mean that definite and definitive type of higher sight, or apprehension, which objectivises the things which are perceived: which, in fact, make *things* of them, as objective, in their own degree, as are the ordinary phenomena of the physical plane.

There is, however, another type of clear-seeing, which we may term *subjective* clairvoyance. In this type, there is a form of perception, perhaps more accurately termed *apprehension*, which does not objectify that which is being observed, but which rather feels or cognises it in a more subtle, and a more interior manner. Let a simple illustration suffice.

Whilst relatively few people are able to *see* auras, so that they become perfectly objective, far more seem to be able to "sense" auras, and to *know*, without actually *seeing*, what are their general characteristics, such as size, quality, colour, and so forth. They appear to see, quite literally, with the "mind's eye."

In both cases of clear-seeing, the wise and experienced student will be extremely cautious and prudent, and will always take a strictly conservative view, either of what he sees—*or thinks he sees*—or of what he feels—*or thinks he feels.* Whilst it would be highly foolish, and contrary to all the canons of scientific method, to ignore, or to discount too severely, that which is seen or apprehended, it is equally as foolish, and certainly more dangerous, to accept rashly, and without careful corroboration, everything that is seen or apprehended. The student must, in entering the unknown, strive to maintain that careful balance, between caution and rashness, which alone leads to true knowledge, and keeps him on that "middle path" which has so often been described as narrow as the edge of a razor.

As mentioned in a previous volume, to have attempted to give proofs of the statements made in these books would have been, for many reasons, quite impossible, or at least impracticable. For a very large proportion of the contents of these volumes, rigid, intellectual proof could most certainly *not* be given, because it is not at present available. Comparatively few things—some would say no things—can be proved absolutely: facts, phenomena, observations, statements, are one thing; proof of those facts, etc., and, still more, *ability to appreciate such proof*, are a totally different thing. Men do not as yet seem to have been able to devise a system of proving whether certain things are true or are not true, a system as reliable, shall we say, as is a pair of scales for ascertaining weights of objects.

And yet, amongst all the phenomena of life are many things, of supreme importance, upon which man *must* form an opinion, if he is to live as a rational being, and direct his life truly. He cannot afford to wait until clear, unequivocal proof is forthcoming. To do so is to incur the risk of rejecting, merely on account of insufficient proof, information which, if true, may be of immeasurable importance and value to him.

Only one attitude seems reasonable and just. We must, as just said, make up our minds one way or the other, even when proof is *not* forthcoming. When intellectual proof happens to be deficient, it is often as stupid to disbelieve, as to believe. There is a superstition of disbelief, as there is a superstition of belief: and it is doubtful from which form of superstition the human race at the present time suffers most.

Proof, to-day, perhaps always, is an individual matter for each man. There is a theory, and it is a theory by no means unsupported by evidence and by experience, that it is possible for a man so to train himself that, when a true fact is presented to him for the first time, something within him leaps to greet it, and he knows it is true. We may call this intuition, or anything else we choose: it has many names: but it is a phenomenon open to any one to observe, and to test for himself as a true phenomenon.

As Dr. Besant has said: "As that higher sense in you which knows truth at sight gradually unfolds, you will be able to take in more and more of the truth. Then there will grow up in you a deep inner conviction, and when a truth is presented to you, you will know it is true. This sense corresponds to eyesight on the physical plane. It is the faculty of buddhi, pure reason." (*Talks on the Path of Occultism*, p. 210.)

So, the wise man observes instances of this phenomenon in himself, and in others, and, recognising its tremendous and far-reaching importance, deliberately sets to work to train and perfect the faculty in himself. Obviously it can become of incalculable value to him, more particularly in his psychological and spiritual life.

Strange and extraordinary, perhaps even impossible, as many of the statements made in these four books may seem, to some readers, it would surely be a wiser policy (seeing that they are all made by sincere and honest investigators) *not* to reject them, merely because they cannot be proved, but, if they do not awaken a responsive thrill that feels them to be true, to set them aside for the time being, to "file" them for "future reference." Whereas, if they do awaken that responsive thrill, which, in those who have developed the faculty referred to above, is often quite unmistakable, they may be accepted, tentatively at least for the time, as probably true.

More and more students of occultism are finding that, as time goes on and they develop their own inner powers, they are able to verify for themselves many statements which, years or months previously, they had accepted in this manner, on the authority of others.

So much for the abstruse and complicated question of proof of the teachings of the Ancient Wisdom, in its guise of modern Theosophy.

Turning to the ethical aspect of what has been said in these four books, the reader will no doubt have observed that moral and ethical considerations, arising from a study of the occult constitution of man, have been touched upon only occasionally, and quite secondarily. This has been done deliberately, the view having been taken that facts speak for themselves, and point their own moral. If man is constituted as described, if he has etheric, astral, mental and causal bodies of the nature stated, surely there can be no two opinions as to the way in which he ought, even in his own interest, to live and to conduct his relations with other men, and with the world in general. Whether he does so or not is, of course, his own affair entirely.

And now a few words directed more specifically to occult students, and to the general method of approach to the subjects dealt with in these four volumes.

The Ancient Wisdom can no doubt be presented in many ways, ways utterly diverse from one another. A mechanic would present them in one fashion : an artist in quite another way : a scientist would describe them in a manner very different from that which a poet or a mystic would adopt. According to the types or temperaments of men, and their qualifications and knowledge, so will be their presentations of the eternal verities.

Hence, there may be danger for one in the method of presentation of another. To be quite specific, the presentation adopted in these books many would say is mechanical, even materialistic. So be it : but, in the nature of things, there must be a mechanical and a material aspect of every phenomenon, no matter how spiritual, for there can be no spirit without matter. But the true occult student will guard against shutting himself up in any rigid mechanical system. Whilst his "tidy" mind may delight in categories, and precise tabulations of facts, yet he must not let these become a prison-house, with barred windows, limiting and restricting his views to certain narrow directions only.

Dissection, analysis, categorisation are necessary for the intellect: but they are, after all, but scaffolding by means of which the structure, complete in all its parts, is raised. Moreover, as H. G. Wells has admirably stated: "these things—number, definition, class and abstract form—I hold, are merely unavoidable conditions of mental activity; regrettable conditions rather than essential facts. The forceps of our minds are clumsy forceps, and crush the truth a little in taking hold of it." (*First and Last Things*, Book I, "Metaphysics," page 19.)

The structure of knowledge is one whole, made up, it is true, of its manifold parts, yet greater than the arithmetical sum of all its parts, and, in its totality, fulfilling a function which none of its parts, nor any group of its parts, can perform.

So with man: we may, for purposes of study and understanding, divide him into Monad, Ego and Personality, his bodies into physical, etheric, astral, mental, and causal: yet the man himself *is no one of these things, nor even all of them together*. These are all but means through which he expresses portions, aspects, or functions of himself: but he himself "remains," an entity, a mystery, if the truth be told, different from, and greater than, all of these categories into which we divide him.

Bishop Leadbeater (in *The Science of the Sacraments*, page 547) gives an analogy which may be useful here. If an electric current be made to flow round a bar of soft iron, through a coil of German-silver wire, and within a tube filled with mercury vapour, it will give rise respectively to magnetism, heat, and light. The current is the same, but its manifestations vary according to the nature of the matter through which it is acting. So with man : the current of life flowing in him is split up into different varieties of manifestation, according to the bodies through which it expresses itself. We study the bodies in turn, and their methods of functioning : but the man himself, that which results in consciousness of various kinds in the various bodies, is the noumenon behind all these external phenomena : and, be it noted, just as the true nature of electricity still eludes our scientists, so does man himself, in his true nature, still elude us.

Hence, it is quite conceivable, nay probable, that it would be possible to give a fair and full presentation, shall we say solely from the point of view of consciousness, rather than of form, of the truths of the Ancient Wisdom, without any mention of ātmā, buddhi, manas, or the hosts of other technical terms with which these pages are so liberally sprinkled. The real student, the genuine lover of truth, will recognise truth, no matter in what guise, or in what "jargon"—to use an unpleasant word—it may be expressed, or *veiled*. But let him, above all things, be tolerant and kindly : all roads lead to the one goal : let each pilgrim find and follow his own path, offering goodwill, friendship and kindliness, without stint and without patronage, to pilgrims who prefer to follow other paths.

In view of what was said above, regarding the inherent defects of intellectual processes and categorisation, the student must, *à fortiori*, guard himself against placing too much faith in diagrams, useful as these may be to the labouring mind. Let the student by all means employ them as scaffolding, as ladders up which he climbs, but let him be on his guard lest they become cages which imprison him. Here is a test : if his understanding be genuine, and full, the synthetic conception, which he has generated, will belong to a world far above the world of form or diagram : but, the moment he casts his conception into the lower, categorising mind, it will project itself into countless forms and shapes, varying according to the materials he selects, from his store of knowledge, for the expression of that which is, in its own nature, incapable of being imprisoned in any graph, no matter how ingenious or appropriate. Diagrams, like all forms of categories, are admirable servants, but tyrannical masters.

It is the hope of the compiler that the years of work he has spent on these volumes will help to bring to many of his readers at least as much clarification of ideas, and, above all, enthusiasm and ever-deepening love for the Brahmā-Vidyā, the noble science, the knowledge of God and of man, as they have brought to the compiler himself. From knowledge comes understanding: from understanding comes that serenity and peace which are so immeasurably greater than all knowledge and all understanding.

"The value of knowledge," wrote Dr. Annie Besant, "is tested by its power to purify and ennoble the life, and all earnest students desire to apply the theoretical knowledge acquired in their study of Theosophy to the evolution of their own character and to the helping of their fellow-men. . . . The emotion which impels to righteous living is half wasted if the clear light of the intellect does not illuminate the path of conduct; for as the blind man strays from the way unknowing till he falls into the ditch, so does the Ego, blinded by ignorance, turn aside from the road of right living till he falls into the pit of evil action. Truly is Avidyā—the privation of knowledge—the first step out of unity into separateness, and only as it lessens does separateness diminish, until its disappearance restores the Eternal Peace."

INDEX

PRINTED AND MADE IN GREAT BRITAIN BY
FLETCHER AND SON LTD NORWICH

PRINTED AND MADE IN GREAT BRITAIN BY
FLETCHER AND SON LTD NORWICH